D1596778

SPACES OF ENSLAVEMENT

New Netherland Institute
Exploring America's Dutch Heritage

For more than three decades, the New Netherland Institute (NNI)—an independent nonprofit nongovernmental organization—has cast light on America's Dutch roots. Through its support of the translation and publication of New Netherland's records and its various educational and public programs, NNI promotes historical scholarship on and popular appreciation of the seventeenth-century Dutch mid-Atlantic colony. More information about NNI can be found at newnetherlandinstitute.org.

SPACES OF ENSLAVEMENT

A HISTORY OF SLAVERY AND RESISTANCE IN DUTCH NEW YORK

ANDREA C. MOSTERMAN

CORNELL UNIVERSITY PRESS
Ithaca and London

Published in association with the New Netherland Institute

First published 2021 by Cornell University Press

Library of Congress Cataloging-in-Publication Data

Names: Mosterman, Andrea C., author.
Title: Spaces of enslavement : a history of slavery and
    resistance in Dutch New York / Andrea C. Mosterman.
Description: Ithaca [New York] : Cornell University Press,
    2021. | Includes bibliographical references and index.
Identifiers: LCCN 2020056471 (print) | LCCN 2020056472
    (ebook) | ISBN 9781501715624 (hardcover) |
    ISBN 9781501715631 (ebook) | ISBN 9781501715648 (pdf)
Subjects: LCSH: Slavery—New York (State)—History—
    17th century. | Slavery—New York (State)—History—
    18th century. | Slavery—New York (State)—History—
    19th century. | Slaves—New York (State)—
    Social conditions—17th century. | Slaves—New York
    (State)—Social conditions—18th century. | Slaves—
    New York (State)—Social conditions—19th century. |
    Spatial behavior—Social aspects—New York (State)—
    History—17th century. | Spatial behavior—Social
    aspects—New York (State)—History—18th century. |
    Spatial behavior—Social aspects—New York (State)—
    History—19th century. | Dutch—New York (State)—
    History—17th century. | Dutch—New York
    (State)—History—18th century. | Dutch—New York
    (State)—History—19th century.
Classification: LCC E185.93.N56 M67 2021 (print) |
    LCC E185.93.N56 (ebook) | DDC 306.3 / 620974—dc23
LC record available at https:/ /lccn.loc.gov/2020056471
LC ebook record available at https:/ /lccn.loc.gov
    /2020056472

To my parents,
Maria Helena Wolbers (1937–2005) and Johannes Theodardus Mosterman

CONTENTS

ACKNOWLEDGMENTS

During the many years that I have worked on this project, I have relied on the help and encouragement from colleagues, institutions, friends, and family. Without them, this book would not exist.

Early on in the process, I was fortunate enough to receive the mentorship from several remarkable scholars. Linda Heywood and John Thornton encouraged me to study the history of slavery in Dutch New York, and their continued guidance proved essential to this study. Lois Horton was one of the very first people to support my research, and she has remained an important influence. In the Netherlands, I received significant encouragement from Dienke Hondius.

Conversations with Brendan McConville and Allison Blakely helped me frame this study when it was still in its early stages. Since then, multiple people have aided me with my research: Michael Douma, Russell Gasero, Charles Gehring, Wendy Harris, Jeroen van den Hurk, Jaap Jacobs, Helene van Rossum, Francis Sypher, Janny Venema, and David Willem Voorhees helped locate or translate documents. Sherril Tippins scanned documents at the Albany County Hall of Records when I was not able to travel to New York.

Several people have read my work and given me invaluable feedback. Wim Klooster, Richard Boles, Dirk Mouw, D. Ryan Gray, and Graham Russell Hodges read all or parts of this manuscript at its various stages. Special thanks go to my good friend Melissa Graboyes, who was kind enough to read and comment on an earlier version of this manuscript. I am similarly grateful for the New Orleans–based writing group that I have been a part of: without the thoughtful comments from Laura Rosanne Adderley, Nikki Brown, Guadalupe García, Elisabeth McMahon, Angel Adams Parham, and Sharlene Sinegal-DeCuir this book would have looked very different. All of these people have helped me improve my research and writing tremendously.

I could not have completed this research without the assistance of archivists and librarians at the Brooklyn Historical Society, New-York Historical Society, Gilder Lehrman Collection, New York Public Library, New York State Archives, New York State Library, Albany Institute of History and Art, Ulster

County Clerk Archives Division, Historic Huguenot Street Archives and Library, Reformed Church of America Archives, Jacob Leisler Institute, Nationaal Archief in the Hague, and Stadsarchief Amsterdam. Equally important has been the help I received from clergy, church historians, and administrative staff at the Reformed Church of America churches I visited, and from the various site managers and guides who showed me around historic homes. Special thanks go to Cordell Reaves, who organized visits to some of these sites.

Several associations and institutions have made this research possible. The Society of Colonial Wars, the Gilder Lehrman Institute, the New York State Archives, the New York State Library, Boston University Graduate School, Boston University History Department, the American Historical Association, the University of New Orleans Muckley Bequest, and the Reformed Church of America all provided crucial financial assistance. Support from the New Netherland Institute (NNI) has been especially important. NNI has given me opportunities to workshop my research with peers, meet wonderful scholars, and share my work with the wider public. I am honored to have this book appear in Cornell Press's New Netherland Institute Studies series.

Over the years, I have come to rely on several colleagues and friends for advice, feedback, and fellowship. I have spent many hours discussing New York and Dutch Atlantic history with Liz Covart, Deborah Hamer, Jared Hardesty, Erin Kramer, Dennis Maika, Nicole Maskiell, and Sarah Mulhall Adelman. Their friendships enriched me as a historian. The camaraderie of fellow BU grads David Atkinson, Anne Blaschke, Kathryn Cramer Brownell, Estelle Pae Huerta, and Ginger Myhaver have been similarly invaluable.

I owe much to my colleagues and students at the University of New Orleans (UNO). I am especially grateful to James Mokhiber for his friendship, Mary Niall Mitchell for her mentorship, and Robert Dupont for his steady support of my research. Thanks also go to the UNO librarians who helped me access numerous books and articles.

Michael McGandy, my editor, deserves special mention. He first reached out to me when this project was still in its early stages, and his guidance and support have proven absolutely crucial.

Finally, I could not have completed this book without the unwavering support from family and friends. Mariska Jansen, Jenevièvre Telles, Marit Smit, Monique Havinga, and Nynke Boersma welcomed me into their homes on my many research visits to the Netherlands. Jessica van der Laag often watched my daughter while I was in the archives. My love for books and history originates with my mother. She passed away when I just started this project, but she continues to inspire my work. The encouragement I received from my father, stepmother, and siblings proved absolutely crucial in being able to continue this research. My children and stepchildren—Assane, Ousseynou, Aminata, Mariama, and Saliou—have provided mostly welcome distractions from writing and research. They remind me daily of what is most important. Lastly, I could not have done this without my husband, Masse Ndiaye. Not only has he spent many hours listening to me talk about my research, he has also helped me develop several of the concepts that I write about in this book. I am forever grateful for his love and support.

ABBREVIATIONS

AIHA	Albany Institute of History and Art
BHS	Brooklyn Historical Society
GLC	Gilder Lehrman Collection
IISG	International Institute of Social History
IRSH	International Review of Social History
Nat. Arch.	National Archives of the Netherlands
NYCMA	New York City Municipal Archives
N-YHS	New-York Historical Society
NYPL	New York Public Library
NYSA	New York State Archives
NYSL	New York State Library
RCA	Reformed Church of America Archives
SAA	Stadsarchief Amsterdam
TVGESCH	Tijdschrift voor Geschiedenis

SPACES OF ENSLAVEMENT

Introduction

A Spatial Analysis of Slavery in Dutch New York

When studying slavery, it is important to consider the spaces of enslavement. I first came to this realization when I visited the Maison des Esclaves, or house of slaves, at Gorée Island, Senegal (see Figure 0.1). As I entered the space where enslaved men were once held, I instantly felt physically ill, a reaction that completely took me by surprise. At that point, I had studied the history of slavery for years. Yet, that moment when I stood where these men were once held affected me in ways no primary source document or scholarly book had. As I imagined the sounds, sights, and smells of the space, that holding cell—its small size, thick walls, and only a loophole that provided some light and fresh air—told a story of enslavement and human trafficking that is rarely captured in written sources.[1]

It was this experience that led me to consider the spaces enslaved people in Dutch New York inhabited and frequented more carefully. What did the cold, damp cellar Sojourner Truth grew up in look, feel, sound, and smell like? How did Mary, Hannah, Mell, Cate, Harry, Hechter, Powel, and the children Syrus, Jan, Jacob, Hannah, and Poll find rest in the small, dark garrets that served as their living quarters? Where in the Kingston church would Elisabeth have worshipped after she became a full member in 1750? Was she sitting with her enslavers, or was she restricted to back benches where she could barely hear the minister preach? How had Dean, Bet, and Pompey been able to circumvent Albany's watchmen when they made their way to Peter Gansevoort's house

FIGURE 0.1.   Maison des Esclaves, Gorée Island, Senegal. Picture by author.

and set it on fire with the hot coals they were carrying? These were some of the questions that guided the research for this book.

I began to visit these spaces of enslavement in New York homes, churches, and towns. Instead of entering historic homes from the front, I would enter from the back as its enslaved inhabitants would have. I would walk through the cellars where many of them lived and worked, and I would visit the garret spaces that regularly served as their sleeping quarters. Instead of using the main stairwell, I would walk down the steep and narrow service stairs when possible. Thanks to Joseph McGill's Slave Dwelling Project, I was able to spend the night in one of the garret spaces at Stenton Hall, a Georgian-style home that much resembled eighteenth-century mansions that belonged to Dutch

New York elite families.[2] In the churches I visited, I would look for the benches that were reserved for Black worshippers in an effort to gain some perspective of what they would have been able to hear and see from those seats. Doing so helped me think about the history of slavery in early New York's Dutch communities in new ways.[3]

Thus, spatial analysis became the core form of research for this study. As several scholars have noted before me, spatial control proved a central element of enslavement.[4] Enslavers sought to limit and control enslaved people's movements and activities through, among others, systems of monitoring, enclosing, segregating, and patrolling. Enslaved people's resistance to their bondage included their efforts to escape or modify these spaces and expand their mobility and activities within them. In so doing, enslaved people developed "alternative ways of knowing" and navigating these spaces.[5] This book examines such spaces of enslavement in Dutch New York. On the one hand, it looks at the ways in which Dutch Americans used their dominance over these spaces to control and surveil enslaved people. On the other hand, it shows the ways in which enslaved New Yorkers resisted such control. Not surprisingly, these spaces of enslavement meant significantly different things to the free and enslaved people who inhabited or frequented them.

The subject of slavery in Dutch New York has gained significant scholarly attention over the past few decades. Several studies have examined the particularities of slavery in seventeenth-century New Netherland—the Dutch colony in present-day New York, New Jersey, Delaware, and parts of Connecticut and Pennsylvania—where several enslaved Africans accessed the court, owned property, and even obtained (conditional) freedom. The subject of slavery and the Dutch Reformed Church has also received significant scholarly attention. Historians like Graham Russell Hodges and Patricia Bonomi have examined enslaved New Yorkers' participation in this denomination. Leslie Harris, Thelma Wills Foote, Craig Steven Wilder, Joyce Goodfriend, and Shane White, among others, have examined slavery and the lives of the enslaved in New York City, and in recent decades, a growing number of scholars, including A. J. Williams-Myers and Michael Groth, have investigated slavery in the Hudson Valley. These studies are part of growing scholarly and popular interest in the history of slavery in the northern colonies and states.[6]

Through the use of spatial analysis, this book adds a new perspective to the growing number of studies that examine slavery in New York. This book argues that sustaining a system of enslavement necessitates strategic spatial control. Thus, as reliance on enslaved labor expanded in the region, Dutch Americans increasingly used their dominance over spaces to control, contain, segregate, and monitor the men, women, and children they enslaved within them. In fact, it was in part due to an initial lack of such spatial control that enslaved men and women were able to access the courts, church, and public spaces during the Dutch colonial period.[7] Whereas the absence of spatial control in the seventeenth-century Dutch colony enabled enslaved people to expand their participation in the community and eventually challenge their enslavement, they no longer had such opportunities when Dutch American slaveholders developed various strategies to control, regulate, and segregate spaces. Indeed, as this study shows, such systems of spatial control and regulation, which were common in plantation societies, also existed in places like New York.

The Dutch West India Company first brought enslaved laborers to its North American colony New Netherland only a few years after the first Europeans settled there in 1624.[8] The company used the labor of these enslaved men and women to cultivate the land and build an infrastructure. During these early years of colonization, most enslaved people were considered company property, but as the colony and its European settler population expanded, more of these individuals purchased enslaved workers. Indeed, over the course of the seventeenth century, a growing number of individuals held people in bondage. This trend continued into the eighteenth century, long after the English takeover of the colony in 1664. In the region the English named New York, this expansion did not end until the late eighteenth century. With the advent of the state's first gradual abolition legislation that passed in 1799, slavery finally came to an end in 1827.[9]

During the two centuries of slavery in the region that would eventually become New York State, this system of human bondage affected every part of society. Enslaved people could be found in all parts of the region, and their labor was used for a wide variety of tasks. As Anne-Claire Merlin-Faucquez's research demonstrates, free New Yorkers from all ethnic backgrounds and socioeconomic ranks participated in and benefited from slavery.[10] Nevertheless, the larger implications of slavery in New York society have often been underestimated, in part because many free New Yorkers never enslaved people and slaveholding families commonly held fewer than five people in bondage. Even the more prosperous families rarely enslaved more than twenty people. Moreover, New York never had a Black majority or a successful plantation system that relied on the labor of enslaved men and women. But when considering the mechanisms necessary to hold people in bondage, it becomes clear that these nevertheless permeated every part of society.

This study began as an analysis of slavery in Dutch New York, an effort to uncover how slavery and the lives of the enslaved might have been different in these communities. Over time, however, it became increasingly clear that when it concerned the control of spaces to sustain or strengthen the system of slavery and limit resistance, New York's Dutch communities much resembled others. Sure, enslaved and free people in these communities often spoke the Dutch language, worshipped in Dutch Reformed churches, and ate Dutch American foods, but Dutch American enslavers' participation in human bondage, their slaveholding practices, justifications, and regulations were really not that different from enslavers elsewhere in the Americas. Similarly, the ways in which enslaved New Yorkers resisted their enslavement resembled resistance in other areas.[11]

This book focuses on the interactions between Dutch American slaveholders and enslaved New Yorkers, but of course not all Dutch Americans held people in bondage, and the social stratification of New York society proved more complex than a simple dichotomy of enslaved and enslaver. Poor and often indentured white men and women regularly lived in close proximity to enslaved people, and they interacted with each other in the region's streets, taverns, and marketplaces. Various scholars have researched these complex social dynamics in early American communities.[12] This study does not deny that these interactions occurred or that such social stratification existed but instead focuses on the relationships between enslavers and the people they enslaved, as well as the ways in which the system of slavery impacted society at large.

Slavery in Dutch New York

Research for this study centers on New York's Dutch communities. For the Dutch colonial period, this study draws on sources pertaining to the entire colony of New Netherland but with an emphasis on the town of New Amsterdam, the colony's main settlement in the most southern part of Manhattan. For the period from the English takeover of the region in 1664 to the abolition of slavery in the 1820s, research focuses on Kings, Ulster, and Albany Counties, which were largely Dutch American strongholds. When useful it includes evidence from other parts of the region, especially New York City.

This study identifies people as Dutch American if these European descendants were part of Dutch American communities, spoke the Dutch language, were members in the Dutch Reformed Church, or identified themselves as Dutch American. Many of these men and women descended from colonists who were ethnically Dutch, but some of their ancestors originated elsewhere in Europe and traveled to America by way of the Netherlands, or they became Dutch American through intermarriage. Consequently, this study recognizes Dutch American predominantly as a cultural identity.

Although the region first came under English control in 1664, Dutch American identity and culture survived for many generations. In some predominantly Dutch American communities, such as Kingston and Flatbush, Dutch Americans continued to speak the Dutch language until at least the early nineteenth century. Dutch Reformed churches generally held services in the Dutch language until they began to integrate English services in the late eighteenth century, and Dutch Americans took steps to ensure that their children could speak and read Dutch.[13] Of course, their culture was not static. Political, religious, social, and economic changes, such as the Revolution and Awakenings, significantly impacted Dutch American communities. Yet, their American identity did not replace their deep cultural Dutch roots.

The region's enslaved men, women, and children came from diverse backgrounds. The first generation of enslaved Africans who were brought to New Netherland predominantly originated in West Central Africa and parts of the Iberian Atlantic. They were what Ira Berlin called "Atlantic Creoles": they had a multicultural, creolized, and often cosmopolitan background.[14] From 1665 through 1775, more than seven thousand African captives disembarked in New York on board at least seventy-two ships, several of which were owned by Dutch descendants.[15] Many of these enslaved men, women, and children were forced to board these ships in Madagascar, the Gold Coast, and the Senegambia. In fact, from 1665 through 1704 all recorded ships that imported African captives into New York directly from Africa, carrying over one thousand men, women, and children, originated in Madagascar.[16] In the eighteenth century, at least seven slave ships transported more than five hundred enslaved people from the Gold Coast and more than seven ships brought over seven hundred captives from the Senegambia area. Importantly, these estimates provide very little information on the total number of enslaved men, women, and children who originated in these regions. For over half of the known ships that brought African captives to New York, no clear place of origin has been identified.[17]

In addition to the enslaved people who were shipped to New York directly from the African continent, many enslaved people arrived on board ships that originated elsewhere in the Americas.[18] Some of them would have been born in the Americas, while others would have been brought from Africa to New York via mainly English colonies in the Caribbean. From 1701 through 1770, over a third of all enslaved people who arrived in New York did so via the Caribbean.[19]

New York's enslaved population also included a significant number of Native Americans. In fact, frequent references to enslaved Native Americans in colonial legislation suggest that their enslavement was not uncommon in the region, even though a 1679 law prohibited the bondage of New York's indigenous populations and granted freedom to Native Americans who had been brought into the colony from other parts of the Americas after they had been there for six months.[20] Thus, New York's enslaved population consisted of an ethnically diverse mix of men, women, and children of African *and* Native American descent.

Spaces of Enslavement

As the words *slavery*, *bondage*, and *captivity* indicate, restricting people's mobility proves integral to enslavement. Historian Stephanie Camp rightly points out that in slavery, "space mattered: places, boundaries, and movement were central to how slavery was organized and to how it was resisted."[21] Thus, spatial analysis can be used to better understand how enslavers used space to control the people they enslaved, and it can reveal how enslaved people resisted in these spaces. In fact, spatial analysis has proven an especially useful method to reconstruct the histories of those people whose voices are rarely found in the archives. Their stories can emerge more clearly from an analysis of the spaces they inhabited.

In a 1967 lecture titled "Of Other Spaces: Utopias and Heterotopias," Foucault suggested that "the present epoch will perhaps be above all the epoch of space."[22] Indeed, since his now famous speech, spatial analysis has made a significant impact in various disciplines, including history. In fact, literary scholar Robert Tally noted in 2013 that "a recognizable *spatial turn* in literary and cultural studies (if not the arts and sciences more generally) has taken place."[23] This spatial turn has affected multiple disciplines and includes wide-ranging approaches of analyzing space or interactions within spaces, what Tally identifies as the "multilayered and interdisciplinary debates concerning space, place, and mapping."[24]

This spatial turn has been influenced greatly by the work of various twentieth-century scholars who explored the importance of spatial analysis in the humanities and social sciences. Henri Lefebvre introduced the concept of "social space." In his book *The Production of Space*, he argues that it is important to consider what occupies a space, because "space considered in isolation is an empty abstraction."[25] Michel Certeau explores the relationship between space and place in his now famous work *The Practice of Everyday Life* when he writes, "Space is a practiced place." As an example, he explains that the street, which is "geometrically defined by urban planning[,] is transformed into a space by walkers."[26] In other words, people give meaning to places and transform them from purely mathematical, natural, or physical into social spaces.

Many of these early theorists of space and spatial analysis explored the connections between power and space. Foucault identifies cartographies of power in which he examines how space and power intersect; in fact, Foucault suggests that consideration of space should be central to an analysis of power.[27] Similarly, Lefebvre argues that no space remains untouched by the "exercise of hegemony." Yet, although he acknowledges that space serves as a "means to control," such control is never complete.[28] Spatial analysis of slavery similarly reveals that control and power largely determined the ways in which enslaved and free people organized, navigated, and experienced these spaces.

Not surprisingly, historians of slavery have increasingly turned to spatial analysis. In fact, Foucault's writings on heterotopic spaces and the panopticon model of surveillance, first introduced by Jeremy Bentham, proved influential in slavery studies.[29] Over the past decades, developments in mapping, cartography, and Geographic Information System (GIS) have further encouraged research that looks at slavery from a spatial perspective. For instance, in her 2005 study of the 1741 New York City conspiracy, Jill Lepore uses GIS to map the city, its enslavers, their wealth, and where the fires that led to fears of an impending slave revolt occurred. In doing so, she succeeded in telling a more nuanced story of what happened during those months. More recently, Vincent Brown mapped the different stages of Tacky's 1760 revolt through which he was able to show "that the insurrection was in fact a well-planned affair that posed a genuine strategic threat" to the British.[30] In her study of unfree labor in New Orleans, Rashauna Johnson uses mapping to trace the cultural and social lives of enslaved New Orleanians.[31]

The fields of archeology, architectural history, and women and gender studies have played a similarly important role in advancing spatial analysis as a way to obtain new insights into the history of slavery in the Americas. In archeology, consideration of space and spatial organization naturally plays a role, and so it is not surprising that archeologists James Delle, Theresa Singleton, and Terence Epperson, among others, have used spatial analysis to interpret archeological findings. Through their analysis of artifacts, their placements, and plantation layouts, they have been able to provide important new perspectives of slavery and the lives of enslaved peoples.[32] Similarly, architectural historians like Dell Upton have used analysis of the built environment to gain a better understanding of the role architecture played in efforts to control enslaved people. Yet, some of the most innovative scholarship on slavery and space has been conducted by scholars in women and gender studies, a field that has long considered the important connections between gender and space. Katherine McKittrick, Marisa Fuentes, and Stephanie Camp have all used spatial analysis to reconstruct the histories of enslaved women.[33]

Several scholars have addressed shifting or conflicting meanings of certain spaces. Elizabeth Maddock Dillon demonstrates in her study of Olaudah Equiano's autobiography how the meaning of certain spaces changed depending on Equiano's circumstances. For instance, he considered the ship on which he was transported across the Atlantic as a young enslaved man as a "hollow place," a space of pain and suffering. Yet, when he later worked as a sailor, the ships he sailed on became spaces of meaning to him.[34] Ann Stoler's work further shows how people might experience the same spaces or interactions very differently. In her book *Carnal Knowledge and Imperial Power*, she demonstrates that Dutch colonists often remembered interactions with the Indonesian men and women who worked in their homes very differently from how these Indonesians remembered them: "Whereas the Dutch invocation of family ties conjured an enclosed realm of cozy intimacy, former servants who spoke of being treated like family evoked their stance of respectful fear and deference."[35] Enslaved men, women, and children in Dutch New York likely experienced such intimate interactions similarly dissimilar.

The painting of a Van Rensselaer child with an enslaved boy perfectly captures how enslaved and free Dutch Americans might have occupied the same spaces, yet their circumstances and thus experiences in them proved distinct (see Figure 0.2). The Van Rensselaer family had the artist, thought to be John Heaton, portray this member of their family with the intent to have his image saved for posterity. Thus, the young boy looks proud and prosperous, dressed in a high-quality and colorful dress. The color of his orange dress also appears in the sky, the mountain, and the sleeve of an enslaved boy who is placed behind him, as if to suggest that all of this belongs to him. The enslaved boy is wearing dark clothes and almost becomes invisible, like a shadow on a dark background. In fact, a shadow of the Van Rensselaer child on this boy signals that he stands in the shadow of this child. Clearly, the enslaved child is depicted here as a symbol of the Van Rensselaer family's wealth and status. Although these children are placed within the same space, it is evident that their roles and experiences there were vastly different.[36]

As the above discussion illustrates, spatial analysis encompasses a wide variety of methods and interpretations. For instance, archeologists will use the location of an artifact to help reconstruct its use and meaning, literary scholars might use narrative cartography in their analysis of a novel or autobiography, and anthropologists will consider what a space means to the people they study. Some of these methods are predominantly qualitative, whereas others are largely quantitative. The analysis in this book combines such qualitative methods to reconstruct the history of slavery and the lives of the enslaved in Dutch New York. This study uses analysis of the built environment to see how

FIGURE 0.2. *Child of the Van Rensselaer Family and Servant.* Attributed to John Heaton. Albany, NY, c. 1730. Current repository: Ms. and Mr. Rockefeller.

people related to these spaces and modified them, the location of places and people and how that influenced their experiences, and the meaning of spaces for the free and enslaved people who inhabited and frequented them.

The spatial analysis at the heart of this study shows the important ways in which control over or regulation of spaces changed over time. Whereas very little spatial regulation of enslaved people existed in the Dutch colony of New Netherland, such control in these spaces became increasingly important to sustaining slavery in the region now called New York. Because enslaved people in New Netherland encountered few restrictions on their access to, among others, the public space, church, and court, they were able to participate in these spaces in ways that would become increasingly challenging over the course of the long eighteenth century. A consideration of geography further shows that close proximity to the various institutions facilitated participation in these spaces in ways that were unattainable to enslaved men and women who lived in more remote parts of the colony. Because enslaved people had only limited mobility, space and geography mattered.

Such spatial analysis also demonstrates that enslaved people in these Dutch communities resisted their bondage daily. They circumvented systems of patrol and surveillance, and they regularly pushed the limits of their permitted mobility. They modified the spaces they inhabited, and they challenged restrictions on their religious and cultural practices. When keeping the spaces they inhabited and frequented in mind, it becomes evident that they created alternative ways of knowing and navigating these spaces. These enslaved men and women knew how to avoid being caught by watchmen who patrolled the streets, and they understood when and how they would be able to escape their enslaver's surveillance to participate in prohibited activities. Stephanie Camp has termed such resistance "rival geographies," alternative geographies created by enslaved people in which they resisted their enslavers' control over their movements and activities.[37]

This book centers on various spaces of enslavement in Dutch New York. The first two chapters focus on the Dutch colonial period. Chapter 1 explores the importance of enslaved laborers in Dutch efforts to settle the colonial space—the region they called New Netherland. Chapter 2 examines how some of the company's enslaved laborers took advantage of the lack of spatial control in the Dutch colony and their close proximity to each other and several important institutions. This chapter argues that because these enslaved men and women were able to access, among others, the court and church, they were able to advance their social standing.

Chapters 3 through 5 each analyze a separate space of enslavement during the long eighteenth century: the public space, the home, and the church. Chapter 3 shows that as slavery expanded in the eighteenth century, authorities increasingly restricted enslaved people's activities and movements in New York's public spaces. This chapter also explores how enslavers utilized the celebration of Pinkster, the Dutch version of Pentecost or Whitsuntide, to support the system of enslavement. Yet such control was never complete, and enslaved people developed endless ways to escape or circumvent it, thus creating geographies of resistance. Chapter 4 demonstrates that over the course of the eighteenth century, Dutch American architecture began to include a more intentional ordering of domestic spaces to house enslaved men, women, and children and their labor in these homes. It further investigates the rival geographies enslaved people created in these spaces, and it explores the dual nature of these homes, as these buildings had very different meanings to their free and enslaved inhabitants. Chapter 5 turns to the region's Dutch Reformed churches. It shows that these churches and membership in them became tools of enforcing social power in these communities, which proved crucial in sustaining slavery. This chapter also demonstrates that enslaved people created alternative ways to continue religious worship when excluded from or segregated within these churches.

In all, this study shows how considerations of geography and space can contribute to our understanding of slavery. Such analysis requires an interdisciplinary approach, but this work also relies on a wide array of archival sources, from account books to church records, located in multiple archives across the United States and The Netherlands. Importantly, however, these archives rarely hold records that were produced by the enslaved people themselves.[38] Consequently, historians who rely on the archives often struggle to piece together the history of slavery and the lives of enslaved women, children, and men. Through its interdisciplinary approach and spatial analysis, this book is able to tell a more complex history of enslavement in Dutch New York.

CHAPTER 1

Enslaved Labor and the Settling of New Netherland

On January 24, 1641, Manuel de Gerrit de Reus awaited execution for killing Jan Premero. At the time, both men were enslaved by the Dutch West India Company in New Netherland. Although de Reus and eight other enslaved men—Cleijn Antonij, Paulo d'Angola, Gracia d'Angola, Jan de Fort Orange, Antonij Portugies, Manuel Minuit, Simon Conge, and Groot Manuel—had confessed to the murder, de Reus drew the lot that determined he should be the one to be punished for the crime.[1] Several New Amsterdam settlers gathered on this cold January day to witness his hanging, but when his body fell both nooses around his neck broke and he miraculously survived. The amazed spectators now pleaded with the colony's council to pardon de Reus, arguing that this turn of events was evidence of divine intervention. The council agreed to spare his life, but its objectives for doing so probably originated in more pragmatic concerns: pardoning de Reus and his accomplices saved the company from losing several of its most valuable laborers.[2]

These men belonged to a small group of enslaved men and women who were considered particularly important to the colony. Brought to the region only a few years after the first Europeans settled in the area in 1624, they had contributed to its development during the early years of Dutch colonization. They were Christians who attended Dutch Reformed Church services, and the company considered them "loyal servants."[3] Even though New Netherland did not develop a successful cash crop economy that relied on enslaved labor, the presence of enslaved workers nevertheless played a crucial role in developing the colony. Enslaved workers helped build infrastructure, including the fort, roads, and palisades of its main settlement, New Amsterdam. They also cultivated the land, thus providing the company with much-needed provisions, and at times they took up arms to help protect the colony. Indeed, the company used them to help populate the colonial space at a time when it struggled to attract Dutch settlers.[4]

Thus the significance of the colony's enslaved people like Manuel de Gerrit de Reus extended far beyond their actual labor: the company used the promise of enslaved laborers to attract potential European settlers, and, more importantly, enslaved Africans helped populate the area and keep it in firm control of the Dutch. The company understood that it needed a settler population to claim the region—the colonized space—that would become New Netherland, and following the example of the Dutch East India Company (VOC), the West India Company (WIC) that controlled New Netherland imported enslaved peoples to help do so. Not surprisingly, then, the company would have welcomed the chance to spare the life of one—or several—of these enslaved men.[5]

Historians have often underestimated the enslaved laborers' importance to the WIC in New Netherland, in large part because their significance did not originate solely in the work they produced.[6] This chapter argues that enslaved men and women proved crucial to the company's colonial project in New Netherland, because their presence and contributions were instrumental in company efforts to claim this space for the Dutch. It examines enslaved Africans' significance in the settling of New Netherland, discusses their contributions to the colony's development, and shows how the company implemented hierarchies of enslavement to enforce their cooperation in Dutch colonial development.

Only three years after having confessed to killing a fellow enslaved man, several of the men, including De Reus, obtained a conditional freedom often referred to as half-freedom.[7] At first glance, it may appear odd or unusual that these men, who escaped execution only a few years prior, were able to obtain such a half-free status. A closer look at these men and what they meant to the company shows that the company did not need them to remain in bondage; in fact, they may have been able to obtain this conditional freedom because the company believed such a status would help them control the colony's enslaved population more effectively. Using enslaved people to settle new territories, as the company did in New Netherland, came accompanied with significant risks, which the company may have tried to mitigate by developing a mechanism of control and regulation through hierarchies of enslavement: enslaved men and women who served the company loyally had an opportunity to obtain a conditional freedom, whereas those who resisted their bondage risked a life in bondage and possible chain labor. With these various degrees of unfreedom, the company tried to force a certain degree of loyalty from the people it held in bondage, a loyalty necessary when partly relying on enslaved people to claim the colonial space.

Claiming Space

Dutch colonization in New Netherland and the significance of enslaved laborers in doing so can best be understood when placed solidly within the context of global Dutch expansion in the seventeenth century. The West India Company in North America did not operate in a vacuum. Instead, seemingly local decisions often proved reflective of more global trends. During the seventeenth century, both the Dutch West India Company and the Dutch East India Company conquered and settled various territories in the Atlantic and Indian Ocean regions. Although they were separate companies that operated in different parts of the world, their main objectives and tactics were often very similar.[8]

The WIC and VOC are frequently described as either militaristic machines or mercantile companies. Yet, acquiring territory proved a crucial element of the companies' military and economic success. Thus, the companies, whether it was the VOC or WIC, developed various systems to claim colonial spaces.[9] As Gerrit Knaap points out, how one perceived the Dutch East India Company's main objectives depended largely on where one was located. In the Dutch Republic, the VOC may have appeared a predominantly commercial enterprise, but when observing the company from Ambon, Indonesia, it clearly functioned as a political authority.[10] Similarly, whereas people in the Dutch Republic may have considered the West India Company's objectives in New Netherland primarily commercial, the Munsee who lived on Manhattan prior to Dutch colonization would undoubtedly have disagreed.

Indeed, claiming territory or colonial space became a central element of these companies' missions, and they developed various approaches to do so effectively. Among others, the companies used legal claims to assume colonial space. The Dutch, who only recently had been able to free themselves from the yoke of Habsburg oppression, often portrayed America's indigenous populations as "natural allies" in their continuous fight against their Spanish foes.[11] Thus, instead of using violence at the offset, the Dutch West India Company in North America used Dutch law to negotiate what it claimed were legal purchases of indigenous peoples' lands. However, these indigenous peoples did not see these agreements as transfers of territory but rather as permissions for the Dutch to access the land. As Erin Kramer explains, New Netherland's indigenous populations continued to farm and hunt on the land the Dutch now claimed was theirs.[12]

In addition to such supposed legal claims, the Dutch asserted their control over newly conquered territory through modifications of the natural and built environment. In the VOC's Cape Town settlement, for instance, the company's garden worked by enslaved people served as "a more direct claiming of the landscape."[13] In places like Batavia in Indonesia and New Amsterdam in North America, Dutch-style vernacular architecture and city planning, including canals, not only helped make these settlements feel and look Dutch, they also proved a powerful tool of asserting Dutch control over these foreign spaces.[14]

Importantly, the companies understood it was necessary to have a supportive population to firmly maintain Dutch control in foreign territory. While the WIC's charter stated in its preamble that the company's primary objective was advancing trade, the charter's second article reveals the importance of settler populations in doing so when it detailed that the company "must advance the peopling of those fruitful and unsettled parts."[15] Of course, these territories were not really "unsettled." Instead, the East and West India Companies regularly displaced, massacred, or oppressed indigenous populations. In the Banda Islands, for instance, the VOC had the majority of its original inhabitants slaughtered, starved, and deported.[16] A massacre at that scale did not happen in New Netherland, but WIC officials certainly did not hesitate to kill, enslave, or displace the region's indigenous populations when deemed necessary. When the Munsee of Manhattan and surrounding regions continued to use land the Dutch claimed to own, relationships between them and the Dutch quickly escalated. The company considered itself the rightful owner of the land, and thus demanded tribute and attacked the Munsee, destroying entire villages, when they did not respect Dutch claims to the land.[17]

The WIC and VOC explored various avenues to establish settler populations in these spaces to help keep them in firm control of the Dutch.[18] Although the companies promoted their overseas colonies, they generally struggled to motivate Dutch migration to these faraway places. Thus, both the WIC and the VOC developed wide-ranging tactics to attract and maintain settlers.[19] For instance, as Deborah Hamer and Leonard Blussé show, the VOC in Batavia encouraged marriages with indigenous women as a way to tie VOC soldiers and *freeburghers* to the region.[20] The companies also relied on non-Dutch European populations to claim these colonial spaces. Alison Games explains that the Dutch often practiced "cohabitation," in which they let conquered European colonists stay in a now Dutch colony, in part to ensure control over the colonial space.[21] Such was the case in Suriname and Brazil, where the WIC allowed English and Portuguese settlers to stay after these colonies had come under Dutch control. At times, the companies also accepted non-Dutch European settlers to come into their colonies and establish settlements to help with colonization.[22] In New Netherland, for instance, company officials allowed some English settlements even when they worried these colonists might challenge Dutch sovereignty in the region.[23]

When it proved too challenging or costly to attract or retain European settlers, the companies looked to non-European populations. In Batavia, Amboina, and Taiwan, the VOC relied in part on Chinese immigrants.[24] The VOC used various tactics to attract these migrants to the Dutch colonies, promising Chinese migrants who came to Taiwan land and tax exemptions. Consequently, Chinese migration to Taiwan became so substantial that according to historian Tonio Andrade this Dutch colony essentially became "a Chinese colony under Dutch rule."[25]

The companies also used forced migration to supplement free settler populations. In fact, as Pepijn Brandon and Karwan Fatah-Black point out, the Dutch "came to appreciate the enslavement of non-Europeans on a more systematic basis as a way to build their empire."[26] Already in 1623, Jan Pieterszoon Coen wrote, "There is nothing, I say again, that will do the Company more service and profit than the purchase of a large number of slaves."[27] Increasingly, East India Company officials like Coen considered slavery an effective method to populate their colonies.[28] Thus, after Dutch officials had rid the Banda Islands of their original inhabitants, it largely replaced them with enslaved laborers.[29] In Batavia, the VOC imported large numbers of enslaved people from, among others, Coromandel.[30] Consequently, as Remco Raben explains, the enslaved population in VOC-controlled cities like Batavia quickly reached 50 percent.[31]

Both the Dutch East India and West India Companies applied various strategies to secure their claims of colonial spaces. But laying claim of foreign territory effectively required a settler population, and both the WIC and VOC often struggled to motivate Dutch migration to these places. The VOC began using enslaved people to settle conquered territory in the early seventeenth century. Not surprisingly, when the West India Company could not attract enough European colonists to its North American colony of New Netherland, it similarly relied on enslaved people to help claim this space for the company.

Populating New Netherland

Disregarding the indigenous populations, the Dutch often described New Netherland as empty space that needed to be populated. Nicolaes van Wassenaer, for instance, wrote in his *Historisch Verhael* that the region's land "could not be properly cultivated in consequence of the scantiness of the population."[32] The company needed people to populate the land, but due to the relative prosperity of the Dutch Republic, the hazardous journey to unknown frontier lands did not appeal to many Dutch men and women.[33] Thus, the company sought various ways to populate the land with settler populations. Following the examples of the VOC and the Portuguese before them, the WIC considered importing enslaved Africans to help settle the colony.[34]

To attract settlers to New Netherland, the company laid out a plan for colonization in the "Charter of Freedoms and Exemptions," ratified by the States General in 1629. The company offered patroonships to investors who would send fifty adults to their estates within the first four years of settlement.[35] However, except for Rensselaerswijck, these patroonships largely turned out to be failures, and by 1639 only about six hundred Europeans had settled in New Netherland.[36] In an effort to further encourage migration, the company offered benefits to immigrants such as the right to participate in the fur trade. It also opened up the region to English migrants from Rhode Island and New Haven to further boost the population. Because immigration remained low by 1644, the States General—the Dutch Republic's governing body—proposed that the transatlantic journey to New Netherland should be made more affordable to colonists, and it suggested that a significant number of farmhands and slaves should be transported to the colony to help develop the region's agriculture.[37]

When Dutch servants did agree to travel to the colony, they often did not stay permanently, and some of them did not even complete their contract.[38] Colonist Thomas Chambers of Rensselaerswijck, for instance, complained in 1651 that his servant Adriaen van Bil refused "to serve out his term and wastes and neglects his time, claiming to be free."[39] Jacob Bouwensen had traveled to the colony as a servant of Johannes Winckelman, but once in New Netherland, Bouwensen breached this agreement when he contracted his labor to someone else.[40] Three company servants—Jan Claesz from Bellekum (ship carpenter), Bastiaen Symonsz Root (sailmaker), and Meyndert Gerritsz (house carpenter)—fled the colony in 1647. They made it to New Haven, where, to the company's dismay, English authorities protected them.[41] And they were not the only servants who ran away. The frequency with which indentured servants fled their masters during the Dutch colonial period led the council in

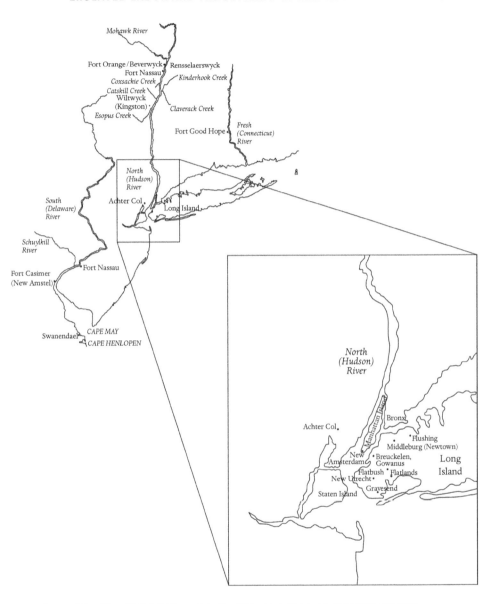

FIGURE 1.1.   Map of Dutch Settlements in New Netherland. Drawing by Jeroen van den Hurk.

1640 to forbid anyone to harbor, feed, or assist these runaway servants in any way, because, the company claimed, their frequent escapes caused unharvested foods to spoil in the fields.[42]

Immigration finally increased more significantly in the 1650s when economic prosperity in the Dutch Republic declined, making migration to New

Netherland more appealing.[43] At the same time, the colony received several settlers from Dutch Brazil after the Dutch lost control over this South American colony in 1654.[44] Consequently, by 1655 the colony's European population reached about 3,500 people.[45] European migration continued to increase during the last fifteen years of the Dutch colonial period, bringing New Netherland's European population to somewhere between seven and eight thousand people in 1664.[46]

To supplement the colony's population and further promote Dutch immigration, the company and the States General facilitated and at times requested the importation of enslaved Africans into New Netherland.[47] They promised to provide the patroonships with twelve enslaved men and women for the advancement of the colony.[48] These enslaved laborers could attract potential colonists, and they would help cultivate the land.[49] A 1644 company report suggested that it would be beneficial to bring enslaved laborers from Dutch Brazil to New Netherland because this would be less expensive than attracting Dutch farm workers who, according to the report, could only be persuaded to leave the Dutch Republic for a lot of "money and promises."[50] On several occasions, the directors of the company emphasized that enslaved workers were sent to New Netherland for agricultural purposes, and for that reason they were not to be sold outside of the colony.[51] When in 1653 Juan Dillian of Curaçao requested permission to bring African captives to Curaçao instead of New Netherland, the colonial council denied this request, explaining in a letter to Lucas Rodenburch, vice director at Curaçao, that "the company would much rather see the population promoted first in New Netherland. For which reason all servants are to be kept there as much as possible, and must not be sent out of the country."[52] For the same reason, the company directors promised to send enslaved laborers to the colony in 1659, but only under the condition that they would be used to cultivate the land instead of being transported elsewhere.[53]

Even as late as 1664, by which time the colony's European population had grown significantly, the company directors again instructed Director General Petrus Stuyvesant that the enslaved Africans who arrived in New Netherland on board the ship *Gideon* should not be taken outside of the colony.[54] Initial correspondence between the company and Stuyvesant stipulated that the *Gideon* would transport three hundred African captives to the colony, a third of whom were supposed to help cultivate the land of the New Amstel—or Nieuwer-Amstel—colony, a territory by the Delaware River that previously was under Swedish control and now belonged to the city of Amsterdam. Thus, the city of Amsterdam also recognized that enslaved Africans could help settle and develop its colony.[55]

It should not be surprising that the West India Company, or the city of Amsterdam, would look toward importing enslaved Africans to help settle the region they called New Netherland. The VOC was doing so successfully in its colonies, so surely it could work elsewhere. Although the number of enslaved people in New Netherland never reached the percentage of enslaved inhabitants it did in places like Batavia and Amboina, they certainly played an important role in West India Company efforts to claim this space for the Dutch.

Slave Trade

The demand for enslaved people promoted a steady importation of African captives into the colony. Generally these enslaved men, women, and children were brought into New Netherland in relatively small groups through intercolonial trade, as was the case in most seventeenth-century North American colonies.[56] Sometimes they had been captured from Portuguese or Spanish ships by privateers or pirates who then brought them to New Netherland. Geurt Tijsen, for instance, was accused of selling African captives in New Netherland whom he had taken from a Spanish ship.[57] Indeed, Johannes de Laet estimated that by 1636 the West India Company had captured as many as 2,356 African captives on board Spanish ships.[58] Only two Dutch slavers transported more than 200 African captives to the colony: 't Witte Paert in 1655 and Gideon in 1664.

The WIC largely controlled the slave trade with New Netherland, but by the 1640s growing demand for enslaved laborers among Dutch settlers led a group of New Netherlanders to request permission to import African captives themselves. By 1652, the company directors in Amsterdam decided to allow such imports by individual settlers as long as they abided by certain regulations. In the end, however, no settler-sponsored transatlantic slave trade journeys occurred during the Dutch colonial period. Dutch merchants did fund the journey of 't Witte Paert in 1654–55, but to the company's dismay, most of the African captives who arrived in New Netherland on board this ship were transported to the English colonies in the Chesapeake. To discourage such exportation of enslaved laborers, the company determined that a duty should be paid for enslaved laborers who were transported out of the colony.[59]

As more individuals in New Netherland began to rely on enslaved labor, a local slave trade emerged. Individual slaveholders bought and sold enslaved workers in private agreements or at public sales. In March of 1656, for instance, Maria Verleth sold enslaved women at a public auction in New Amsterdam.[60] The company also sold enslaved men, women, and children at public sales.

One of these auctions took place in New Amsterdam in May of 1664 when the company sold thirty enslaved men, women, and children. At this public sale, William Maerschalck, Adriaen Vincent, Nicolas Verleth, and Jacob Leisler or Leyseler, who would later lead the now famous Leisler's Rebellion, purchased enslaved people from the company. In a letter to Vice Director Beck, Director General Petrus Stuyvesant boasted that some of these people were sold for as much as 600 guilders.[61]

At times, the company sold enslaved people in return for much-needed provisions. In 1664, for instance, the company bought meat and bacon "to be paid with negroes."[62] When the company received a number of enslaved laborers from Curaçao that same year, it sold the weakest among them at auction to the highest bidder in return for food provisions.[63] Although these auctions usually occurred in New Amsterdam, at least one public sale took place in Beverwijck (now Albany) in 1659 when three men and one woman, all of whom were enslaved by Cornelis Martensen Potter, were auctioned.[64] Settlers who purchased these enslaved Africans brought them to their homes or farms, thus dispersing them across New Netherland and sometimes beyond the Dutch colony.[65]

The enslaved men, women, and children who were brought to New Netherland came from various African, European, and American regions. Most of them arrived from West Central Africa where Dutch merchants had established important trade relations.[66] Temporary Dutch control of Luanda in present-day Angola from 1641 to 1648 further promoted Dutch trade with this West Central African region. Enslaved Africans who had been captured from Portuguese ships by Dutch or French privateers also often originated in West Central Africa, which further solidified their predominance among New Netherland's enslaved population. Other areas that supplied captives to Dutch slavers included the Senegambia, the Gold Coast, and the Slave Coast. Especially in the second half of the seventeenth century, enslaved men, women, and children from these West African areas became more numerous in the Dutch colony.

Most enslaved laborers who were brought to New Netherland had experienced the traumatizing Middle Passage from Africa to the Americas at some point during their journey to the Dutch colony. Dutch slave ships traveled from various African locations to Brazil (under Dutch control from 1630 to 1654) or the Dutch Caribbean and Curaçao, which would become a Dutch slave depot in 1659, in particular.[67] At least 13 percent of the African captives transported on board these seventeenth-century Dutch slave ships did not survive the infamous Middle Passage.[68] In addition to the poor conditions on board these ships, including a lack of food, crowded spaces, and unhygienic conditions, slave ships could fall victim to privateers, pirates, or natural disasters. Moreover, their horrific circumstances brought some enslaved people to take their own life when they had the rare opportunity to do so.[69] Thus, the transatlantic and intercolonial slave trade that transported enslaved men, women, and children to New Netherland so that the company could claim this space more effectively came at a very high cost of human life.

Enslaved Labor

Enslaved men and women were more than just additional bodies that populated the colonial space. The challenge to attract free Dutch colonists and reliable Dutch servants made the labor of enslaved Africans all the more important. The men and women enslaved by the company helped build the colony's infrastructure and fortifications, such as Fort Amsterdam, clear the land, develop its agriculture, and tend to the livestock.[70] During times of war, enslaved men were often armed to help defend the colony.[71] For instance, when the Dutch fought the area's Munsee during Kieft's War (1643–1645), armed enslaved men helped secure Dutch settlements. During these years of warfare, Willem Kieft guaranteed Cornelis van der Hoykens, the colony's *fiscael* (a local official responsible for upholding of company rights), that all of the company's enslaved laborers would be at his command.[72] Not only did enslaved workers complete crucial parts of the colony's infrastructure, they were tasked with work that European settlers would rather avoid because they were either physically taxing or considered demeaning.[73]

Because the company mainly employed enslaved laborers in physically strenuous labor, it preferred strong, young men. In 1657, the company advised Stuyvesant to teach its enslaved workers certain trades, such as carpentry, brickmaking, and coopering, as had been common practice in, for instance, Brazil, but Stuyvesant responded that these men would not be capable of learning such trades.[74] Two years later, when Stuyvesant requested that eighteen to twenty enslaved men be sent to New Netherland from Curaçao, he stressed that they should be "stronger and more masculine" than the few they had previously received, suggesting that these enslaved workers were predominantly used for strenuous physical labor.[75]

Enslaved men who worked in chains likely produced some of the most physically tasking labor, such as the digging of canals. Their circumstances were so severe that working alongside them became a form of punishment in the colony. The first time the colonial council sentenced someone to work along company slaves was in 1639 when Gysbert Cornelissen received this sentence for public disturbance and hurting a soldier.[76] In 1642, this punishment made its way into the colony's ordinances when the council decreed that those who were found guilty of certain crimes, including murder and desertion, should be sentenced to "work with the negroes in the chain" ("*in de ketting gaan*").[77] Since then, several men received this punishment. In 1654, for instance, the court sentenced Elias Emmens to work with the company slaves for one year, and four years later, in 1658, the council sentenced Nicolaes Albertsen to have his head shaved, receive a public flogging, have his ear pierced, and work with the company slaves for two years.[78] Albertsen was among several men who were sentenced to work with the company slaves that year.[79]

The records do not reveal how common this practice was in New Netherland or which enslaved people were subjected to labor in chains. In some VOC colonies, such *kettinggangers* (chain laborers) were a special class of enslaved people, generally war prisoners or enslaved men who were put in chains for disciplinary purposes.[80] In fact, individual enslavers could request the VOC to place enslaved men in chains temporarily. These *kettinggangers* were doing the most physically challenging labor, and they often slept in guarded barracks that were locked at night. Although the New Netherland records provide little insight into the conditions of *kettinggangers* in this colony, it likely resembled the practice in the VOC colonies.

The company also used enslaved laborers to assist local officials and complete tasks that the European settlers resisted doing. Among others, the company assigned enslaved men to apprehend and return runaway servants and slaves. In 1654, for example, the colony's council sent enslaved men to Long Island "to attack and return some escaped servants and runaway negroes."[81] In Beverwijck, the *schout*—a local official responsible for law enforcement—often received the assistance from one or more company slaves in tending the guardhouse fire or to act as jailer.[82] Enslaved men often served as public executioners, a job that the Dutch especially loathed: Jan "the Negro," for instance, had been hired to execute Wolf Nijssen, and the council identified the executioner responsible for Manuel de Gerrit de Reus's hanging as a Black man.[83] The company also considered employing one of the enslaved men to oversee others when the directors of the company advised Petrus Stuyvesant in 1663 that "one of the oldest and most competent slaves" could serve as overseer for the company's remaining seven or eight enslaved laborers in New Amsterdam. They suggested that an enslaved man could be persuaded to take on this job if he would be promised his freedom in return.[84]

When the company was not using their labor, it sold enslaved workers or hired them out to individual settlers or colonial authorities. Settlers could lease enslaved laborers or complete farms or boweries called *bouwerijen* from the

WIC; in so doing, the company avoided having to provide for its enslaved workers at times when it did not need their labor.[85] In 1644, for instance, the company hired Maria, daughter of Groot Manuel, out to Nicolaes Coorn for four consecutive years. During that time, Coorn had to provide her with food and clothing.[86] In November of 1661, the city of New Amsterdam requested "four capable [*bequame*]" enslaved men, and a month later the council provided the city with three laborers under the condition that the burgomaster, or mayor, feed and clothe them.[87] Such practices became so common that at one point the company could not find enough enslaved workers when it needed them because these laborers had been rented out to others. On December 19, 1656, for instance, the company directors wrote to the director general and council that they "were surprised to learn that altogether too many of these Negroes are employed in private service."[88] In 1658, Jacques Corteljou resisted orders to return an enslaved man he had hired from the company because he relied on the man's labor.[89] Evidently, some of these settlers became significantly dependent on the labor of enslaved workers.

Not surprisingly, an increasing number of individuals purchased enslaved laborers, whose labor they used for a wide variety of tasks. Most of these enslavers lived in New Amsterdam and its surroundings.[90] Some enslaved Africans tended to these settlers' farms, while others worked on docks, in domestics, in lumber, or they assisted artisans in the workplace. During the 1650s, shipmaster Egbert Van Borsum required an enslaved man to assist him with the ferry, and Pieter Taelman had two enslaved men labor on his tobacco plantation.[91] Settlers also used enslaved workers to run errands for them, as did Cornelis Van Ruyven, who had an enslaved man carry supplies from Manhattan to his wife in Midwout, Long Island.[92] In rare cases, individual enslavers tasked enslaved laborers with the capture and return of servants or enslaved laborers who fled. Jan Janzen van St. Obin, for instance, ordered one of his enslaved workers to return a runaway servant in September of 1659.[93]

Although enslaved Africans often performed physically taxing work, some of them had specialized skills that proved especially valuable to free settlers. Correspondence between Jan Baptist van Rensselaer and his brother Jeremias van Rensselaer, for instance, showed that Jan's enslaved laborer Andries was a skilled horse trainer. Initially, when Jan Baptist returned to *patria*, he asked his brother to sell all his belongings, including Andries. Soon after, however, Jan Baptist sent another letter to his brother requesting that he "please send him [Andries] over in the first ship and contract for his passage at the lowest price possible. I need him very much at Cralo [the family estate in the Dutch Republic] to take care of my horse." Toward the end of the letter, Jan Baptist once again urged his brother to "not forget to send the Negro." Not surprisingly, he expressed great disappointment when Andries did not arrive in the Netherlands "as everything was ready for his arrival."[94] Before Jeremias had received Jan Baptist's request to send Andries, Jeremias had boasted in a letter to his brother that Andries had "taken care of the horses and has done it so well that during my time the horses have never looked so fine."[95] Not surprisingly, then, Jeremias refused his brother's request for Andries, claiming "it would be nothing but foolishness to try to have him serve in a free country, as he would be too proud to do that." While Jeremias's praise of Andries dissipated now that the possibility of losing him loomed, he acknowledged his interest in keeping Andries, stating that he "could not spare him very well."[96]

Andries had likely learned how to care for horses in his African homeland. Van Rensselaer's description of Andries as a proud, "tall and quick fellow" suggests that he may have been of Senegambian descent, since he used adjectives Europeans often used to describe Senegambians. The Jolof kingdom had a well-trained, highly skilled cavalry, and horses in this area required special care to survive the region's climate.[97] Whether or not Andries had learned to train horses in Africa or the Americas, he was among the enslaved Africans whose specialized skills were considered especially valuable in New Netherland.

Enslaved men and women proved essential to the colony's development not only because their mere presence helped claim this space for the Dutch. They were at times armed to protect the colony, helped build public works and infrastructure, and cultivated the land, providing the company and free colonists with much-needed labor and provisions. Not surprisingly, an increasing number of individual settlers in the region relied on enslaved laborers. In all these capacities, these enslaved women, men, and children proved crucial in Dutch efforts to solidify their control over the region.

Hierarchies of Enslavement

On February 25, 1644, only three years after he survived his hanging, Manuel de Gerrit de Reus, together with ten fellow company slaves—Paulo Angola, Groot Manuel, Cleijn Manuel, Simon Congo, Antonij Portugies, Gracia, Piter Santomee, Jan Francisco, Cleijn Antonij, and Jan Fort Orange—obtained a conditional freedom that also became known as half-freedom. These men and their wives received their freedom under the condition that they pay yearly fees of "30 *schepel* [a Dutch measuring unit equal to about ¾ bushel] of maize it be wheat, peas or beans, and a fat hog," render their services available to the company whenever it needed them, and their children—including those who were not yet born—would remain at the service of the company as "*lijff eigenen*."[98]

The council proclaimed that if they abided by these conditions, the men and their wives would be "free and at liberty just as other free people here in New Netherland."[99] Indeed, free settlers in the Dutch colony also had to provide their assistance to the company when requested and pay yearly fees for their land. Yet, what clearly distinguished these half-free men and women from free settlers was the fact that their children remained company property.[100]

These men and women were not the only ones to receive such a conditional freedom from the company; in fact, at least forty enslaved men and women would be manumitted conditionally during the Dutch colonial period, although the conditions of their freedom often differed. In 1662, for instance, the company granted freedom to three women under the condition that every week they return to do domestic work at the director general's house. The company also granted freedom to several of the men it enslaved in December of 1663, but it required that they monthly return to labor for the company.[101] Some colonists followed the company's example: Philip Jansz Ringo, for instance, granted freedom to Manuel de Hispanien for an annual fee of one hundred guilders to be paid for over the course of three consecutive years.[102] Ringo stipulated that he would have the right to reenslave De Hispanien if he did not abide by these terms.

These conditional freedoms have received ample attention from scholars. Some historians have argued that these men and women received half-freedom because they were old and thus they were no longer useful to the company.[103] Others have suggested that granting conditional freedom to several of its enslaved laborers proves that slavery in New Netherland was of a milder form.[104] Such suggestions have contributed to the widely influential view that slavery in New Netherland was different from slavery elsewhere, that it resembled indentured servitude, and that it was not very important to the development of the colony. Close examination shows, however, that providing a conditional freedom was a logical and rather pragmatic step for the company; in fact, it demonstrates these enslaved laborers' continued importance to the colony's development. Half-freedom proved an opportunity for enslaved people who served the company loyally to obtain a conditional freedom. But what happened to enslaved men and women who were not considered loyal servants? Certainly, they forfeited their chances of such a freedom, and they may even have been condemned to working in the chains as *kettinggangers*. Thus, with these various degrees of enslavement, the company tried to force a certain degree of loyalty from the people it held in bondage, necessary when partly relying on enslaved people to maintain control over the colonial space.

With half-freedom, the WIC created an in-between status: the conditionally freed men and women were neither enslaved nor free, and their fate still depended on the goodwill of the company. Whatever the conditions of their freedom were, these freed people continued to have varying obligations to their former enslaver, in this case the WIC. For the company, the most significant benefits of such manumissions were threefold: (1) it would still have access to their labor when it needed it, (2) the freedmen and women continued to cultivate the land and help keep this area in firm control of the Dutch, and (3) such conditional manumissions created a hierarchy of enslavement, which the company used to force loyalty from the men and women it held in bondage.

The freedmen were still required to help the company whenever it needed them, a common practice in the colony where men generally could be called upon by authorities for assistance. In May of 1653, for instance, company officials requested that all healthy men, including the freedmen, help fortify New Amsterdam.[105] Moreover, by demanding yearly dues from the freedmen, the company ensured that these men would cultivate the land they received and share part of their harvest with the company. In so doing, the company continued to reap the benefits of their labor. Moreover, by giving them land in Manhattan and by keeping their children in bondage, the company effectively tied these families to the region, which meant they would still contribute to Dutch colonial efforts. Although the company may not have used these children's labor, these children were still considered company property, and several families would eventually petition the company for the children's freedom.[106]

Importantly, granting such a conditional freedom was not exclusive to this Dutch colony, nor was it unprecedented or uncommon. In both the Greek and Roman worlds, they had a specific term to refer to such freedmen and freedwomen: the *apeleutheroi* in ancient Greece and the *paranomê* in the Roman Empire. Like the half-free people in New Netherland, these freedmen and freedwomen became a distinct class of people who had obtained a conditional freedom but who were still obligated to their former enslavers.[107] In fifteenth- and sixteenth-century Spain, freedwomen and freedmen were similarly obliged to pay respect to their former masters by assisting them when necessary. Failure to do so could result in reenslavement.[108] A similar conditional freedom could also be found in Dutch East India Company territories. In Batavia, for instance, freed people continued to have certain responsibilities to their former enslavers.[109] Often, these societies used such opportunities to obtaining a conditional freedom to strengthen a system of enslavement.[110]

That the West India Company would follow these examples should not be surprising. Dutch-Roman law often used Roman legal examples to help sort out new legislative circumstances. At its core, New Netherland's judicial system rooted in Dutch-Roman law, which combined Roman law with elements of Germanic customary law.[111] In addition to consulting Roman legal examples, East and West India Company officials also tended to model colonial practices on those of the Portuguese and Spanish who had come before them.[112]

Like De Reus, several enslaved people found ways to improve their circumstances in the Dutch colony. It is important to acknowledge, however, that most of New Netherland's enslaved people never obtained conditional or complete freedom.[113] The majority of enslaved men and women lived in bondage until they died. Amplification of the half-free status has obscured their experiences. Using enslaved laborers to help claim the colonial space was not without risk. Why would enslaved men and women support and even help protect their enslavers? The company may have created a hierarchy of enslavement to help sustain such a system of bondage and colonization. It is likely that the company used the threat of chained labor to discourage resistance from the men and women it enslaved in the same way that it used half-freedom as a reward for so-called loyal service.

At the time of the botched hanging, Manuel de Gerrit de Reus had been enslaved by the company for at least fifteen years.[114] During those years, he became an active participant in the Dutch Reformed Church, and he had used the colony's judicial system successfully to obtain unpaid wages. Only three years after he miraculously escaped execution, he and ten fellow enslaved men, several of whom had confessed to killing Jan Premero, obtained a conditional freedom that came to be known as half-freedom.[115] According to the council minutes, the company granted them this conditional freedom because they were Christians, had been loyal to the company, and had long been promised their freedom.

Why did De Reus and his accomplices escape execution? And why were they able to obtain a conditional freedom only a few years after they had killed another enslaved man who was considered company property? De Reus and the many other enslaved Africans who toiled for the Dutch West India Company and individual colonists proved integral to the colony's survival. Not only did they complete a large part of the necessary labor, but they also settled the land, helped protect the colony, and could be used to attract Dutch settlers. Thus, the company used these enslaved men, women, and children to effectively claim the colonial space they called New Netherland when they failed to attract enough Europeans to do so.

But using an enslaved population for such colonial purposes was not without risk. The company needed a system that would keep these enslaved people from undermining the company's colonial aspirations, and it looks like the company developed a hierarchy of enslavement to do so. The company provided a select group of enslaved people with conditional freedom and plots of land, ensuring that these African descendants cultivated and populated New Amsterdam's land while also serving the company in times of need. At the same time, other enslaved men were forced to work in chains, forced to do some of the most physically tasking labor. Such a hierarchy of enslavement, similar to what was used in VOC colonies, appears to have been an important strategy to use enslaved people to help claim space for the company in foreign territories.

CHAPTER 2

The Geography of Enslaved Life in New Netherland

After having been forced to labor for the Dutch West India Company for at least thirty-four years, Maijken van Angola petitioned New Netherland's council for her freedom.[1] She first approached the council with two other enslaved women in 1662. Together, they requested that the company manumit them so that they could live in freedom together with the previously freed men and women who resided just north of New Amsterdam. The council granted their request, but under the condition that they would return weekly for domestic work at Director-General Petrus Stuyvesant's home.[2] Within months of their partial manumission, Maijken's fellow petitioners passed away, leaving her to take care of these weekly duties all by herself. She now returned to the council, pleading with the company to have mercy and "consent and allow that she may complete the little life she has left in freedom."[3] This time, the council granted her request without any conditions; after decades of enslavement, Maijken was finally free.

It should not be surprising that Maijken turned to the colony's council to argue for her freedom. As her petitions emphasize, she was Christian and was considered a loyal servant to the company, which had been among the most convincing arguments of previously successful freedom petitions. New Amsterdam's church records indicate that she was well connected and respected in New Amsterdam's Black community, and she had been close to many of the men and women who had obtained conditional freedom before her, including Manuel de Gerrit de Reus. Whereas enslaved men and women elsewhere in the colony often lived in fairly isolated areas, both geographically and socially, New Amsterdam's enslaved population lived close to the church, court, and taverns, and, maybe most importantly, they lived close to each other. For Maijken, living in close proximity to the town's institutions and to other enslaved men and women made it possible for her to attend church, establish close connections with other enslaved men and women, and, eventually, submit her petitions for freedom to the council.

Scholars have explored a variety of reasons why some of New Amsterdam's enslaved men and women, like Maijken van Angola and Manuel de Gerrit de Reus, had been able to attend the Dutch Reformed Church, use the courts to secure wages or defend property, and obtain a (conditional) freedom. Several historians have attributed these men and women's access to such institutions to a milder or relatively fluid and flexible system of slavery in this Dutch colonial society.[4] More recent scholarship has pointed to the importance of their cultural background, Christian faith, and close-knit community.[5] What these scholars have not yet explored, however, is the importance of place, space, and geography. Because enslaved people had very little control over their mobility or the environment in which they lived, the physical and social spaces that they inhabited played an especially important role in the ways they were able to partake in society.

Close examination of the geography and the spaces these people inhabited and frequented shows how these physical and social spaces shaped their lives and their opportunities within this colonial society. Since their access to, among others, the church, public space, and courts had not been regulated or restricted, they could actively participate in these spaces. Thus, these places had not yet become spaces of exclusion, segregation, and control as they would be in the eighteenth century. Importantly, however, only some of New Netherland's enslaved men and women, such as Maijken van Angola and Manuel de Gerrit de Reus, navigated these spaces relatively successfully, and they all lived in New Amsterdam. Close proximity to each other and to the court, council, and church enabled the town's enslaved women and men to participate in these spaces in ways that were usually not available to enslaved men and women who lived in other areas of the colony. Thus, whereas chapter 1 provided a discussion of the company's objectives when using enslaved labor and implementing hierarchies of enslavement, this chapter looks at the ways in which enslaved people navigated these systems and the colonial spaces.

Space and Geography

Although the men and women enslaved by the company lived in different areas of New Netherland, most of them resided in New Amsterdam and its environs. During the early decades of colonization, the majority of the colony's enslaved population belonged to the company, but as the settler population grew, so did the number of free individuals who either hired or purchased enslaved people. While such enslavers lived across the colony, the majority of them resided in the lower Hudson region. Thus, most of New Netherland's enslaved men, women, and children lived in or close to New Amsterdam, where they regularly interacted with each other.

Many of the people enslaved by the company lived in close proximity to each other, often sharing close quarters. When in January of 1641 several enslaved men admitted to the murder of Jan Premero, the court records detailed that they had killed Premero in the woods by their houses (*int bos omtrent haer huijsen*).[6] Their testimony suggests that they lived in several houses in a relatively isolated area, surrounded by forest. They likely lived north of the main settlement at the time as indicated on the Johannes Vingboons 1639 map of Manhattan that placed their houses northeast of the main settlement, in the area of today's East 74th Street (see Figure 2.1).[7]

If the company's enslaved workers lived at this location—about five and a half miles from New Amsterdam—in the 1630s, the company must have relocated them to New Amsterdam by the early 1640s. The murder of Premero may have motivated the company to move them to the main settlement, where they could be watched more closely. On August 8, 1642, Adam Roelants, the first schoolmaster in town, sold a house inhabited by the company's enslaved workers. This sale forced the women, men, and children who lived there to relocate, and it may have been at this time that they moved to the plot that a year later, in June of 1643, was identified as the "lot of the Negroes," which likely remained home to the company's enslaved workers for the next two decades. Both Evert Duyckingh and Touchyn Briel purchased land that bordered this property.[8] Enslaved people still lived there in 1654, when Adriaen Dircksen Coen purchased the grounds around their home.[9] The house remained their residence until at least 1657 when, according to I. N. Phelps Stokes, Coen sold the land around the building to Jacob van Couwenhoven.[10] Deeds sometimes referred to this plot of land on the *Slijcksteeg* as belonging to the company slaves, but the enslaved men and women who lived there did not own the land. When they eventually moved out of this house remains unclear, but they no longer resided there when it was sold in 1662.

FIGURE 2.1. Johannes Vingboons, *Manatvs gelegen op de Noot Riuer*, 1639. This map illustrates the locations of plantations, boweries, and mills in Manhattan and surrounding areas. The slave quarters ('t Quartier vande Swarte de Comp Slaven) are listed under F, which on the map is located just across from Roosevelt Island in the area of what is now East 74th street. Library of Congress, Geography and Map Division, https://www.loc.gov/item/97683596/

Very little is known about the size and quality of these homes, but records provide some information that helps reconstruct the circumstances in which these enslaved men, women, and children lived. When Roelants sold the house they inhabited, the deed referred to it as a *huijsken*, meaning small house. Their home on the *Slijcksteeg* must have been bigger: the 1654 deed that detailed the size of the lot excluding the house indicates that the building measured about 1,080 square feet at most. No surviving documents describe the quality of the home in the 1640s and 1650s, but when the house was demolished in 1662, it was reportedly in very poor condition.[11]

It is difficult to estimate accurately how many people resided in this home.[12] Manuel de Gerrit de Reus and the other men who received their conditional freedom in 1644 likely lived at the *Slijcksteeg* together with their wives and children. By the 1660s, the seven or eight people still enslaved by the company in New Amsterdam may have inhabited this building as well.[13] Although this certainly was not a small home, if most of the people enslaved by the company lived here, which was likely the case considering that it was referred to as *the* house of the company slaves, it housed multiple families, thus leaving little privacy and space to each of them.

Importantly, not all of the people enslaved by the company lived in these homes at the same time. Some of them would have stayed at the *bouwerijen*, boweries or farms, where they worked. In 1641, for instance, Thomas Hall signed a five-year lease of a company farm at *Sapokanikan*, which included two enslaved laborers. When the company sold a bowery to Petrus Stuyvesant in 1651, it consisted of "a dwelling house, barn, hayrick, land, six cows, two horses and two young Negroes."[14] Other men and women enslaved by the company lived with individuals who rented their labor, and in rare cases they may have resided with free Black men or women. For instance, Jan, who was enslaved by the company, lived with Catryn, a free Black woman.[15]

Although the company house on the *Slijcksteeg* was situated in New Amsterdam, it was initially located in a sparsely populated part of the town also referred to as the company's marshes, a swampy area during the early years of settlement (see Figure 2.2).[16] As more colonists began to settle and cultivate this land, the home became more central to the town's layout. On the one hand, their residence in the colonial town made them part of the community. They could more easily attend church services, access the courts, and visit local taverns. In fact, one tavern was located on the corner of the *Slijcksteeg*, only steps from their home.[17] On the other hand, they lost some of the privacy they had when they lived in the woods, north of the colonial town.

The men and women who had obtained freedom from the company received land outside of New Amsterdam by the wagon road, where they

1. Slijcksteeg residence of people enslaved by the company
2. Madaleen Vincent's tavern
3. Rutgersen's tavern
4. City Hall
5. Church at Perel straet
6. Dutch Reformed Church
7. Joghemsen's tavern
8. The commons

FIGURE 2.2. Jacques Cortelyou, *Afbeeldinge van de stadt Amsterdam in Nieuw Nederlandt*. From the New York Public Library, https://digitalcollections.nypl.org. Annotations by the author.

founded the region's first free Black community. As early as July 1643, Domingo Antonij and Catelina Antonij acquired farmland in this part of Manhattan, located in the area of today's Greenwich Village.[18] Manuel de Gerrit de Reus and the other freedmen soon followed when they obtained land in this area in 1644. By 1660, the company had granted land in this area to several freedmen, including Christopher Santome, Salomon Pieters, Assento, Francisco Cartagena, Willem Antonij, Groot Manuel, Claes de Neger, and Pieter Tambour.[19] Some free Black people had property within New Amsterdam itself. Susanna Anthonij Robberts, for example, owned a piece of land on *Prince Straet*, not too far from the company's home on the *Slijcksteeg*.[20] The women and men who resided just north of New Amsterdam lived close enough to the town to maintain relations with its population, both free and enslaved.

Enslaved persons who were held in bondage by individuals usually lived on the land of their enslaver. For instance, Swan Loange, who was enslaved by Govert Loockermans, likely lived at one of Loockermans's properties on *Perel Straet* or Pearl Street. Although they would have fewer opportunities to interact with other enslaved people, records reveal that they were nevertheless able to meet with other enslaved men and women in the streets, markets, church, and taverns. Undoubtedly, it was easier for New Amsterdam's enslaved men and women to do so because they lived in close proximity to each other.

Interactions in the Public Space

Enslaved and freed Africans had a significant presence in New Amsterdam. When traveling through the town's streets, European settlers would pass enslaved Africans working in their garden plots or on the colony's farms. Africans and Europeans lived on properties that bordered each other, frequented the same taverns, and shared common pasturage lands. The men and women who were enslaved by individual settlers often lived and worked on their enslaver's property. Their daily interactions in these spaces made these enslaved men and women a familiar and integral part of daily life in New Amsterdam.

The town's many drinking establishments provided an important space where freed and enslaved Africans met with each other and with the town's European settlers. With her business located on the corner of the *Slijcksteeg* and *Heerengracht*, Madaleen Vincent's tavern was closest to the home where most of the people enslaved by the company lived, but Jan Rutgersen, whose establishment was located just around the corner on the *Heerengracht*, was apparently more popular among the town's enslaved Africans.[21] Another meeting place they frequented was Andries Joghemsen's tavern, which was located on *Perel Straet* or Pearl Street, at the edge of town.[22]

Although there were no restrictions in place that kept enslaved people from visiting taverns or from drinking alcohol, New Netherland's colonial council prohibited the serving of alcohol on the Sabbath and other religious holidays.[23] Nevertheless, New Amsterdam's tapsters were regularly caught serving alcohol to enslaved men on these days. In 1662, for instance, the court of New Amsterdam accused Andries Joghemsen of "irregular tapping on the Sabbath to Negroes."[24] Such was the case when Mattheu, Swan, and Frans—who were enslaved by Cornelis Steenwijck, Govert Loockermans, and Thomas Hall— met for drinks on a Sunday at Joghemsen's tavern. According to their court testimonies, Mattheu started imbibing at the tavern when church was still in service. That afternoon, Frans picked up Swan to join Mattheu at Joghemsen's, where they enjoyed brandy together.[25] It is probably no coincidence that they chose to congregate at Joghemsen's tavern. Not only did Swan likely live near this tavern at one of Loockermans's properties, this establishment was also located relatively far away from the town's church, and so their illicit consumption of alcohol on the Sabbath would have been less obvious to the town's churchgoing residents.[26]

Such daily interactions between the town's free and enslaved residents did not erase the violence and trauma inherent to slavery, which was certainly evident in New Amsterdam's public spaces. For instance, some enslaved Africans who were working on the roads and fortifications would have done so in chains supervised by an overseer. At times, such work gangs of enslaved workers included chained prisoners who were sentenced to work alongside these men.[27] Plus, every now and then there would have been public sales where men, women, and children of all ages were sold to the highest bidder. As early as 1656, individuals sold people they enslaved at a public auction in the town, and during the 1660s, the West India Company organized several such sales.[28] These auctions may have taken place inside the fort, but it is not unlikely that at least some of these sales happened at the stoop of City Hall where auctions often took place. There, anyone could witness these inhumane exchanges at which men, women, and children were sold to the highest bidder.[29] Some of them had just arrived from their African homelands after a traumatizing journey across the Atlantic, while others were transported from American colonies such as Curaçao in often similarly horrifying circumstances. And while enslaved women and nursing children, or sucklings, were usually sold together, children who no longer nursed were regularly separated from their mothers.[30] These auctions would have been chilling reminders of the violence inherent in the system.

African Participation in the Dutch Reformed Church

New Amsterdam's enslaved families became active participants in the town's Dutch Reformed church. They attended church services, married in the church, and had their children baptized there. Certainly, they did not achieve equality within the church. For instance, it is not clear how many of them were admitted as full members, and none of them would have been able to become an elder in the church. Yet, New Amsterdam's church did not exclude them from participating in this space, and thus a significant number of enslaved men and women accessed the church.

Enslaved men and women likely attended church for various reasons. Just like Maijken van Angola, many of them came from West Central Africa where Catholicism had spread widely throughout the sixteenth century. Consequently, by the early seventeenth century, many West Central Africans were Catholic Christians, and thus the enslaved New Netherlanders who originated in West Central Africa were often Christian before they were brought to the Dutch colony. While they would have been Catholic, they likely attended the Dutch Reformed Church because this was their only opportunity to access Christian religious practices, including the sacraments of baptism and communion. They also realized that their participation in the Dutch Reformed Church proved crucial in improving their circumstances in this Dutch colonial society, which may have provided additional motivation to attend the church. Importantly, however, it was because they had not been restricted from participating in these spaces and often lived in close proximity to the church that they were actually able to attend service, marry, and have their children baptized there.

Their involvement in this denomination has received significant scholarly attention.[31] Yet, this scholarship has not taken into consideration the significance of geography and space when it was in fact their close proximity to the town's church buildings that allowed a significant number of these enslaved men and women to participate in the church. Thus, they frequented the often-small church spaces where they attended church services together with white settlers and shared important life events such as marriage and the baptism of their children.

New Amsterdam's surviving church records frequently mention enslaved Africans. About a year and half after the first recorded marriage intention between Egbert van Borsum and Annetje Hendricks, church records listed the marriage intentions of an African couple—Anthonie van Angola and Lúcie d'Angool—on May 5, 1641. They were probably not the first Africans to marry in the church; in fact, both Anthonie and Lucie were widowed at the time of their marriage and since the record mentioned their previous marriages these had likely also taken place in the town's Dutch Reformed Church.[32] Soon after they joined in holy matrimony, Jan Fort-Orangien married Marie Grande, and in 1642 four more African couples tied the knot.[33] African women and men continued to marry in the church throughout the seventeenth century.[34]

These enslaved Africans also baptized their children in the church. As early as 1639, Pieter St. Anthonij had his son Barent Jan baptized in New Amsterdam's church, and several fellow Africans followed. In 1640, the children of Samuel Angola, Emanuel d'Angole, Jan Fort-Orangien, Johan Françisco, and Emanuel van Angola were all baptized. Their baptisms made up almost 15 percent of the total baptisms that took place that year.[35] At least thirty-seven children of African descent received baptism in the church from 1639 through 1647, which was about 11 percent of New Amsterdam baptisms.[36] Importantly, African marriages in the church decreased between 1653 and 1664, when such unions accounted for only 3.8 percent of New Amsterdam's Dutch Reformed Church marriages. Baptisms of Black children also dropped midcentury, and it appears that most, if not all, of the African descendants who were baptized in New Amsterdam's church after 1647 were the children of free people. A change in clergy that served New Amsterdam's population closely coincided with these changes, thus suggesting that they played an important role in enslaved Africans' access to baptism and marriage.[37] Yet, it was enslaved people's close proximity to the church that allowed for their everyday participation in this denomination.

New Amsterdam's enslaved population could reach the church within a short walk. Congregants first created a space for church services in 1626, when François Molemacker constructed a mill that included a room for worship in the attic. Services in this space were held by the *ziekentrooster* (comforter of the sick) Sebastiaen Jansen Krol until Domine Jonas Michaëlius arrived in the colony in 1628.[38] When Everardus Bogardus became minister in 1633, a small wooden church was built outside the fort on *Perel Straet* or Pearl Street, also referred to as *Op 't Water*. Finally, in 1642, a brick church was erected inside the fort.[39] New Amsterdam's enslaved residents would have lived in walking distance of all of these meeting spaces.

Though it is not clear if any African men and women attended services in the room above the mill, they were certainly present in the wooden church on Pearl Street. It was in this church that Anthonie and Lúcie joined in holy matrimony, and that Pieter St. Anthonij had his son Barent Jan baptized. In fact, most of the African men and women who married and baptized their children in New Amsterdam's church would have done so in this building. And though this church must have been more spacious than the mill's attic, European and African church attendants still shared an intimate space.

Surviving church records do not reveal if the African men and women who attended church were restricted to a separate area of these buildings, but their marriage intentions and baptisms appear in the church records alongside those of Europeans. These intentions, including those of African couples, would have been repeated during the town's church service three Sundays in a row for all men, women, and children present in the church to hear. If no one objected to the planned marriage, the couple could go ahead and join in matrimony. Thus, on February 26, 1642, Dominie Bogardus entered the marriage intentions for European settlers Oloft Stephenszen van Wijck and Anneken Loockermans Van Turnhout, as well as for the enslaved Francisco van Angola and Palassa van Angola. Later that year, Bogardus entered Anthonij Ferdinand Van Cascalis in Portugal and Maria van Angola's intention to marry on the same day that Henricus Sibelszen van Langendijck and Marritje Theunis van Naerden expressed their intention to join in matrimony.[40] These intentions of enslaved and free couples were announced on Sundays in front of all congregants.

Africans and Europeans also frequently baptized their children on the same day: Pieter St. Anthonij and Claes Janszen, for example, both baptized their children on October 2, 1639; the next year, on July 1, Emanuel D'Angole and Gerrit Janszen van Aldenburgh had their daughters Pernante and Anneken baptized; Jan van 't Fort Orangien—or Jan de Fort Orange—and Hans Noorman had their daughters baptized on July 22, 1640. All of these baptisms would have occurred in the relatively small and intimate wooden church at Pearl Street. Both European and African witnesses took part in these baptisms, thus making these socially and ethnically diverse events. At the baptism of Jan van 't Fort Orangien's daughter Maria, for instance, Simon Congo and Isabel D'Angola served as witnesses, while at the same time Hans Noorman had Governor Willem Kieft and Teuntje Jeurgien witness the baptism of his daughter Anneken.[41] Such diverse baptisms continued to take place throughout much of the Dutch colonial period.

Church participation helped strengthen the African community and their bonds with white residents as they shared this religious experience and space. Witnesses at the aforementioned baptisms, for instance, became forever linked to these children in ways that resembled the role of godparents in the Catholic Church. In various places in the Americas, enslaved and freed Africans used these ceremonies to create guardian-child ties. According to the Moravian missionary Christian Oldendorp, for example, enslaved men and women in what was then the Danish colony St. Thomas would serve as witnesses at baptisms to forge family relationships that many of them did not have in this colony.[42] Enslaved men and women established similar relationships in New Netherland. In fact, in several cases, these witnesses took over the care of the child when their parents no longer could. Anthonij, son of Cleijn Antonij, for example, came to rely on his godmother, Dorethea Angola, after his mother and stepmother passed away.[43] As Susanah Shaw Romney has demonstrated in her work on New Netherland, enslaved Africans selected men and women whom they considered reliable and respected members of the community to serve as witnesses at their children's baptisms. Consequently, well-respected men and women like Manuel de Gerrit de Reus, Maijken van Angola, and Bastiaen, "Captain of the Negroes," appeared regularly as witnesses for the baptisms of Black children.[44] Because such witnesses played an important role in the child's life, the parents of the baptized child would choose these witnesses carefully.

These baptisms show how New Amsterdam's African population forged close connections with each other, but they also reveal their relations with the town's European population. When Pieter St. Anthonij had his son Barent Jan baptized in Manhattan's church, three fellow Africans—Dominco Anthonij, Jan Françoijs, and Susanna D'Angola—stood witness, as did recent Dutch settler Trijntje van Camp.[45] Samuel Angola had only white men and women—Theunis Craeij, Jan Jacobszen, and Claertje Gerrits—witness the baptism of his son Laurens on January 6, 1640.[46] Jan de Vries witnessed the baptism of several Black children, and when he had his son Jan, whose mother was a Black woman enslaved by De Vries, baptized, both white and Black witnesses attended. Together with three Africans, Domine Bogardus stood witness at the baptism of Phillipe Swartinne's daughter Anna, and Paulus Heijmans, overseer of the company slaves, served as a witness at the baptism of Anthonij, son of Anthonij Ferdinandus.[47] Whatever the circumstances were, their witnessing of these baptisms connected the African and European populations in significant ways.

It would be incorrect, however, to suggest that these enslaved people attended the church only because it strengthened their community and opportunities of freedom. Many of the colony's enslaved Africans who attended church came from West Central Africa, where Catholicism had spread since the King of Kongo, Nzinga Knuwu (or João I), requested baptism in 1491. Although Kongo elites were the first ones to embrace Christianity, over time the religion expanded to the rest of the population, particularly after João's son Afonso I made Catholicism the kingdom's state church. As European descriptions of the area demonstrate, by the late seventeenth century, Christianity had penetrated most of Kongo.[48] The Dutch trader Ferdinand van Capelle described the strong influence Christianity had on the region when he wrote that "in the city Congo there are many churches, where Portuguese papists conduct daily services and other Roman ceremonies"; moreover, he claimed, "every noble has in his village his own church and crosses."[49] Missionaries in Central Africa noted that people in the region were willing to travel long distances to be baptized or to have their children baptized. Capuchin missionary Dionigi Carli, who visited Kongo in the 1660s, pointed out "the poor people coming many leagues to us" for baptism.[50] In the sixteenth century, Christianity also spread in the neighboring kingdoms of Angola, Loango, and Ndongo, and by the seventeenth century, most West Central Africans would at the very least have been exposed to Christianity and many of them would have been Catholic.[51] In New Amsterdam, they continued part of their Christian traditions in the only accepted religious institution: the Dutch Reformed Church.

New Amsterdam's African women and men used their close proximity to the town's Dutch Reformed Church to attend services and marry and baptize in the church. They combined their religious beliefs and practices with the Dutch Reformed religion, while they also forged a common experience with each other and with European settlers. Their participation in the Dutch Reformed Church proved a crucial step toward societal inclusion, and through their marriages and baptisms in the church, they helped legitimize their community and family ties. Importantly, they were able to participate in the church because they had not been excluded from these churches and they lived in close proximity to them.

Family and Community

When Manuel de Gerrit de Reus, Paulo Angola, Groot Manuel, Cleijn Manuel, Simon Congo, Antonij Portugies, Gracia, Piter Santomee, Jan Francisco, Cleijn Antonij, and Jan Fort Orange petitioned the company for their freedom in early 1644, they argued that they required freedom in order to better provide for their wives and children as they had been "accustomed to in the past." The company granted the men and their wives a conditional freedom, and it provided them with farmland north of New Amsterdam.[52] In doing so, the council acknowledged these African families and the responsibilities of these husbands and fathers. At the same time, however, it determined that the children of these men should remain company property, thus continuing its control over these families.[53] These circumstances became typical for Black family life in New Amsterdam. Due to their close proximity to each other, enslaved men and women in this settlement were able to establish close connections and build strong family relationships that were mostly recognized by the company, council, and individual settlers. Yet, the company and individual enslavers often continued to hold sway over these relationships.

Over the years, New Amsterdam's enslaved people were able to build a strong Black community. As the colonial records reveal, the town's Black men and women supported one another when needed, in part by taking care of one another's children.[54] After some of these men and women obtained conditional freedom and settled just north of New Amsterdam, they continued to build on these strong relations. Their close-knit communities had largely been strengthened by their ethnic backgrounds, their common experiences, and the strong family bonds they created through their marriages and baptisms in the Dutch Reformed Church. Just as their participation in the Dutch Reformed Church had become a possibility because they lived close to the church, their community thrived because they lived close to each other.

Because the company and colonial council recognized marital and parental responsibilities, enslaved Africans could use these family ties to improve their circumstances and those of their dependents. When Dorethea Angola's husband pleaded to the council to free her godchild Anthonij, he emphasized that his wife had cared for Anthonij as a mother.[55] Some wed Africans used their marriage to avoid separation. Dutch authorities and settlers not only acknowledged these marriages but at least in some cases also made efforts to keep married couples together, very likely at the urging of these couples and their families. Thus, when in 1664 Jeremias van Rensselaer purchased an enslaved man whom he planned to take to the upriver settlement of Rensselaerswijck, Stuyvesant convinced Van Rensselaer to also purchase the man's wife.[56] Similarly, Dutch settler Govert Loockermans apparently helped keep a couple together when he purchased the freedom of Christina Emanuels so that she could marry Swan Loange, who was enslaved by Loockermans.[57]

Importantly, however, when enslaved and freed Africans established family and community, they never *fully* controlled their lives, nor could they protect the people they loved. Even the men who obtained their freedom in the 1640s could not do the same for their children, and by keeping these children in bondage, the company continued to have power over the people they had freed conditionally. Although most of the children of the half-free men and women grew up with their (extended) family, the fact that they could be taken away always loomed.

At times, daily contact fostered intimate relations between Black and white New Netherlanders. Although they may have been frowned upon, such interracial relations were not prohibited in the colony. In 1638, New Netherland's colonial council proclaimed that everyone should refrain "from adulterous intercourse with heathens, blacks, or other persons."[58] Some scholars have interpreted the colonial ordinance as a ban on interracial relationships, but it focused rather on adulterous intercourse, which was prohibited regardless of ethnic origin.[59] No laws forbade interracial marriages, and not once did the

Dutch colonial council punish people for having interracial relationships, which appeared practice in other Dutch colonies as well. Instructions by Jacob Pietersen Tolck concerning interracial marriages in Curaçao, for instance, noted that marriages with indigenous and Black women would be accepted when these women were educated, baptized, and part of the Christian community.[60] Evidently, Protestant conviction proved more important than racial or ethnic background.[61]

Indeed, some Black and white New Netherlanders joined in matrimony. Harmen Hanszen from Hessen, a German immigrant, married Maria Malaet from Angola in New Amsterdam's church in 1650. In 1663, Jan, "the negro," married Annetie Abrahams, likely the same as Annetje Abrahams who had left Amsterdam on March 29, 1660 aboard the *Vergulde Bever* (Gilded Beaver).[62] One of the colony's most notorious couples were Anthony Jansen van Salee, also known as Anthony Jansen de Turck, Anthony Jansen van Vaes, or Anthony Jansen the Mulatto, a settler of Dutch and African descent, and his Dutch wife, Grietje Reyniers.[63] The various names used to refer to Van Salee point not only to his skin color but also to his Islamic faith.

Although such interracial unions were not prohibited in the colony, they were likely frowned upon. Anthony Jansen van Salee and Grietje Reyniers dealt with frequent accusations of ill-behavior, as is evident from the numerous slander, abuse, and debt-related cases in which they appeared. In a 1638 court case, Remmer Jansen testified that Hendrick Jansen had called Anthony Jansen van Salee a "Turck, a rascal and horned beast."[64] Other charges filed against van Salee concerned physical abuse or unpaid wages. Reyniers, on the other hand, had been accused of pulling "the shirts of some sailors out of their breeches" and having "measured the male member of three sailors on a broomstick." Moreover, she reportedly had screamed in New Amsterdam's fort, "I have long been the whore of the nobility, now I want to be the rabble's whore." Adding to her troubled reputation, her midwife claimed that shortly after Reyniers gave birth to one of her children she asked the midwife if the child looked like her husband or Andries Hudde, suggesting she did not know who the child's father was.[65] These and other accusations led the fiscal in 1639 to request that van Salee and his wife be banned from New Amsterdam so that "the few people here in New Netherland may live together in peace."[66] Van Salee and Reyniers moved to Long Island, but their relocation did not bring an end to their conflicts with authorities and other settlers.[67] And even though none of the charges against them referred to their mixed marriage, it likely contributed to their troubled reputation.[68]

Importantly, not all of the colony's interracial relationships were consensual. Sexual relations between free and enslaved people could never be separated from coercion and struggles for power or autonomy. Thus, when Captain Jan de Vries had a son with a woman he held in bondage known as Elaria but sometimes referred to in the records simply as Swartinne (*Black woman*), her bound condition prohibited her from giving consent to the man who claimed to own her.[69] Enslaved men also fell victim to sexual aggression, as was evident in 1648 when Harmen Meyndertsz van den Bogaert was accused of sodomizing Tobias, an enslaved boy, at Fort Orange.[70] The records rarely reveal the more specific circumstances of sexual encounters between enslaved and free people. On Monday, March 27, 1656, Jan Gerritsen, brewer, complained in New Amsterdam's court that Elias Silva had delayed or detained (*opgehouden*) an enslaved woman who belonged to Gerritsen and had "carnal conversation with her." Silva claimed that he had done no such thing, and it appears the case was dismissed. The records suggest that authorities never questioned the enslaved woman who was the subject of these accusations.[71] Within a system of human bondage, enslaved men and women had few opportunities to protect themselves and their loved ones from sexual aggression.

Close proximity to each other and to the town's white population proved both useful and challenging. Because they lived close to each other, New Amsterdam's enslaved men and women were able to forge close relationships, start families, and build a strong Black community. Still, the company and individual enslavers often asserted their control over these relationships, even in their supposed benevolent acts to keep these families together.

The Court

On September 4, 1664, eight "half-slaves" petitioned New Netherland's colonial council to grant them full freedom. At the time of their request, Ascento Angola, Christopher Santome, Peter Petersen Criolie, Anthonij Criolie, Lewis Guinea, Jan Guinea, Solomon Petersun Criolie, and Basje Pietersen held this conditional legal status unique to the Dutch colony. Earlier that year, the Dutch West India Company had granted them freedom under the condition that they would regularly return to perform work for the company.[72] In their 1664 petition, they argued that because New Amsterdam's fort was close to being finished and "this summer two ships with a large number of negroes have arrived," they, humble servants who had served the company faithfully, should receive their full freedom. Not coincidentally, they submitted their petitions on the same day that the English demanded the Dutch surrender of the colony after four English warships had been stationed off the coast of Manhattan since August 28. In fact, these men directly linked the urgency of their petition to the "arrival of the English ships and soldiers."[73] They feared that if they were surrendered in their current conditionally freed status, the English might reenslave them. Certainly, while freed Africans could be found throughout the early modern Atlantic, including the English colonies, the conditional freedom that became known as half-freedom was a de facto legal status particular to the Dutch colony.

These freedmen had used their access to the colony's judicial system to obtain this conditional freedom, and now they petitioned the colony's council to grant them full freedom. Clearly, these men had access to the colony's courts. The Dutch colony had no laws that barred enslaved people from participating in the legal system, and New Amsterdam's enslaved population lived close enough to the council and court to actually bring cases or submit petitions. Much has been written about New Netherland's enslaved men and women navigating the colony's legal system to protect their property, fight for unpaid wages, and even secure their freedom, but scholars have not yet sufficiently addressed the importance of proximity to these courts.[74]

Except for the patroonship Rensselaerswijck—the Rensselaer family patroonship in the Upper Hudson area—the Dutch West India Company controlled New Netherland's judicial system.[75] By 1664, sixteen inferior courts operated in the colony.[76] While inferior courts handled minor offenses, major crimes such as prostitution, adultery, murder, sodomy, and smuggling required consideration by the colonial council in New Amsterdam. Initially, the council, in addition to being the High Court responsible for the colony's executive decisions, also considered local civil and criminal cases. When New Amsterdam obtained a town charter in 1653, the city magistrates took over local criminal cases, and the council now served as a high court for all but one of the colony's local courts. A similar move had come into effect for civil cases only a few years earlier.[77] Schepenen, municipal court of justice members, and a schout, a local official also responsible for law enforcement, ran the local courts. High cases were brought before the director and council, where the fiscael served as prosecutor.[78] Unlike courts in the English colonies, New Netherland's judicial system did not use a jury. The courts often met weekly, which secured immediate attention to various cases and petitions. Petitioning could be used to bring about changes in government or to solve certain problems.[79]

New Netherland's legal system did not grant enslaved people access to New Netherland's courts or consider them legally equal to their free counterparts; instead, equal treatment of enslaved and free people in the colony's judicial system resulted from the lack of laws concerning slavery and slaves' legal status.[80] Thus, enslaved men and women had not yet been restricted from these spaces, and they assumed equality before the law by using the absence of such restrictions. In fact, through their participation in the colony's courts, enslaved men and women forced the courts to consider issues concerning slavery; in doing so, they inadvertently helped shape the colony's legal system.

Due to the absence of restrictions and their close proximity to the courthouse, New Amsterdam's Black population, both free and enslaved, could participate in the colony's judicial system, and they often did so successfully. In 1638, for example, the court sided with Antonij Portugies when he demanded compensation from Anthoniy Jansen van Salee for the damages he had done to Portugies's hog.[81] Manuel de Gerrit de Reus appeared in the court as early as 1639 when he won a court case against Dutch settler Henric Fredericksen van Bunninck for the fifteen guilders he had earned but not yet received.[82] Four years later, De Reus appeared in the colony's court again, this time to testify on behalf of Cleijn Manuel, whose cow had been struck by Jan Celes, an English colonist.[83] The court resolved that Celes pay Cleijn Manuel, an enslaved man, for the damages he had done; in addition, the council threatened Celes with banishment if he ever did anything like that again.[84] These and additional cases show how De Reus and other enslaved men successfully used the colony's courts to protect their property or wages.

Not coincidentally, Manuel de Gerrit de Reus, Cleijn Manuel, and Antonij Portugies lived close to each other, close to the colony's council, and close to New Amsterdam's courthouse. Some scholars have pointed out that their uses of the courts would have been informed by their cultural background, but their intimate relations with each other and their close proximity to the courts would have played an equally or maybe even more important role. Many of these enslaved Africans lived only blocks away from the colony's council, which was located inside the fort. Similarly, New Amsterdam's municipal court, located at City Hall on Pearl Street, was in walking distance from where these enslaved men and women lived. Moreover, records reveal that the enslaved men and women who were enslaved by the company and thus often shared close quarters were most active in the colony's judicial system. Through these interpersonal connections, they were able to share information on how to improve their circumstances, including effective ways to navigate the courts.

Enslaved Africans' participation in courts throughout the early modern Atlantic demonstrates that many of them knew how to work these judicial systems to their advantage.[85] Among others, the men and women whom Ira Berlin has called "Atlantic Creoles" had been exposed to European cultures and institutions in Africa or the Atlantic, and they used these experiences to navigate colonial legal systems.[86] West Central African societies generally had structured judicial systems that often resembled European legal systems.[87] Not surprisingly, enslaved West Central Africans, such as Maijken van Angola and

Manuel de Gerrit de Reus van Angola, were among the most active participants in the courts. Similarly, enslaved men and women who came from the Iberian Peninsula or who had been born in the Americas played an active role in the colony's legal system. Yet, while their background helped them navigate colonial courts, it was their close proximity to these courtrooms and to each other that allowed them to actively apply their judicial knowledge.

Living a Life in Bondage Outside of New Amsterdam

In 1652, Claesje, one of the few enslaved women who lived in Rensselaerswijck, appeared before the local court for accusations of theft.[88] She declared that she had in fact stolen certain goods from her enslaver, Sander Leendersz, including candles, blankets, clothes, butter, and combs, which she then sold to Jan Michielsz and Jacob Luyersz. Upon admission to the theft, she claimed that in exchange for the stolen goods she had received, among others, "an old undershirt" from Jacob Luyersz and Jan Michielsz. More importantly, however, Claesje testified that she had stolen these goods because Jacob Luyersz had promised her he would take her to New Amsterdam where "she would then get a husband."[89] Evidently, Claesje longed for such an intimate relationship and the opportunity of starting a family, and she understood that she might have a better chance of doing so in New Amsterdam.

Although many enslaved men and women in New Amsterdam were able to establish family and community, forging such intimate relations proved challenging and often nearly impossible for enslaved people who lived elsewhere in the colony. Many of them struggled to establish family and community because they lived in remote locations where they had only few opportunities to interact with fellow Africans. The company and individual enslavers frequently rented out or sold the men and women they claimed to own, which greatly complicated these enslaved people's efforts to take part in an African community or establish intimate relations.[90] For individuals like Claesje, isolation and frequent relocation made it especially challenging to sustain any personal relations, let alone a family life.

Church participation also proved much more challenging for enslaved men and women who did not live in New Amsterdam or its vicinity. Even though several congregations organized in other parts of the colony, including Flatbush, Rensselaerswijck, Beverwijck, and Esopus, it would have been difficult for enslaved Africans who lived in the colony's more rural areas to attend church services regularly.[91] Stuyvesant understood this challenge and so, in an effort to ensure that his workers would have access to religious services and teachings, he directed the building of a chapel for the people who labored on his bowery, including the enslaved workers.[92] From 1660 to 1664, while a minister at Long Island, Selijns officiated at Sunday evening services in Stuyvesant's chapel, weather permitting, and he actively catechized at the bowery on days that there were no services.[93] In most cases, however, enslaved Africans in more remote locations would have had to travel long distances to attend church service or receive catechism.

Enslaved men and women who were located in more remote areas of the colony also had few opportunities to access the colony's courts. During the 1650s, for instance, enslaved Africans in Pavonia and Staten Island would have had to travel to New Amsterdam because these territories fell under New Amsterdam's jurisdiction. Enslaved men and women in Wiltwijck and neighboring settlements had to use the court of Fort Orange until Wiltwijck received its own court in 1661.[94] The absence of local courts in these settlements rendered it difficult or nearly impossible for an enslaved population with little control over their mobility to have reliable access to the colony's judicial system. Not only did travel to the colony's courts require time and means, enslaved men and women also needed cooperation from their enslavers to be able do so. Consequently, only a few Africans appear in the surviving court records of local courts outside of New Amsterdam, and only a few of these enslaved people appeared before the colony's council. When they did appear in the courts, they were mostly there because they had been accused of crimes, as was the case with Claesje.

Whereas New Amsterdam's enslaved population had been able to take advantage of their close proximity to, among others, the town's church, court, taverns, and each other, enslaved men and women who lived in more rural and often isolated areas of the colony did not have these opportunities available to them. Without much time or means to travel to the colony's courts or churches and with few other enslaved people close by, it proved incredibly challenging to access these institutions or build a community in the ways many of New Amsterdam's enslaved women and men had been able to do.

When Maijken van Angola obtained her freedom in 1664, a substantial community of free Black people lived by the wagon road, just north of New Amsterdam. This community originated in New Amsterdam's earliest enslaved population, most of whom were held in bondage by the Dutch West India Company. While still enslaved, many of these men and women shared close quarters in this colonial town, which allowed them to build strong relationships. Equally important, they lived in close proximity to the various institutions they accessed, such as the church and the court. They had been able to take advantage of the fact that the Dutch colony had no legislation in place that restricted them from accessing the court, the church, and public spaces. In doing so, they not only became a familiar part of the town's daily life, they also were able to improve their circumstances, unlike their counterparts in the more rural parts of the colony where they often lived in socially isolated conditions and at too great of a distance to access churches and courtrooms. Indeed, spatial proximity and geography played a crucial role in the opportunities the colony's enslaved people were able to create for themselves and their families.

New Netherland's legislators and European settlers did not impose clear spatial restrictions on the Black population; consequently, their interactions in the various colonial spaces were often spatially intimate and relatively friendly. Enslaved men and women like Maijken used these circumstances to expand the limits of their bondage. In doing so, they were able to own and protect property, participate in the church, create strong connections with other enslaved men, women, and children, and eventually obtain their freedom. As Domingo Angola, Maijken's husband, would soon discover, however, such interactions and opportunities would become increasingly rare when European settlers progressively began to limit spatial access for free and enslaved Black men and women in the late seventeenth century.

CHAPTER 3

Control and Resistance in the Public Space

In March of 1671, New York City's Mayor's Court summoned Domingo and Manuel Angola, both free Black men. Several residents had complained that these men regularly harbored enslaved and servant laborers, which according to the complaint caused "great damage to their owners." In an effort to stop them from "harboring" such laborers, the court warned them that they risked losing their freedom if they did so again.[1] This warning must have had a chilling effect on the town's free Black community. Both Domingo and Manuel had obtained their freedom when the region was still under Dutch control, and they owned land in Manhattan's free Black community outside of New York City, the colonial town that was called New Amsterdam only a decade ago. Both men had become prominent members of this free Black community. In fact, the last time Domingo Angola, husband of Maijken van Angola, appeared in the court, it was to obtain freedom for his stepdaughter Christina.[2] Yet, here they were, summoned to the court and threatened with reenslavement, a warning that the circumstances of free Black New Yorkers became increasingly precarious.

The court's warning to these men signified important early efforts by the city and its slaveholding residents to control the Black population, efforts that would expand over the course of the long eighteenth century. Though there were a few interruptions to English control after they first took over the region in 1664, by the late seventeenth century they effectively controlled what was once New Netherland. The white population in the region now named New York grew significantly over the course of the eighteenth century. With that expansion, the number of slaveholding and thus enslaved individuals also increased considerably, especially in communities along the Hudson River, in Manhattan, Staten Island, and in parts of Long Island. Men, women, and children were held in bondage across the region, in all types of households, working in wide-ranging tasks.[3] Although New York's enslaved population never exceeded 20 percent of the total population, it reached about a third in some of these areas.[4] More importantly, over the course of two centuries, slavery came to affect all parts of New York society.

With slavery an integral part of New York society, free, white New Yorkers saw it as imperative that they develop a system that helped control and regulate the enslaved population. As Ira Berlin points out, New York had the "trappings" of a slave society: it implemented slave codes, restricted manumissions, and responded to various acts of resistance.[5] Indeed, most of New York's public spaces became "white space" in which Black people were tolerated, but only if they could be controlled. In these white spaces, Black people were always considered suspect, and at any moment they could be subjected to searches, interrogations, or even violent attacks.[6] Thus, public spaces in the town, and in the region, became more distinct "white space" as defined by Elijah Anderson, over the course of the long eighteenth century.[7] Even the majority Black community where Domingo and Manuel Angola lived would be monitored.[8]

This chapter examines how white New Yorkers turned the area's public spaces into "white space" through, among others, architecture, legislation, and surveillance. It looks at the ways in which white New Yorkers tried to control the enslaved population in the public space, and how enslaved people managed to escape such control, even if only temporarily. Within the region's public spaces, this meant that the movements of enslaved people were always contained, controlled, and monitored. In order to do so, enslavers created geographies of control: pass systems, surveillance, patrols, curfews, public punishments, and limitations on the number of enslaved people who could gather in public spaces were all used to control New York's Black population. Enslavers also utilized celebrations like Pinkster, the Dutch version of Pentecost or Whitsuntide, to support the system of enslavement. Yet, such control was never complete, and enslaved people developed endless ways to escape or circumvent it, thus creating geographies of resistance or "rival geographies," as Stephanie Camp calls them.[9]

These dynamics in the public space were neither unusual nor exceptional. In fact, they were quite common in American slave societies. Indeed, it is the fact that these activities in New York much resembled those of other areas that is important here. Although slavery and the enslaved population may appear peripheral to New York society in the long eighteenth century, the extent to which the enslavement of Black New Yorkers shaped New York's public spaces shows that the opposite was true. Enslaved people and the institutions that enslaved them proved integral to New York society. Thus, even though New York never became a full-fledged slave society, at least not according to traditional definitions, slavery and the enslaved population deeply affected New York's culture, legislation, and politics.[10]

Whereas men like Domingo and Manuel Angola had been able to obtain their freedom, own land, and build a free Black community during the Dutch colonial period, by the late seventeenth century such opportunities became sparse for enslaved men and women. They rarely had the same access to the various institutions, and their movements and activities in the public space were increasingly regulated and surveilled. Thus, these public spaces became white spaces that free and enslaved Black people were forced to navigate but in which they were always watched closely.

The Expansion of Slavery in Dutch New York

White New Yorkers of all backgrounds relied on the labor of enslaved people, but slavery appeared especially widespread in some of New York's predominantly Dutch communities. Although freed Africans were among the founders of some Kings County communities—today the New York City borough of Brooklyn—by the early eighteenth century almost all of the county's Black residents were enslaved. This enslaved population made up almost 15 percent of the region's total population in 1698. The institution of slavery continued to grow in Kings County over the course of the eighteenth century, and by 1790, about a third of Kings County's population lived in bondage (see Figure 3.1).[11] Similarly, the enslaved population in Ulster County increased significantly in the eighteenth century. Wiltwijck court records mention enslaved people as early as the 1660s, but they appear to have been a relatively small number.[12] By 1723, however, enslaved people made up 19 percent of Ulster County's total population, and they continued to be a substantial part of the county's population until the abolition of slavery in 1827.[13] In the area of Albany County, the population included several enslaved men, women, and children during the Dutch colonial period, and their numbers increased substantially during the long eighteenth century. While Albany County's enslaved population reached just over 5 percent of the county's total population in 1790, the county had the

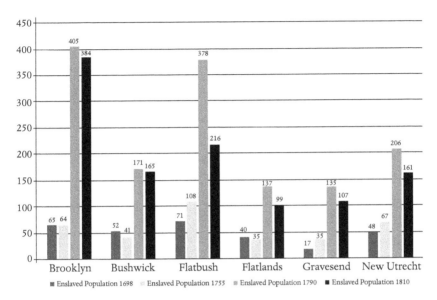

FIGURE 3.1. Kings County Enslaved Population in 1698, 1755, 1790, and 1810. Note that the 1755 census only recorded enslaved adults. If children had been included in that census, these numbers would have been significantly higher. Graph created by author.

largest enslaved population of all of New York's counties at the time (see Figure 3.2).[14]

Home to the region's first enslaved and later free Black community, New York City continued to have a significant Black population in the eighteenth century. There, free and enslaved Black residents reached almost 20 percent of the total population in 1737. While many Dutch Americans were among the city's enslavers, free New Yorkers of all ethnicities and religious convictions held people in bondage.[15] Unlike any other part of the region, New York City also had a substantial free Black population by the late eighteenth century, when about a third of its Black residents were free.

Most often enslavers in these communities held fewer than five people in bondage, but there were certainly slaveholders who enslaved more people at any given moment. Ulster County's 1790 census records demonstrate that in some towns the number of slaveholders who enslaved five or more people was quite substantial. In Hurley, 40 percent of the town's enslavers held five or more people in bondage, and in Kingston this number reached 48 percent of its slaveholders.[16] Albany County included some of New York's largest slaveholding estates, including Stephen Van Rensselaer, who reported fifteen slaves; Volkert Dow (or Douw), who counted fourteen enslaved people as part of his household; and Francis Nichols of Watervliet, who held eighteen people in bondage.[17]

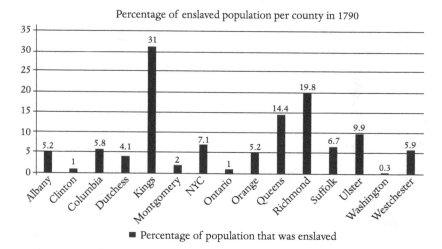

FIGURE 3.2. Percentage of the population that was enslaved per New York county, according to the 1790 census. Graph created by author.

Enslaved men, women, and children in these communities were forced to complete a wide variety of tasks. By the mid-eighteenth century, most Dutch American farmers grew crops—such as flax, wheat, and corn—for regional and international trade.[18] Enslaved laborers toiled on these farms, but they also assisted artisans in the workplace, ran errands for their enslavers, worked in domestics, and labored on the docks, especially in the vibrant merchant communities of Brooklyn, New York City, and Albany.[19]

The importance of enslaved laborers did not go unnoticed to the region's visitors. Alexander Coventry, for instance, noted in his late eighteenth-century journal that among the Dutch farmers in the Coxsackie region enslaved people "did all the work on the farm, and in the house."[20] When William Strickland traveled through the region, he suggested that "the oldest slave manages the lands, directs the cultivation of it and without consulting him the master can do nothing."[21] Such descriptions attest to white New Yorkers' growing reliance on enslaved people's labor.

In an effort to keep the free Black population small, eighteenth-century legislation implemented manumission regulations that discouraged them. As detailed by the 1712 "Act for preventing Suppressing and punishing the Conspiracy and Insurrection of Negroes and other Slaves," enslavers were now required to pay a two-hundred-pound manumission fee, and they had to pay these freedmen and women a yearly fee of twenty pounds, supposedly to ensure that they would not fall into poverty.[22] Consequently, New York's free African American population remained small throughout the eighteenth century. Even when slavery and abolition became hotly debated topics in the late eighteenth century, 82 percent of New York's African American population remained enslaved. Most counties counted only a few free Black families, and only New York City had a considerable free Black population.[23]

Even though New York's legislators passed the "Act for the Gradual Abolition of Slavery" in 1799, it would take decades for slavery to come to a complete end.[24] In most of Kings County, for instance, the enslaved population continued to make up about 20 percent of the population in 1810.[25] The 1830 Federal Census provides further evidence that even after the state's abolition of slavery it had not yet come to its complete demise. According to this census, seventy-six men, women, and children still lived in bondage, two of whom were in Albany County, seventeen in New York County, and twenty-six in Montgomery County. Even in 1840, New Yorkers reported four enslaved people to the census, three of whom lived in Brooklyn.

Over the course of the long eighteenth century, slavery had become an integral part of New York society, and it continued to be well into the nineteenth century. Free New Yorkers from all social and ethnic ranks benefited from the labor of enslaved people, including many Dutch descendants. Consequently, efforts to sustain the system permeated every part of society. Whether it was in Albany, Kingston, or New York City, enslavers always sought ways to control the men, women, and children they held in bondage.

Geographies of Control

When Benjamin Franklin left Philip Schuyler's Albany mansion in May of 1776, Mrs. Schuyler insisted that he let Lewis, one of the men enslaved by the Schuylers, drive him to New York City in a post-chaise. Once he arrived safely at his destination, Franklin wrote to Schuyler that he was glad he took the offer because "part of the Road being very stoney and much gullied, where I should probably have overset and broke my own Bones; all the Skill and Dexterity of Lewis being no more than sufficient."[26] Evidently, Schuyler, a prominent Dutch descendant and major general in the Continental Army, regularly relied on Lewis to transport Schuyler family members and their guests. Although Lewis would travel many miles independently, out of sight of his enslaver, Schuyler trusted that he would return without any major divergences. Schuyler assumed that the system that he and fellow white New Yorkers had put in place helped control and contain the movements and activities of enslaved people in the public space.

As the number of enslaved people increased and more white New Yorkers, many of whom were of Dutch descent, relied on the labor of enslaved people, their interests in developing ways that would help control and regulate the movements and activities of these enslaved women, men, and children in public spaces expanded. Over time, white New Yorkers established a system of legal restrictions, surveillance, patrols, and public punishments that helped turn public spaces into geographies of control. Increasingly, Black New Yorkers' activities in these white spaces were deemed illegitimate unless they could prove otherwise. Thus, Black New Yorkers, whether free or enslaved, navigated controlled and white-dominated public spaces in which their activities were always considered potentially criminal.[27]

By the latter part of the seventeenth century, New York authorities began to pass legal restrictions on the activities of free and enslaved Black New Yorkers. Whereas some enslaved Africans in New Amsterdam had been able to access the colony's courts to protect property, secure wages, or obtain freedom for themselves or their families, such opportunities became rare by the late seventeenth century. The Duke's laws, named after the Duke of York James Stuart and implemented by the English after they took over the region, formally codified slavery in the colony's laws, and the New York assembly and local courts soon began to pass legislation in an effort to control and contain the region's enslaved population.[28] In doing so, legislation became an effective tool of enslavement.

New York authorities passed several acts that prohibited enslaved men and women from congregating in public spaces and forbade free New Yorkers from trading with enslaved laborers without consent of their enslavers. A 1682 ordinance prohibited enslaved New Yorkers from leaving their enslaver's property without his or her consent, and in 1684 the general assembly resolved that they should not be allowed to engage in trade without permission.[29] In November of 1702, the colonial council passed its first comprehensive act "for Regulateing of Slaves," which, among others, regulated trade with enslaved people, permitted enslavers to punish enslaved people, and prohibited enslaved people to meet in groups larger than three.[30] Over the course of the eighteenth century, the colonial assembly and local councils continued to curtail enslaved people's movements and activities in the public space through implementation of strict regulations. The 1706 "Act to Incourage the Baptizing of Negro, Indian and Mulatto Slaves" stipulated that enslaved New Yorkers could not serve as witness in cases concerning free people.[31] A 1709 law prohibited the sale of strong liquor to enslaved men and women.[32] After the 1712 New York City slave revolt in which enslaved New Yorkers killed several enslavers, "An Act for preventing Suppressing and punishing the Conspiracy and Insurrection of Negroes and other Slaves" prohibited enslaved people to meet in the colony's public spaces with more than three people at the same time.[33]

Local courts passed similar slave codes in an effort to contain and control enslaved people. As early as 1707, New York City's council determined that the city's enslaved men and women would not be allowed to meet with more than four fellow enslaved men and women at a time.[34] Bellmen of the city were to check the city's streets "every hour in the night" and apprehend "all disturbers of the peace."[35] After the city's 1712 revolt, the city's Common Council prohibited "Negro and Indian slaves above the Age of fourteen years from going in the Streets of this City after Night without a Lanthorn and A lighted Candle."[36] In an effort to limit theft and illicit trade, the city's council also passed laws that prohibited enslaved New Yorkers from trading goods in the city's markets. In Albany and Ulster counties, legislators passed similar legislation to help regulate and control their enslaved populations.[37]

Enslavers' efforts to curtail enslaved people's mobility and enforce control over them in public spaces extended beyond legislation. White New Yorkers used the built environment to assert their supposed undisputable dominance over the public space.[38] Through design and planning, as well as social and cultural practices, white New Yorkers signified that these public spaces belonged to them. In the region's Dutch communities, the central location of Dutch Reformed churches signaled the community's dominant religion. Dutch American design of homes and streetscapes further reinforced that they defined these communities' social and cultural foundations. Through practice and legislation, they also determined the behavioral norms in these public spaces. Thus, within these communities, enslaved men and women were always deemed outsiders even if these were the communities in which they were born and raised.

Through enforcement of the various laws and prohibitions in these public spaces, enslavers sought to intimidate enslaved people. As Marisa Fuentes points out in the case of Barbados, architectural structures such as the gaol, whipping post, and execution gallows served as important symbols of power and control.[39] Barry Higman similarly argues that it was not unusual for Caribbean towns to contain "visible symbols of public terror in the shape of workhouses, jails, cages, stocks, and treadmills."[40] New York authorities placed such structures in similarly strategic public spaces. In the city of Albany, for instance, authorities positioned the gallows and prison on the hill where now the state capitol is located, an area visible from the town. The permanent and public presence of these symbols of discipline and punishment became constant reminders of these communities' power structures.[41]

Enslaved people often endured public punishments, intended to instill fear into enslaved men and women, at these locations. When in 1676 Baltus confessed to having violently attacked several people in the streets of Kingston, he received an especially horrendous sentence: "His right hand shall be cut off, his legs and arms shall be broken and directly thereafter he shall be hung to the gallows as an example for others."[42] Similarly, after Tham of Hurley was found guilty of killing an enslaved woman of the same town in 1696, he was "sentenced to be hanged till dead, to have his throat cut and then be hanged in a chain for an example to others."[43] The mangled bodies of these men and women were placed in public spaces to convey a clear message to others. Enslaving communities across the Americas used such public displays of discipline and punishment to force control over its enslaved population, and New York was no different.

Dutch American communities in the region also employed architectural designs that enhanced control of public spaces. As explained in Oscar Newman's theory of "defensible space," certain building styles can discourage prohibited behavior in the public spaces. Newman argues that such architectural design can create "defensible space" through, among others, "real and symbolic barriers" and architecture that facilitates surveillance.[44] Although he developed his theory in the context of 1970s urban planning, his concept of defensible space proves useful when examining slavery and public spaces. For example, Newman contends that windows that oversee entrances and common spaces help keep areas safe, because neighbors can then recognize any unusual behavior or potential intruders.[45] Such building practices became integral to Dutch American towns like Albany. In fact, Newman uses a traditional Dutch home that resembles the architecture of eighteenth-century Albany houses as an example of defensible space (see Figure 3.3). Stoops at the entrances of these homes signified the transition between the private and public space. In many of these towns, Dutch Americans built their houses close to one another with windows that provided a good overview of the streets, which reinforced what Newman identified as "territorial claim by providing unmistakable surveillance from within the dwelling."[46] Within these communities where most people knew their neighbors and their daily routines, it would have been difficult to traverse the streets unnoticed. Many of these Dutch American towns, often inadvertently, developed a system of surveillance similar to Foucault's theory of the panopticon in which the surveilled often internalize such surveillance, leading them to always feel as if they are watched, which influences behavior.[47]

In addition to such informal systems to control Black people in public spaces, slaveholders also organized patrols or vigilante services. Especially at night and in rural areas such forms of surveillance proved crucial to limiting the activities of enslaved people in the public space. To this end, enslavers in Ulster County organized the Society for Apprehending Slaves in 1796. Based in Shawangunk, the society accepted members for an annual fee and each

FIGURE 3.3.   James Eights, *View of North Pearl Street just north of State Street in Albany, NY*, ca. 1850. First published as *North Pearl Street, from Maiden Lane Northward* in George R. Howell, ed., *History of the County of Albany, N.Y., from 1609–1886. With Portraits, Biographies and Illustrations* (New York: W. W. Munsell & Co., Publishers, 1886), 668.

member would be required to "enter in a book to be kept by the Secretary the name or names of such slave or slaves as he intends to put in charge of the society." These members could call on the society's riders to apprehend any of the registered men or women who might try to escape their bondage.[48] Thus, these enslavers created a community-based system to keep enslaved people from fleeing successfully.

Communities implemented curfews and pass systems to further their control over enslaved people. Church bells often served as a reminder that a night curfew was about to start, as was the case in Albany, where at 8 o'clock the Dutch Reformed Church bell alerted residents of the town's curfew.[49] In an effort to enforce curfews and generally avoid criminal activities at night, towns often required enslaved people to carry lanterns, and they employed watchmen to patrol the streets.[50]

Enslaved women and men had to obtain permission from their enslavers to navigate public spaces.[51] Sylvia Dubois, an enslaved woman in New Jersey's Dutch communities, gave an unusual insight into the various tactics communities employed to control the enslaved population:

You see that in those days the negroes were all slaves, and they were sent nowhere, nor allowed to go anywhere without a pass; and when anyone met a negro who was not with his master, he had a right to demand of him whose negro he was; and if the negro did not show his pass, or did not give good evidence whose he was, he was arrested at once and kept until his master came for him, paid whatever charges were made, and took him away. You see, in those days anybody had authority to arrest vagrant negroes. They got paid for arresting them and charges for their keeping till their master redeemed them.[52]

Similar practices occurred throughout New York. In fact, New York legislation encouraged free individuals to detain Black men and women if their activities in the public space appeared illegitimate. In 1713, New York City's council passed "A Law for Regulating Negro & Indian Slaves in the Night Time," which, among others, detailed that "it Shall and may be lawfull for any of her Majesties Subjects within the said City to Apprehend such slave or slaves not having such Lathorn [lantern] and Candle."[53] And in 1726, the city's council stipulated that free, white people who found an enslaved person breaking the laws should be rewarded by this person's enslaver.[54] Importantly, enslaved New Yorkers' mere presence in public spaces without permission from their enslavers could be considered criminal behavior.

In some cases, simply being accompanied by a white person gave legitimacy to Black activities in the public space, as is evident from a 1730 oyster-racking ordinance. Claiming that enslaved people had racked so many oysters that none were left for white New Yorkers, the law stipulated that when Black men were racking for oysters, they had to be accompanied by at least one white man. Thus, the presence of white people made this a visibly permitted activity for Black New Yorkers in white space.[55]

The region's enslavers used "runaway slave advertisements" to help identify the men, women, and children who attempted to escape their bondage. Thus, these advertisements proved useful tools for surveillance. As Shane White points out, print was used to enforce "the slave system."[56] In these articles, the people who fled their enslavers were described in great detail, thus exposing their most intimate characteristics.[57] For instance, an advertisement that searched for Jacob, who fled George Wray of Albany, described him with great specificity:

about 23 Years old, 5 Feet 6 Inches high without Shoes, has a Scar on the right Side of his Forehead, another on his left Temple, both just in the Edge of his Hair, two large Pock Marks on the upper Part of his left

Cheek, high Cheek Bones, had a Hair Mole under his Chin, but has lately cut the Hair off it; the Calves of his Legs remarkably high, stoops forward in walking, speaks English very well, some French, and a little Spanish, of an insinuating Address, very apt to feign plausible Stories, has a stammering in his Speech when in Liquor, and may call himself free.[58]

Other advertisements provided similar intimate details of the men and women they were searching. Jack, who escaped John Raff of Albany, had an "outward Bend in his right Foot, which obliges him to brace the hind Part of his Shoe round his Ancle to keep it up, both his Great Toes are nearly frozen off."[59] When Philip ran away the ad that looked for him mentioned that he had "a scar on his left foot just above the large toe."[60] These advertisements show that enslavers studied their enslaved laborers' bodies and behaviors, and they shared these details with the rest of newspaper-reading New York in the hopes that such information would help them retrieve the people who had fled. For the enslaved men and women described in these advertisements, such detail limited their chances of successfully escaping their enslavers and put them at risk of random investigation of even the most intimate parts of their bodies.

Even after enslaved men and women obtained their freedom, their former enslavers still might try to regulate their movements. Hillitje DeWitt's early nineteenth-century correspondence illustrates such efforts most vividly when she directed family members in New York City to discourage Nan and Joe, who had recently obtained their freedom from the DeWitt family, from visiting Rochester because "there is a number of Black ones belonging to this family that are Slaves & likely to Remain so, & for Nan & Maybe Joe too, to come parading all the way up here, free people, it would make these here discontented & Sulky."[61] Evidently, Hillitje worried Nan and Joe might cause an uprising among the people she still held in bondage, and so she tried to control the movements of this couple even after they had become free.

New York's enslaving class created a system that helped control, regulate, and surveil the region's enslaved population and to some extent its free Black population in the public space. Although these efforts extended beyond Dutch American communities, Dutch American enslavers participated in or encouraged the implementation and enforcement of such regulations, symbols, and structures on local and regional levels. Whether it concerned public punishments as was the case with the execution of Tham of Hurley, publications of detailed runaway slave advertisements like the one that searched for Jacob from Albany, or organized slave patrols similar to Ulster County's Society for Apprehending Slaves, Dutch Americans often led the creation of geographies of control.

Geographies of Resistance

When in November of 1793 a fire that started at the barn of Peter Gansevoort destroyed twenty-six Albany homes, Albany authorities arrested two enslaved girls—Dean and Bet—and an enslaved man named Pomp.[62] While in custody, Bet confessed that Pomp had asked her and Dean to help him ignite the fire.[63] Although we will never know to what extent her admission of guilt was coerced, her testimony does reveal how she and other enslaved Albanians navigated the town's streets in ways that avoided systems of surveillance.[64] Bet's confession detailed such alternative ways of navigating Albany's streets when she described that they climbed a wall and traveled through the city via alleyways and backyards. They also timed their movements through the city according to the watchmen's schedule.[65] Moreover, she explained that most of their communication with each other and between Pompey and the two men who apparently had promised to pay him if he set Gansevoort's house on fire had occurred in alleyways and during Sunday's church services. Her vivid description shows that enslaved New Yorkers often created geographies of resistance within the communities and areas in which they lived.

That enslaved men and women navigated these communities differently should have come as no surprise to the authorities. For instance, a 1740 New York City law that prohibited enslaved men and women to trade corn, peaches, and other fruit in the city detailed that enslaved New Yorkers had been selling produce in the public streets as well as in "houses, out houses & yards."[66] Moreover, enslaved men and women often lived and worked in cellars and behind their enslavers' living spaces, which would have given them a different perspective of the towns and villages they inhabited. Yet, as Bernard Herman noted in the case of Charleston, white people often believed that they controlled their environment. They assumed that enslaved people traversed the city in the same ways that they did.[67] Enslaved men and women used their enslavers' false confidence to navigate their communities unnoticed. Especially at night, free New Yorkers had very little control or oversight over the backyards and alleyways through which enslaved people moved. In rural areas, enslaved men and women would have traveled on back roads or other alternative routes to hide any unpermitted travel and activities. Thus, enslaved New Yorkers regularly circumvented the mechanism implemented to ensure white control of public spaces.

Enslaved men like Lewis, who had transported Benjamin Franklin from Albany to New York City, often labored in the region's public spaces, and they frequently used these assignments to expand such unsupervised moments. No one would have noticed if Lewis extended his ride back to Schuyler Mansion briefly so that he could include a quick visit with family or friends who lived along the route or if he used this opportunity to circulate messages or even packages.[68] Men like him gained extensive knowledge of the physical and social landscape, which helped them navigate the public space even when they did not have permission to do so. In fact, William Strickland suggested in his journal that enslaved men in Dutch American communities often had a better understanding of their environment than the people who enslaved them when he wrote, "I have several times called at Dutch houses to make enquiries, when the owner, unable, though otherwise willing, to give the information, has called for Con, or Funk his oldest Slave, to answer my questions, or point out the road to the place I was going not perhaps distant more than a very few miles."[69] With knowledge of their environments, these enslaved people were able to create geographies of resistance in which they resisted their enslavers' control over their movements and activities in these public spaces. Although enslavers were acutely aware of the fact that these enslaved men could use such brief moments in the public space to escape their oversight, they needed their enslaved laborers to work in public spaces, and they believed that the systems of control and surveillance they had put in place would at least curtail any prohibited behavior.

Free New Yorkers tried to limit the activities and mobility of their enslaved laborers through legislation. Yet, as the many court cases reveal, legal restrictions could not stop enslaved people's activities in the public space. Even though their activities were firmly regulated, restrictions were not always strictly enforced, and thus enslaved men and women often met in public spaces even when such activities were prohibited.[70] Enslaved New Yorkers gathered in groups, traveled the streets after curfew, purchased alcohol, and traded goods. In 1710, for instance, New York City's courts accused Catherine Elbertse of entertaining enslaved men "without the privity or knowledge of their Masters or Owners."[71] While in New York City, William Livingston complained that one of the men he enslaved would "be abroad at nights after the family was a bed, & we would never find by what avenue he went or return'd."[72] Similarly, Ulster County petitioners explained that because enslaved people often broke the law "in the silent hour of the night" there were few people who witnessed their crimes.[73]

Various sources discuss the predominantly male get-togethers of enslaved New Yorkers in public spaces. In 1690s New York City, for instance, a group of enslaved people were accused of making "a great noise and disturbance" in the evening.[74] In 1710, charges against Elizabeth Green, who entertained enslaved New Yorkers, claimed these enslaved people from the South Ward "feast and revell in the night time."[75] Sometimes, enslaved people used abandoned buildings for late-night gatherings. In the 1730s, for instance, enslaved New Yorkers regularly met at "the little wooden house belonging to Widow Wilkinson upon Golden Hill in the East Ward" of New York City.[76] Although white New Yorkers prohibited such get-togethers and contained general mobility of enslaved men and women in the public space, they could not stop these activities from occurring.

Whether it was in urban or rural New York, court records reveal that plenty of free New Yorkers engaged enslaved men and women in prohibited activities. In 1697, for example, Anthony Bosselyn and John Wels, both of Marbletown, were indicted for selling alcohol to enslaved men "without the consent of their masters."[77] Mattys Slecht of Kingston pleaded guilty to selling "several pots of beer" to enslaved men in 1716.[78] The frequency with which local and regional authorities reenacted legislation that prohibited trade with enslaved people and selling alcohol to them suggests that many ignored such bans. Indeed, one act noted that "many Mischiefs have been Occasioned by the too great Liberty allowed to Negro and other Slaves."[79] The continued occurrences of illicit trade by enslaved men and women brought a group of Ulster residents to petition the State Assembly for "a more effective Law to prevent trafficking with Slaves." In part, their 1792 petition complained about "the scandalous custom of many of the citizens of this state of trading with the said slaves."[80] Thus, often with the collaboration of the free New Yorkers, enslaved New Yorkers defied their enslavers and the social and spatial restrictions imposed on them.[81]

Such activities were undoubtedly difficult to stop because they offered enslaved laborers rare opportunities to congregate while temporarily escaping the "master class," and the free New Yorkers who traded with them or sold them alcohol benefited financially from these exchanges.[82] Clearly, truancy was common among enslaved New Yorkers, but some of them used their knowledge of the physical and sociopolitical landscape to create a more permanent escape from bondage. For much of the eighteenth century, men and women in Albany County, for example, took advantage of the area's close proximity to the Iroquois Nations and New France colony to flee. When in 1786, three enslaved men ran away, their enslavers feared that they "will doubtless make their way to the Indians, as they are very good Hunters, they will doubtless become as one of them."[83] Such efforts to escape caused authorities to pass a law as early as 1705 in an effort to "prevent the running away of Negro Slaves out of the City and County of Albany to the French at Canada."[84]

During times of war, and especially during the American Revolution, enslaved New Yorkers took advantage of the political turmoil. Graham Russell Hodges shows in his analysis of New York and New Jersey runaway slave advertisements that the number of men and women who tried to free themselves increased significantly during the American Revolution.[85] When Vermont abolished slavery in 1777 and Massachusetts followed in 1784, these states became destinations for some enslaved New Yorkers. For example, when an enslaved mother named Bett ran away with her children, they were thought to have fled to the neighboring free state of Massachusetts, which was especially close to Albany.[86] These enslaved men and women understood the sociopolitical landscape and physical geography, and they often knew how to navigate these to escape their enslavement.

Enslaved men and women also defied their enslavers' efforts to control their movement through the use of travel passes. At times, enslaved men and women took advantage of the travel passes they received, or they forged such papers to escape their bondage. When the enslaved woman Deb got "permission to seek a master," a common practice in Dutch American communities where enslaved people were tasked with finding a new enslaver, she used this opportunity to run away.[87] Similarly, according to an 1805 runaway slave advertisement, Jack, who had fled his enslaver in Albany, would "probably shew a paper permitting him to look for a master."[88] An 1815 runaway slave advertisement in the *Albany Register* searched for Caesar, "a black man, having got leave of absence from his master to join in the amusements of Pingster Holidays, with a promise that he would come back on the Tuesday following, but he has not yet returned."[89] These enslaved men and women used the pass system their enslavers had put in place to control them to legitimize their movements in the public space.

Although New York's enslavers developed various tactics to control the movements and activities of the people they enslaved in the public space, these geographies of control were never foolproof. Indeed, enslaved New Yorkers found multiple ways to expand their mobility. They created geographies of resistance, alternative ways of knowing and navigating public spaces that helped them escape their enslavers' control, even if only temporarily.

Pinkster

On June 29, 1803, the *Daily Advertiser* of Albany published a description of its Pinkster—the Dutch version of Pentecost or Whitsuntide—festival. It detailed a parade through the streets of Albany that was led by a Black man known as King Charles. According to the article, he was "master of ceremonies, whose whole authority is absolute and whose will is law during the whole of the Pinkster holidays."[90] The days-long celebration that followed included games, music, dancing, and drinking. Similar African American Pinkster celebrations took place in Dutch American communities from Schenectady to Brooklyn. While it appears peculiar that an African king had complete authority and enslaved men, women, and children were allowed to congregate, drink, and dance in the public space, a close examination reveals that Pinkster resembled celebrations led by enslaved people across the Americas.

The earliest descriptions of Pinkster as a distinct African American celebration date back to the late eighteenth century, when slavery in New York reached its peak. During the celebration, enslaved men, women, and children in the region's Dutch communities would gather in large groups, play music, dance, and drink alcohol, apparently even excessively if they liked to do so. But why did slaveholders allow enslaved men, women, and children to take time off and celebrate in the public space for several days, doing those things that they were restricted from doing the rest of the year? Some scholars have suggested that allowing brief periods of freedom during Pinkster was a way for enslavers to avoid resistance. Historian Shane White, for example, argues that Pinkster served as "a safety valve allowing a cathartic release from the pent-up frustrations both of the long winter and of the institution of slavery."[91] Similarly, Graham Hodges contends that Pinkster celebrations "created a momentary equality and community among Africans and Dutch and was a safety valve for household tensions."[92] Indeed, similar regulated celebrations proved integral to maintaining slavery in other parts of North America, whether it was Election Day in New England, General Training Day in New Jersey, Sunday meetings in New Orleans's Congo Square, or local "frolics" on southern plantations.[93] Such celebrations, akin to Pinkster, proved integral to sustaining slavery in slaveholding societies.

Crucial to these celebrations, the slaveholding class determined the location and parameters of the celebration and observed the festivities. While Pinkster appeared to be led by enslaved people, it was only possible with permission of the people who held them in bondage. Regardless of these limitations, Pinkster became one of the few opportunities during which enslaved New Yorkers could freely meet with family and friends in the public space, and thus this celebration became an especially powerful tool for them to create community, spend time with loved ones, and celebrate a shared African heritage.[94]

The history of Pinkster and how it became such an important celebration to enslaved New Yorkers proves complex. In the Dutch Republic, Pinkster was both a religious and a folk celebration. Although Dutch authorities wanted to end the more popular celebrations that often accompanied these religious holidays, it appeared too challenging to completely abolish these days.[95] New

Netherland's authorities also strongly opposed such revelries, but many of these traditions, including Shrove Tuesday, Maydays, and New Year's celebrations, survived in the region.[96]

The folk festival connected to Pinkster became a popular event in many of the region's Dutch communities. Traditionally, this celebration came out of several nonreligious spring celebrations of which Pinkster was the last one before summer.[97] Early descriptions of Pinkster in North America emphasized the social aspect of the holiday. Already in 1680, Jasper Dankaerts mentioned the Pinkster celebration in the colony when he wrote, "Pinxter (Whitsunday). Domine Niewenhuyse having recovered from his sickness, we went to hear him preach . . . 10th, Monday. The second day of Pinxter. We had several visitors whom we received with love and affection, each one according to his circumstances."[98] Gabriel Furman's history of Pinkster in Long Island similarly focused on the holiday's social role: "Dutch inhabitants of Long Island . . . celebrated it by treating their friends to an abundance of good cheer, among which, and peculiar to this festival, was the 'Soft Wafels [waffles],' and by riding in parties about the country making visits."[99] Both descriptions show that the Pinkster holiday served as an opportunity to spend time with family and friends.

Over the course of the eighteenth century, Pinkster descriptions began to mention enslaved men and women who participated in the celebrations. Alexander Coventry, for instance, noted in his journal that Cuff, whom he enslaved, left to celebrate Pinkster, "a festival or feast among the Dutch." Coventry then explained, "It is all frolicking to-day with the Dutch and the Negro. This is a holy day, Whitsunday, called among the Dutch 'Pinkster,' and they have eggs boiled in all sorts of colors. . . . And the frolicking," he continued, "is kept up among the young folks, so that little else is done to-day but eat eggs and be jolly."[100] Similarly, in 1797, William Dunlap identified Pinkster at Passaic Falls, New Jersey, as a Dutch holiday during which "blacks as well as their masters were frolicking and the women & children look'd peculiarly neat and well dressed."[101] Although enslaved people already took part in Pinkster activities, it was not until the early nineteenth century that the festivities were depicted as large celebrations that appeared to be predominantly African American.

The African American Pinkster celebration may appear unusual, but regulated celebrations by enslaved women, men, and children were not uncommon in North American communities. In fact, Stephanie Camp argues that organized events of entertainment served as a way "to control black pleasure by allowing it periodic, approved expression." She explains that in order to ensure that these celebrations remained harmless enslavers would be "attending and surveilling the parties."[102] Similarly, Saidiya Hartman suggests that enslavers used these "innocent amusements" as a way "to cultivate hegemony, harness pleasure as a productive force, and regulate the modes of permitted expression."[103] In Dutch New York, Pinkster proved similarly integral to successfully sustaining slavery.

Pinkster festivals became controlled celebrations in seemingly carefully chosen locations where enslaved people gathered under white surveillance. For one, the celebration was commonly restricted to a specific area of the town or city in which it was celebrated, probably so that the festivities could be monitored more effectively. According to James Fenimore Cooper's semiautobiographical novel *Satanstoe*, Pinkster in New York City was celebrated on the commons, close to the gallows and the African burial ground.[104] Likewise, in Albany the celebration took place near the town's prison and the gallows on what became known as Pinkster Hill. Reportedly, Pompey, Dean, and Bet were executed there in 1794 for their presumed role in the Albany fire.[105] Shane White claims that the celebration took place close to the gallows to "emphasize the functional role that the festivities played in reinforcing the social order."[106] Thus, enslaved celebrants would have had constant reminders of the consequences if they extended their temporary liberty beyond the carefully orchestrated social and physical parameters of the celebration.

That white New Yorkers observed and surveilled the festival is apparent from descriptions of the celebration by these white spectators. In an 1857 *Harper's Magazine* description of Albany's Pinkster celebration, an Albany citizen recounted his childhood memories of Pinkster: "Pinkster Hill! What pleasant memories of my boyhood does that name bring up!"[107] Alexander Coventry and William Dunlap both described Pinkster as a festival that Dutch *and* African Americans attended. Moreover, James Fenimore Cooper noted in *Satanstoe* that during a Pinkster celebration in New York City, "hundreds of whites were walking through the fields, amused spectators."[108] An article published in the *Albany Centinel* and reprinted in the *Daily Advertiser* provided further proof that white people were present when it mentioned that as part of the tradition the Pinkster king would collect revenue from the Black and white celebrants: "This consists in a levy of one shilling upon every black man's tent, and two upon every tent occupied by a white man."[109] The "Pinkster Ode," an early nineteenth-century poem attributed to Absolom Aimwell (probably a pseudonym), referred to the diverse crowds: "Now, there will be, the eye to lure, / All the world in miniature. / Men of every grade you'll see, / From lowest born to high degree. / Indians from the west will come, / And people from the rising sun. / There you'll see brave mountaineers—/ The independent Vermonteers."[110] The ode then listed the various socioeconomic and ethnic groups that attended the festivities.

North America's Pinkster celebrations also resembled various inversion traditions, which played an important role in maintaining social order in hierarchical societies. Reversing worlds served as a central element in various African,
American, and European celebrations: those who were in power allowed those
in lower social positions to have absolute authority for a short time period.[111]
In his work on Christmas celebrations, Daniel Miller traces reversal as well as
elections of kings back to Roman feasts. With regard to reversal, he states that
in "both Saturnalia and Kalends we find the master feasting the slave and . . .
this is merely the most extreme example of a sense of inversion from ordinary norms."[112] Miller also explains that these celebrations often included other
elements such as the election of a king who would be in charge of the festivities. Likewise, upside-down behavior played a role in a number of precolonial
African traditions as detailed by Evan M. Zeusse, who points out that these
practices often carried religious significance.[113]

In the Netherlands, the medieval folk celebration of Pinkster also included
such elements of inversion. Historian Marc Wingens explains that in Amsterdam people elected the most beautiful girl of the neighborhood to be the *Pink-
sterbloem* (Pinkster flower) during the Pinkster celebration. This young woman
would be crowned with a *Pinksterkroon* (Pinkster crown) made of leaves and
flowers.[114] She would go from door to door to collect money to fund the festival. Comparable inversion practices in which those people who had least social and political power were in charge of the festivities played a role in
Pinkster celebrations across the Dutch Republic.[115]

The nineteenth-century texts that discuss Pinkster in North America describe a similar celebration. In fact, the North American Pinkster festivals in
which enslaved men and women were in charge could be seen as a direct con-
tinuation of Dutch Pinkster celebrations. During Albany's Pinkster, King
Charles (or Charley) was the master of ceremonies, and according to some
descriptions this king, clad in British military costume, paraded through the
streets of Albany and collected revenue from participants.[116] The "Pinkster
Ode" detailed the king's central role in the festivities: "Of Pinkster, who pre-
sumes to sing, / Must homage pay to Charles the King: / For Charles, like
Israel's mighty Saul, / Is nobly born, well made and tall."[117] Thus, it appeared
as if Black New Yorkers received unmediated authority during these festivities. But while it seemed as if those who usually had the least social power
commanded the celebration, the leading classes always contained and controlled such inversion rituals.

Although white New Yorkers served as important observers of the celebration, some early nineteenth-century sources began to complain about the
participation of "a certain class of whites" in Albany's Pinkster festival.[118] These

complaints suggested that some white people became more active participants instead of spectators. In one of its more outrageous descriptions, an *Albany Centinel* article complained, "Here lies a beastly black, and there a beastly white, sleeping or wallowing in the mud and dirt."[119] The multiethnic aspect of Pinkster became so problematic that Albany's council felt the need to restrict white participation in the celebration in July of 1804:

> No white person shall during the Whitsuntide Holiday erect or put up any Boothe Hut or Tent within the said City near to or where the Negroes shall erect or put up theirs, nor shall any white person expose for sale any beer, Cyder, mead, spirituous liquors, or cake, crackers or any kind of refreshment at the place or places where the Negroes shall meet to carry on their said amusements, under the penalty of $5 for every offence.[120]

In fact, several historians have argued that it was increased white participation in Albany's Pinkster celebrations that would eventually lead to its abolition in 1811.[121]

It remains unclear why there were no earlier sources that so vividly depicted the elaborate Pinkster festival as the early nineteenth-century sources did. Interestingly, most descriptions of its New England counterpart, Negro Election Day, also date back to the late eighteenth and early nineteenth centuries.[122] Perhaps most white authors initially found such celebrations unworthy of detailed reporting. Both Peter Burke and Jonathan Prude have argued that before the late eighteenth century there was no interest in describing the activities of the poor and enslaved. Instead, they focused on the "ladies and gentlemen." Prude contends that even "travel accounts before the late eighteenth century generally skipped over the lower orders or conflated them with all 'people' of a region."[123] Certainly, this focus on "high" rather than "low" culture could explain the absence of detailed Pinkster descriptions in the early eighteenth century. It is also possible that these predominantly African American Pinkster celebrations simply did not exist in the early eighteenth century. James and Lois Horton, for example, have suggested that African influences in the North, which were crucial in the development of these celebrations, became more influential in the second half of the eighteenth century when larger numbers of African captives were imported into the region.[124]

Although these may have been contributing factors, it is also possible that the more elaborate late eighteenth-century and early nineteenth-century Pinkster celebrations came out of an increasingly paternalistic approach to slavery that became more prevalent during this period. Although slavery in New York still expanded in the late eighteenth century, Enlightenment thought and revolutionary rhetoric had challenged the continued enslavement of fellow human beings. Paternalism served as a justification for their enslavement because it suggested that white people were not just superior, they also knew what was best for Black men, women, and children. Plus, as more enslaved New Yorkers considered manumission or an escape from slavery a real possibility, Pinkster may have been an attempt to mollify such efforts and tie enslaved men, women, and children more thoroughly to local communities. To this end, Dutch American enslavers allowed enslaved men, women, and children an opportunity to celebrate and not pay attention to the many laws that restricted their movements and activities in the public space through a festival they controlled and surveilled.

Such paternalistic attitudes were evident in the early nineteenth-century descriptions that noted Black participants' supposed laziness and excessive alcohol consumption during the celebration, a tool often used to degrade Black people. An 1804 article in the *Albany Centinel* called "Death of Capt. Shawk" provided an especially detailed account to illustrate these so-called weaknesses of Black men:

> Upon that great Dutch holiday, which they call *Pinxster*, [Captain Shawk] would dress himself in his best clothes, and indulge too much in idleness with his fellow blacks. This was the season in which he was most likely to be overcome with liquor. It is observable that whatever objections the blacks have to religion, they readily embrace, and are extremely fond of holidays; and wou'd be still more so, were they increased to double the number. This part of religion operates as a charm upon them; and may be one reason why the Dutch encourage the observance of such days. The servants wander abroad, drink, and frolic, all in honour of Pinxster; and have a licence and opportunity of committing excess and lewdness which they have not upon any other day.[125]

Such stereotypical depictions of Black New Yorkers helped whites feel superior to their Black counterparts who according to such descriptions could not control themselves.[126] Robert Ross discusses similar portrayals of the Khoikhoi in South Africa by European colonists: in drama, literature, and drawings, the Khoikhoi were often portrayed drunk, which was the "antithesis to respectability."[127] For similar reasons, Rashauna Johnson describes get-togethers in Congo Square as opportunities for free people "to enjoy a curated and contained blackness."[128] Not surprisingly, some of the more famous descriptions of Pinkster were likely exaggerated accounts used to justify the continued enslavement and degradation of Black people.

A Celebration of Family, Friends, and Heritage

Although Pinkster may have been used to sustain slavery in the region, the festival nevertheless proved incredibly important to the enslaved men, women, and children who lived in Dutch American communities, as is evident from several surviving records. Sojourner Truth shared her fond memories of the Pinkster festival in her autobiography, suggesting that she considered returning to her former enslaver, John Dumont, so that she "might enjoy with [her former companions], once more, the coming festivities."[129] During Pinkster, enslaved men, women, and children had an opportunity to escape their bondage, if only for a few days. They would join in all kinds of revelry, sell produce, and simply reconnect with family and friends. As some scholars have explained, the performances at the center of such get-togethers had an important emotional and spiritual meaning and could provide healing for people who experienced daily emotional and physical abuse.[130]

Enslaved New Yorkers often lived in their enslavers' homes with only few other enslaved men and women, and thus they often struggled to build a community. For these men, women, and children, Pinkster served as a rare opportunity to spend time with family and friends. Sojourner Truth's narrative provides an especially chilling description of this important function of the festival during which "all her former companions enjoy[ed] their freedom for at least a little space, as well as their wonted convivialities, and in her heart she longed to be with them."[131] Her longing to join the festivities proved so strong that she even considered returning into slavery. At this point in her life, Truth had been forcefully separated from many loved ones, a typical experience for enslaved men and women in the region. Pinkster, then, gave them something to look forward to: a brief moment during which they could enjoy the company of some of the people from whom they had been separated.

Indeed, Pinkster served as a moment during which enslaved men and women could reconnect with each other; at the same time, they used the celebration to reconnect with their cultural roots. During the celebration, they would rejoice in predominantly African-originated traditions. In fact, for some enslaved Africans in the region, Pinkster must have been a familiar holiday, especially if they came to New York from predominantly Catholic areas in the Americas or Africa. By 1600 Catholicism had become the predominant religion in large parts of West Central Africa.[132] Even though only a few sources mention Pentecost celebrations in these regions, Catholicism in West Central Africa has been well documented. West Central Africans used Catholic holidays to pay their respect to the ancestors, as was the case with the All Souls' holiday. On this holiday, as well as on Holy Thursday, a procession would pass by churches and tombs, where the participants would light candles for the dead.[133] According to John Thornton, "Central Africans argued that it was best to attempt this form of mediumship in the presence of physical remains of the ancestor."[134] Thus, it should not be surprising that Angolans usually visited the tombs of the dead during All Souls' Day.[135]

The importance and even physical presence of the ancestors integral to these West Central African celebrations was also evident in Pinkster festivities, which often took place close to African burial grounds. The "Pinkster Ode" mentions the proximity of Albany's Pinkster Hill to the ancestors when it rhymed: "Now if you take a farther round / You'll reach the Africs' burying ground."[136] But the similarities do not stop there. Various popular celebrations in West Central Africa carried elements similar to Pinkster. By far the most important Catholic celebration in the Kingdom of Kongo was St. James Day. This holiday commemorated the victory of the Christian Kongo King Afonso I over his pagan brother Mpanzu a Kitima, a symbol of the establishment of Christianity in the kingdom.[137] In Kongo, royal tax collectors collected state revenue and a large military review would take place.[138] This holiday connected the power of the ancestors with this world through the person of the king, also known as the *Mani Kongo*. St. James Day was a day of great celebration in Kongo, with parades, military dances, and various other festivities. Like Pinkster, it celebrated connections to the spirit world, had a king at the center of its festivities, and was accompanied by a collection of revenue. In his work on Pinkster, Jeroen Dewulf highlights that elements of Pinkster celebrations also resembled Kongolese sangamentos during which, as Cécile Fromont explains, Kongolese confraternities "elected kings and queens, sent off ambassadors, staged mock battles with sticks or fake swords, and collected funds." West Central Africans exported these activities to various parts of the Americas, including New York.[139]

Various West African cultures similarly knew celebrations that resembled, at least in part, Pinkster. In his descriptions of the Gold Coast, Willem Bosman mentioned that people there held a festival that took place at the end of harvesting time and one that he claimed served to expel the Devil, both of which he compared to a Dutch fair.[140] In a description of Cape Coast, Jean Barbot described a yearly festival on a date assigned by the king of Fetu when people from all over the region would gather for an eight-day celebration. As part of the festivities, a supreme court, which included the king, resolved disputes that the local courts had been unable to settle.[141] Several scholars have connected the central role of the king in New England's Negro Election Day to such West African traditions. Many of these kings or governors had Akan names, including Governor Quash Freeman of Derby, Governors Cuff and

Quaw of Hartford, Roswell Quash Freeman of Derby, and Quash Piere of New Haven.[142] In fact, Joseph Reidy linked Election Day to the Ashanti Adae ceremony during which the king would lead a procession.[143]

Pinkster descriptions mentioned African-originated music and dance as important elements of the celebration. The *Albany Centinel* article, for example, claimed that after revenue had been collected, "sports of various kinds commence in what the different Negroes call *Toto*, or the Guinea dance."[144] According to another account, "The dances were the original Congo dances, as they danced in their Native Africa." The author of the text then provided an elaborate description of the music and dance of Albany's Pinkster celebration:

> The music consisted of a sort of drum, or instrument constructed out of a box with sheep skin heads, upon which old Charley did most of the beating, accompanied by singing some queer African air. Charley generally led off the dance, when Sambos and Philises, juvenile and antiquated, would put in the double-shuffle-heel-and-toe breakdown, in a manner that would have thrown Master Diamond and other modern cork-onions somewhat in the shade.[145]

Likewise, the "Pinkster Ode" mentioned the music and dance that were part of the festival: "All beneath the shady tree / There they hold the jubilee. / Charles, the king, will then advance, / Leading on the Guinea dance."[146]

The music and dances integral to these Pinkster celebrations were likely expressions of African American religious life.[147] Several descriptions by Capuchin missionary Dionigi de Carli point to music as part of West Central African religious rituals. After De Carli baptized a young woman he named Anne, for instance, spectators "made a ring and took her in the midst of them, dancing, playing on their instruments, and crying, 'Long live Anne, long live Anne.'"[148] In another account, De Carli described how after their baptism some Central Africans "fell a playing upon several instruments, a dancing, and shouting so loud, that they might be heard half a league off."[149] Such descriptions showed the central role of music and dance in these West Central African religious experiences.

Pinkster festival participants also performed ring dances that are considered an important part of African religious rituals. The "Pinkster Ode" noted these ring dances when it rhymed, "Afric's daughters full of glee, / Join the jolly jubilee. / Up the green and round the ring, / They will throng about their king. / Dancing true in gentle metre, / Moving every limb and feature."[150] Sterling Stuckey demonstrates that such traditions survived in the Americas because most Africans included some variation of a ring dance in their religious worship.[151] Like the ring shout, various African practices and traditions emerged in New York's Pinkster celebrations. Enslaved New Yorkers had few opportunities to share such traditions with other Africans and African descendants, making the Pinkster festival incredibly valuable to its Black celebrants.

Even though Dutch Americans likely used Pinkster to sustain slavery through this temporary yet controlled celebration, the festival proved crucial to enslaved people's emotional, social, and physical well-being. Not only did it give them an opportunity to meet with friends and family, it also gave them a chance to celebrate their heritage and religious beliefs. Not surprisingly, then, most enslaved New Yorkers cherished the celebration, and in some communities they continued to celebrate it into the late nineteenth century.[152]

Although Domingo and Manuel Angola had been able to obtain their freedom and become landowners in seventeenth-century Manhattan, their eighteenth-century counterparts would not have the same opportunities. Over the course of the eighteenth century, Dutch New Yorkers' increased reliance on the labor of enslaved people necessitated implementation of stricter regulations within public spaces. Whereas enslaved Africans in the seventeenth-century Dutch colony faced few restrictions on their movements in public spaces and access to public institutions, their eighteenth-century counterparts were forced to navigate a society in which their every move was controlled and surveilled and their access to public institutions often became severely limited or altogether prohibited. Public spaces became white space that enslaved people were required to access but where their activities and movements were closely monitored.

Even though enslaved people never became the majority of the region's population and the economy did not rely solely on enslaved labor, the slaveholding class's efforts to control enslaved New Yorkers in the public space much resembled that of slave societies elsewhere in the Americas. In an effort to control and contain enslaved people's access to and movements in public spaces, New York's enslavers created geographies of control by implementing, among others, legal restrictions, surveillance, and patrols. Yet, they could never fully control the movements and activities of enslaved New Yorkers, who developed alternative ways of knowing and navigating these public spaces, thus establishing geographies of resistance. Enslaved people moved through backyards and alleyways, and they timed their movements to avoid patrols. Even the carefully controlled Pinkster celebrations became opportunities of cultural, social, and in some cases physical resistance for Dutch New York's enslaved men, women, and children.

CHAPTER 4

Enslavement and the Dual Nature of the Home

Years after she had obtained her freedom, Sojourner Truth recounted some of the most heartbreaking memories of her enslavement in Dutch New York in her autobiography. Truth, then still called Isabella Baumfree, grew up in the home of her enslaver, Charles Hardenbergh of Swartekill in Ulster County. Together with the other people held in bondage by this Dutch American family, Truth, her brother Peter, and her parents, Bomefree and Mau-Mau Bett, lived in the dark, cold cellar of the house. She described these living quarters in her autobiography when she wrote that "its only lights consist[ed] of a few panes of glass, through which she thinks the sun never shone, but with thrice reflected rays; and the space between the loose boards of the floor, and the uneven earth below, was often filled with mud and water." When Charles passed away, his family manumitted Truth's parents and let them stay in the "dark, humid cellar" that for years had served as their living quarters, but Truth, who was only nine years old at the time, and her younger brother Peter were sold at auction. With their forced departure, her parents were separated from the last children they still had by their side.[1]

Although Truth and her family lived in the home of their enslaver, they experienced this space very differently from the people who held them in bondage. To them, this building could never be a true home or a safe haven. In fact, Truth's parents were acutely aware of the fact that the Hardenberghs had the power to break up their family at any time. Before the Hardenberghs sold Truth and her brother at auction, her parents had already been forcefully separated from at least eight other children. In her narrative, Truth describes moments when they would sit by "a blazing knot" in "their dark cellar" and she would listen to her parents "recalling and recounting every endearing, as well as harrowing circumstance that taxed memory could supply, from the histories of those dear departed ones, of whom they had been robbed, and for whom their hearts still bled." When recalling these events, Truth noted that she wished "all who would fain believe that slave parents have not natural affection for their offspring could have listened as *she* did" to these stories of love and loss.[2]

Few records discuss the experiences of enslaved New Yorkers in the great detail that Truth's autobiography does, but the surviving records do illustrate that her experiences much resembled those of other enslaved men, women, and children in the region. Although the enslaved population never reached 50 percent of New York's total population, in several of New York's Dutch communities the majority of Dutch American families enslaved people in their home. In Kings County, the number of households with enslaved laborers was especially large: by 1790, 72 percent of the Flatbush households included enslaved laborers, and in New Utrecht it almost reached 75 percent of families. Only in the town of Brooklyn did the number of slaveholding families not reach the majority, but at 48 percent it came very close (see Figure 4.1).[3] In Ulster County, where Truth grew up, the percentage of slaveholding families differed significantly per township. Whereas in Middletown just over 2 percent

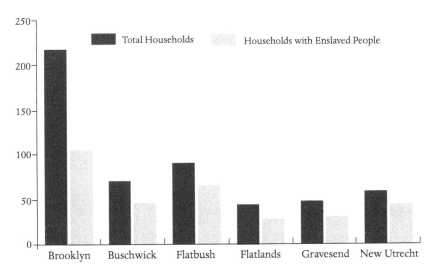

FIGURE 4.1. Total number of Kings County slaveholding families per total families in 1790, based on the 1790 Federal Census. Graph created by author.

of households included enslaved men and women in 1790, as many as 53 percent of Hurley families, 39 percent of Kingston families, 32 percent of Rochester's households, and 23 percent of New Paltz families held people in bondage. In Albany County, the number of slaveholding households was largest in the city of Albany and Rensselaerswijck.[4] When looking at these numbers, it becomes evident that a large number of free, white New Yorkers lived with enslaved men, women, and children in their home or on their grounds.

While many Dutch American families enslaved people in their homes, scholarship on slavery in these houses remains very limited.[5] Undoubtedly, the fact that few documents describe their relationships in these intimate spaces accounts for the limited scholarship that tackles this part of the history of slavery in the region. Yet, when incorporating analysis of the built environment and archeological research, a reconstruction of this history becomes possible. This chapter examines slavery and the lives of the enslaved in these Dutch American houses, considering the home a physical, social, and emotional space. Over the course of the eighteenth century, Dutch American enslavers increasingly considered where to house the people they held in bondage as they began to spatially segregate the work and living spaces of these enslaved people from the main living quarters. Many of these Dutch Americans organized their homes in ways that helped them control these enslaved people as well as assert their own status and dominance. Enslaved men, women, and children often inhabited the cold cellars or drafty garret spaces that in no way resembled the living spaces of their enslavers. Within these domestic spaces, enslaved men and women sought to create rival geographies.[6]

This chapter also examines the home as an emotional and social space. When doing so, the dual nature of these homes becomes clear: whereas the home generally symbolized domesticity, family, leisure, and prosperity for Dutch American families, their enslaved laborers experienced these buildings as spaces of exclusion, bondage, forced labor, abuse, and forced separation from kin. Through analysis of these different meanings, this chapter shows that for their enslaved inhabitants these buildings could never be a true home.

Segregation, Surveillance, and Systems of Control in Dutch American Homes

Whereas sleep and work areas for the enslaved were often haphazardly created in the late seventeenth and early eighteenth centuries, by the latter part of the eighteenth century these considerations had become more central to the layout of homes. Especially prominent Dutch American families who held several people in bondage organized their homes in ways that separated the enslaved laborers' work and living quarters from the family's main living spaces. These enslavers also structured their homes and grounds so that the movement of the men, women, and children they enslaved could best be controlled and surveilled. Much like their southern counterparts, architecture in these Dutch American communities proved a powerful tool in controlling enslaved people and the labor they produced.

While influenced by Dutch building styles, Dutch American homes differed per region and changed over time due to, among others, climate, environment, building materials, and Anglo-American influences. Dutch American farmhouses in western Long Island, for example, were usually wooden-clad, whereas stone farmhouses were more common in the mid-Hudson region, and farmhouses in the upper Hudson area were usually brick-sheathed.[7] In urban areas, like Albany and New York City, Dutch colonists preferred the narrow, brick townhouses with gable fronts that resembled Dutch medieval architecture.[8] Equally important, however, were the social and cultural circumstances that influenced Dutch American architecture. The system of slavery and class distinctions affected local architecture. By the mid-eighteenth century, for example, the area's elites often built Georgian-style homes that had become popular among North America's most well-to-do families.[9]

As an increasing number of Dutch American households relied on enslaved workers, they began to consider where these enslaved men, women, and children would live and labor more carefully. Research of the Hendrick I. Lott home in Flatlands, Kings County, reveals where this Dutch American farm family housed their enslaved laborers, and shows that while they initially approached the lodging of their enslaved laborers more haphazardly, they managed their housing more methodically as their numbers increased over the course of the eighteenth century.

Today, the Lott home stands in the middle of Marine Park, a residential area of Brooklyn. This suburban part of New York City was once farmland, largely owned by the Lott family. Johannes Lott, a descendant of Bartel Engelbertszen Loth who migrated to New Netherland in the 1650s, purchased the property in 1719 and built the original structure soon after (see Figure 4.2).[10] In 1800 his grandson Hendrick I. Lott built a new house to accommodate his family and their nineteenth-century lifestyle, and he attached the initial structure to the new house.

The Lott house became home to several generations of the Lott family and the people they enslaved. Very little documentary evidence discusses the enslaved people who lived in this house, though it is clear that the Lott family held several people in bondage over the course of the eighteenth century. In

FIGURE 4.2. Lott family home in Brooklyn, NY. This picture shows the initial structure with lean-to. The larger home, which was built in the early nineteenth century, is now attached to this structure. Picture by author.

1738, Johannes Lott reported three slaves to a local census, and a 1755 census of adult slaves listed two men and two women enslaved by the Lott family.[11] As was common in Kings County, the number of people held in bondage by the Lott family continued to grow over the course of the eighteenth century. By 1790, the family reported eleven slaves, and the 1803 probate records of Johannes Lott's estate listed four enslaved women, three enslaved men, three enslaved boys, and two enslaved girls: Mary, Hannah, Mell, Cate, Harry, Hechter, Powel, Syrus, Jan, Jacob, Hannah, and Poll.[12] Until the early nineteenth century, they likely all lived in the Lott home.

The original home built by Johannes Lott was a salt-box-style house, a one-room building style popular in early American settlements, with a small additional room on the north side.[13] This building had a loft that served as sleeping quarters for members of the Lott family. Much of daily life took place in the main room of the home, allowing for very little privacy for the Lott family and its enslaved laborers. Although the enslaved people who lived and worked in the home did not have clearly designated working and living spaces, the Lott family undoubtedly practiced social exclusion by prohibiting their enslaved laborers' participation in certain daily rituals as a way to mark social difference.[14]

Soon after the initial structure was built, the Lott family added a lean-to that functioned as a kitchen and work area; thus most labor produced by the family's enslaved laborers would have taken place in this lean-to.[15] A small set of stairs with garret spaces on each side led from the lean-to to the loft area where the Lott family sleeping quarters were located (see Figure 4.3). According to archeological findings, these garret spaces served as sleeping quarters for the family's enslaved laborers. The left garret space was ten square feet, four feet high, and had no windows (see Figure 4.4). A chimney ran through this space, which had a hole in it that may have functioned as "a beehive-shaped oven" to both heat up the room and warm up food.[16] A triangle had been cut out of the door to this room, probably for ventilation. The right garret space was a bit smaller and had no heat source.[17] Doors to both these garret spaces had locks on the outside that may have been used to lock up the enslaved laborers at night. These spaces would have been cold and drafty in the winter, and hot and humid in the summer. It would have been impossible to stand up straight in them. In fact, these rooms were so small and inconspicuous that researchers discovered them only a few decades ago. When Hendrick Lott expanded the house in the early 1800s, they likely moved the people they enslaved to an outdoor, brick kitchen.[18] Thus, by the early nineteenth century, the Lott family had probably removed most of the people they enslaved from the main house.[19]

A similar, gradual separation of enslaved laborers' working and living spaces appears to have happened in other Dutch American houses. Ulster County's stone farmhouses, for example, often started as one-room buildings that were expanded over the course of the eighteenth century with several square rooms, attached to each other in a linear arrangement. Commonly, these rooms each contained its own hearth and door to the outside.[20] Initially, Dutch American residents would have shared these spaces with their enslaved laborers, but over time, as they expanded their homes, they commonly removed the people they held in bondage and their labor from the main living spaces, as had been the case with the Lott home. These enslaved men, women, and children would have been relegated to garret spaces, attics, cellars, summer kitchens, or, in a few instances, to slave quarters. In many cases, they would have inhabited the cellar. For instance, archeologists found evidence that Abraham Hasbrouck of New Paltz housed his enslaved workers in his home's cellar, and of course the Hardenbergh family had Sojourner Truth and her family inhabit the cellar of their home.[21] As Truth so vividly described, these cellars were often damp and cold with little light, comfort, or privacy.

In many of these homes, the enslaved laborers' workspaces were moved to the cellar. Cellar kitchens became increasingly common in the region. With

FIGURE 4.3. Stairs from lean-to to the Lott family sleeping area. The garret spaces are located on the sides of these stairs. © Chester Higgins Archive/All Rights Reserved.

FIGURE 4.4. Lott home garret space. Corncobs placed by the enslaved people who slept in this space can be seen on the right where the floorboards have been removed. © Chester Higgins Archive/All Rights Reserved.

the kitchen in the cellar, excessive smoke was kept out of the first floor while the main living spaces of the home benefited from the heat that wafted from the cellar kitchen. Anne Grant, for example, noted that the home at Schuyler Flatts had a "sunk story, where the kitchen was immediately below the eating parlor, and increased the general warmth of the house."[22] Because in many of these New York homes most of the cooking and food preparation were done by enslaved laborers, cellar kitchens also kept the labor of servants and enslaved men and women separated from the main living quarters in the same way that lean-to buildings like the one at the Lott house did.

These developments were not particular to New York's Dutch American homes. In fact, similar changes that removed cooking and service activities to cellars, lean-to buildings, or outdoor kitchens occurred throughout the North American colonies and in Europe.[23] With these changes in architecture, home-owners created separate spaces for domestic labor. In North America, this shift largely excluded enslaved workers from the home's main living spaces. In fact, Dell Upton argues that adding such workspaces in Virginia homes came out of "an analytical desire for order and separation that grew out of and amplified the seventeenth-century division of servant and served spaces."[24] Historian Cary Carson similarly notices this shift in Virginia, noting that "architecture became the instrument of segregation."[25] An increased demand for privacy further promoted the segregation between the enslavers and their enslaved workers.[26] Changes in eighteenth-century New York architecture appear to have had very similar objectives.

At the same time that Dutch Americans increasingly separated the living and working areas of the people they enslaved from the main living spaces, elite families often organized their homes strategically to reflect their wealth, status, and power. As elsewhere in the colonies, Georgian architecture became the most popular building style among these elite families.[27] They moved most labor to dependencies on the sides and back of the home, while the main living areas of their houses became places of leisure and hospitality. These mansions were often located on hills overlooking roads or rivers because it made their homes appear imposing when approached from the river or main roads, and they regularly included tree nurseries and gardens in an effort to demonstrate that they controlled nature.[28] Thus, they used their homes and grounds to reinforce the idea that society's class distinctions were natural and inevitable.

The Philip Schuyler and Abraham Ten Broeck mansions in present-day Albany are clear examples of these building tactics. Philip Schuyler, who descended from several generations of prominent Dutch Americans, was a member of the New York Assembly until 1775 when he was elected delegate to the Continental Congress. He was appointed major general in the Continental Army later that year, and he served as U.S. senator and as a New York state senator. Over the course of his political career, his family became closely connected to many of America's most prominent political figures. The Abraham Ten Broeck family was equally prominent in the region. During the Revolutionary War, Abraham Ten Broeck served in the Albany militia, he was a businessman, and he held the position of Albany mayor from 1779 to 1783 and again from 1796 to 1798. He too came from a long line of Dutch American elites: both his father and grandfather had served as Albany City's mayor. His marriage to Elizabeth Van Rensselaer, sister of the patroon Stephen Van Rensselaer II, further solidified his family's elite status and Dutch roots. Ten Broeck also had a personal connection with the Schuyler family, in part because his daughter Elizabeth married Philip Schuyler's son Rensselaer.

Philip Schuyler and Abraham Ten Broeck were among the largest enslavers of the region. Schuyler owned estates in Saratoga and Albany, largely operated by enslaved laborers. In 1790, he reported thirteen slaves as part of his Albany estate to the first Federal Census.[29] Personal correspondence of Schuyler and his family regularly referred to the enslaved people—including Dick, Bob, Prince, Cato, Cesar, Britt, Bet, Tone, Phoebe, Silvia, and Tom—who cleaned their homes, prepared their foods, tended to their guests, and operated their farm and mill; yet, these letters revealed very little about their daily lives and instead focused predominantly on the various tasks these enslaved laborers completed for the family.[30] Most is known about Prince, the family butler who was known to have "placed every day a Tooth-pick by Mrs. Schuyler's plate."[31] As butler, he became well known by the family's guests, so much so that when in Spain in 1780, John Jay proposed that they use Prince's name, written backward, as a password.[32]

Construction of Schuyler's Albany mansion, then located just south of Albany, took place in the 1760s.[33] The large mansion had two stories, an attic, and a cellar (see Figure 4.5). The first floor included a hall, parlors, and a dining room. The second floor featured bedrooms and a large hallway with windows that overlooked the Hudson River. The home was located on a working farm and functioned as a residence and a place of business, where the family hosted, among others, George Washington and Benjamin Franklin. Attached to the home were a tree nursery and a kitchen on the northwest side and a building that functioned as an office on the southwest side of the main house. These structures were each one story high with small garret spaces. A 7.5-foot-high closed wall with a small roof and four windows that enclosed a work area behind the home connected to these dependencies (see Figure 4.6).[34] The Schuyler family largely restricted the men, women, and children they held

FIGURE 4.5.   Schuyler Mansion, then named The Pastures, built between 1761 and 1765. This was the first Georgian mansion in the Albany area. Courtesy of New York State Office of Parks, Recreation and Historic Preservation.

FIGURE 4.6.   Model of Schuyler Mansion, based on eighteenth-century maps of Albany, archeological excavations of the property, and Philip Schuyler's detailed description of his home and grounds for tax purposes in 1798. Courtesy of New York State Office of Parks, Recreation and Historic Preservation.

in bondage to this enclosed work area and the home's cellar. Most of the enslaved men, women, and children lived in the mansion's cellar, which could only be accessed from the walled yard, as evidenced by an account of a British attempt to kidnap Schuyler, which detailed that one of Schuyler's guards "sought shelter with the negroes in the cellar."[35]

The Abraham Ten Broeck family also lived in a spacious two-story Georgian-style building with a cellar and an attic, and they too built their mansion knowing that it would house enslaved laborers. When Ten Broeck had his new house built in the 1790s, he held twelve men, women, and children in bondage. Just like Schuyler mansion, the Ten Broeck home had a dining room, parlor, and large hallway on the first floor, while family bedrooms could be found on the second floor. Two one-story buildings were built at the sides of the home: most likely a privy had been located on the northwest side of the mansion and a summer kitchen and an office on the southwest side.[36] Although the home did not have an enclosed work area, most labor would have occurred in the building's cellar and at the sides and back of the house.

An archeological report of the home shows that the kitchen, pantry, food storage space, food preparation area, and possibly the living quarters for enslaved people were all located in the home's cellar. The cellar connected to the first floor with a service staircase in the back of the home. These stairs led to a space adjacent to the dining room that likely served as a pantry where the enslaved laborers made final adjustments to the food before they served it to the family and their guests. One cellar exit, located on the southeastern side, close to the front of the home, led directly to the outside where the yard and summer kitchen would have been located. Several enslaved people must have lived in the cellar room that had the best ventilation and was not associated with food preparation or storage, located in the back of the cellar on the most northwestern side, while some of them may have lived in the summer kitchen or the home's attic.[37]

The Schuyler and Ten Broeck families approached the housing of their enslaved laborers' living and working spaces strategically. They had these homes built when they enslaved several men, women, and children. Thus, they developed a strategic ordering of the house and grounds in which they placed the work and living spaces of these enslaved laborers in segregated areas, mainly out of sight from family and guests. Their work and living areas were generally limited to the cellar and the area behind the home. The dependencies at the Ten Broeck home and the wall around this work area at the Schuyler mansion further made much of the enslaved labor invisible. Through this spatial organization, they presented an "ordered and manicured world" to their guests, while hiding the "more cluttered world of the working plantation" behind their home, a practice that was common on southern plantations.[38] In fact, these Dutch American houses resembled many eighteenth-century southern plantation homes. Drayton Hall on the Ashley River in South Carolina, for example, situated its kitchen and slave quarters in the basement, and other southern mansions confined slave quarters and work areas to wings or dependencies.[39] As Kathleen Brown points out in her work on race and gender in colonial Virginia, this spatial organization of the southern plantation homes affirmed these families' gentility and placed slave labor at a "discreet distance from the white family's living quarters."[40] A similar spatial organization is evident in these elite Dutch American homes.

But these families did not only organize these homes to separate the enslaved workers and their labor from the main living spaces, they also created concentrated areas where most of the enslaved people's labor and lives took place as a way to help control the people they held in bondage. This approach is especially evident at Schuyler Mansion where the enclosed work area could be watched through windows at the back of the home as well as from the office, located in the walled area. In some ways, this architectural structure facilitated complete surveillance of the enslaved people's movements in ways that fit the panopticon model of surveillance first introduced by Jeremy Bentham but further developed by Michel Foucault.[41] James Delle has called such constructs on Jamaican plantations "spatialities of surveillance," spaces where visibility helped control the enslaved population.[42] Terrence Epperson has shown how Thomas Jefferson and George Mason implemented such surveillance at their estates, and it appears that the Schuyler and Ten Broeck families practiced similar methods of surveillance and control.[43] In fact, Theresa Singleton has pointed out that wall enclosures, as seen at the Schuyler mansion, combined with "panoptic surveillance" would become well-established methods of control in factories and plantations by the nineteenth century.[44]

In part, such surveillance and segregation were used to keep enslaved people from violent resistance. Even though some Dutch American slaveholders may have thought of themselves as benevolent masters, they still feared resistance from the people they enslaved. Most instances of slave resistance took place as individual acts within the home. The January 1708 murder of the William Hallett Jr. family of Newtown, Long Island, received a great deal of attention in the region. William, his pregnant wife, Ruth, and their five children were all killed in their sleep by two of their enslaved laborers—a Native American man and a Black female. White New Yorkers reeled from the horror, and in October of 1708, the state assembly passed "An Act for preventing the Conspiracy of Slaves," which made special mention of the Halletts' murders.[45] Due to its large scale, the 1712 New York City slave revolt, during which nine white

New Yorkers died, again sent shock waves through these communities. In 1741, anxieties over such resistance led New York's authorities to condemn several men and women to death for allegedly conspiring a revolt.[46] Yet, New York's slaveholders were well aware that they were most vulnerable in their homes. In 1715 an enslaved man named Tom was charged with the attempted murder of his master, Johannes Dijkeman, a tenant farmer at Livingston Manor, and on April 10, 1730, authorities charged a man named Harry with the attempted murder of his enslaver, Zacharias Hoffman of Shawangunk, whom he, according to the court records, had attempted to kill with an ax.[47] Such attacks reminded Dutch American slaveholders of the potential dangers of holding people in bondage within one's home.[48]

While the actual occurrences of violence enacted by enslaved people upon the people who held them in bondage were rare, enslavers created systems of control and surveillance in their homes and on their grounds to avoid or limit such acts of resistance. At the Schuyler mansion, for example, the living quarters of the enslaved laborers had been separated completely from the main living areas. Because the mansion had no staircase that connected the cellar where most of the enslaved laborers lived to the main home, it would have been impossible for enslaved workers to access the main house unnoticed. The walled courtyard ensured that these men, women, and children could not easily exit the premises. At the Lott house, fear of attacks may have motivated the Lott family to place wooden latches on the outside of the garret doors where the people they held in bondage slept. These locks could have been used to lock enslaved people in these spaces at night so that they would not have access to the Lott family members, but they may also have been used to simply control enslaved people's general mobility at night.[49]

While it is not known how common it was among Dutch American enslavers to lock up their enslaved workers at night, it certainly was not unusual for slaveholding families to use locks to protect family and property.[50] William Strickland described in his travel journal how Mrs. Livingston and others secured valuables: "There always is adjoining the drawing room, the breakfast room, or dining room, which serves as a store room and place of safe deposit for the master or mistress of a family. This used to be indispensibly [sic] necessary when slaves were the only servants, in the state of slavery in the first establishment of it in the country, and custom now continues it."[51] Dutch Americans assumed that housing enslaved laborers in the home required extra security.

Analysis of Dutch American homes reveals that whereas Dutch Americans initially approached the housing of their enslaved laborers more haphazardly, over the course of the eighteenth century they developed more deliberate divisions of spaces that relegated their enslaved laborers to separate areas, often below, above, and behind the main living areas. At the same time, they created systems of surveillance and control within their homes and on their properties that much resembled those of their southern counterparts.

Spaces of Resistance

The conditions in which enslaved New Yorkers lived were undoubtedly harrowing. Cellars were often humid and cold, with meager light and ventilation. There, they lived on dirt floors sometimes covered by wooden floorboards. The garret spaces they inhabited had very little space and were largely devoid of natural light. In most cases, they shared small areas with several others and thus they had minimal to no privacy. Yet, the cellars and garret spaces where they lived were also the places where they made love, wept, played, prayed, dreamed, and shared stories as they huddled together on cold winter nights. Sojourner Truth's description of the cellar in which she grew up points to the harsh conditions in which her family lived, but her narrative also reveals that her parents did what they could to create a comforting environment for their children. She recalled the evenings in particular, when they would spend time together either in the cellar gathered around a blazing knot or outside under the stars. During those moments, her parents taught her and her brother life lessons and shared stories about the family members who had been taken away from them.[52]

As was the case with Truth and her family, enslaved New Yorkers always searched for ways to resist their enslavers' attempts to control and monitor their activities. Increasing efforts by Dutch Americans to exclude their enslaved workers from the main living spaces helped these enslaved people to do so. The outdoor kitchens, garrets, and cellars, for example, often became semi-autonomous spaces for the enslaved. Rarely would enslavers tread down the often small and narrow stairs to these cellars or up to the garrets, and in some homes, such as Schuyler Mansion, these spaces would be accessible only from the outside. Historian Jared Hardesty found that enslaved Bostonians often used the kitchen to receive guests; thus they may have seen the kitchen as part of their domain.[53] Bet's confession after the 1793 Albany fire similarly suggests that many of Albany's enslaved men and women at the time considered the kitchen a space with limited oversight. As she explained, she, Dean, and Pompey waited in Volkert Douw's kitchen for the city's watchmen to check the streets before they headed to Gansevoort's home.[54] New York's kitchens, cellars, and garret spaces often served as places where enslaved New Yorkers could escape their enslavers' control temporarily.

Several scholars have researched the ways in which enslaved laborers used their living quarters to resist their enslavers' control, often by finding ways to temporarily escape their surveillance. James Delle's discussion of the "spatialities of resistance" proves pertinent here. He argues that enslaved laborers on Jamaica's coffee plantations created these spatialities when they devised "ways to avoid becoming the disciplined and docile work force that the planters demanded." On these plantations, the yaws house and hospital, where enslaved laborers with the yaws were isolated and treated, became such spaces of resistance because they lacked close surveillance.[55] Similarly, Terrence Epperson shows that while southern planters carefully arranged their property so that they could watch their enslaved laborers, control over these men, women, and children was "not absolute." For example, the entrances to the slave quarters at Carter's Grove plantation in Virginia were positioned in such a way that their movement could be "visually screened from the mansion," but researchers found that inhabitants of one of these cabins had transformed a window at the back of the building into a door, thus making some of their movements unnoticeable. Epperson explains that the creation of this passage shows that there were "both hegemonic and counter-hegemonic conceptions of space within the landscape."[56] He also points to the enslaved men and women who created pits underneath their cabins as ways to hide goods from their enslavers. Epperson identifies these modifications to their living quarters as acts of resistance, as does Theresa Singleton when she points out that enslaved people in nineteenth-century Cuba often "modified their living spaces" without permission from their masters.[57] Undoubtedly, enslaved New Yorkers similarly resisted their enslavers' surveillance and control.

No large modifications to the enslaved people's living quarters have been found in early New York's Dutch communities, but scattered pieces of evidence do reveal enslaved New Yorkers' efforts to create such geographies of resistance in their enslavers' homes. Archeological research at the Lott house, for instance, shows how some of the enslaved men and women who lived in this garret tried to safeguard this space. There, archeologists found various artifacts hidden below the floorboards, including a child's shoe, ritually placed corncobs, and a cloth pouch that contained an oyster shell and part of a sheep or goat pelvis.[58]

The placement of these items close to the chimney and doorways suggests that they served to protect these spaces.[59] Similar cached deposits have been uncovered during excavations at several sites in the South, but research has also revealed such deposits elsewhere in New York. For instance, in his article on apotropaic building practices in New York, Walter Wheeler discusses two caches found at Latting's Hundred, a home in Huntington, New York.[60] Several scholars have connected such charm bags to the *minkisi*—or the singular *nkisi*—of Kongolese people. *Minkisi* served wide-ranging purposes: they could be used to heal people, protect people or places, or inflict harm. These charm bags also resemble the *grisgris*—or *grigri*—that could be found in the Senegambia.[61] There, such pouches were mostly worn on the body for protection, but sometimes they were buried to safeguard a space. Cached deposits contained sacred artifacts that ranged from buttons and shells to animal bones. Their positioning proved equally important in their effectiveness. They are usually found in walls, underneath floorboards, or buried in earth at the northeastern corner of a room or by places of entrée, such as windows, doors, and chimneys, because these were potential access points of evil.[62]

The corncobs that archeologists found under the floorboards of both garret spaces at the Lott home possibly served to ward off evil. Their precise placing remains unclear because rodents may have disturbed them before they were found by archeologists, but they appear to have formed crosses or in one case a five-pointed star. The fact that they had been stripped but with the kernels still intact suggests that they were placed there intentionally, and their placement close to the chimney and doorways indicates that they were placed there to protect these spaces. Similar star-symbolism or ritual placement of corncobs has been uncovered at other New York homes. At the William Brandow house in Greene County, for example, a six-pointed star had been carved on the backside of planks that enclosed basement stairs, and at the Timothy Crane house in Charlton, Saratoga County, a drawing of a star had been hidden in the home's kitchen.[63] In both cases, the location of these stars suggests that they were the work of enslaved people. Research at Johnson Hall, the home of Irish immigrant William Johnson and his Mohawk wife, Molly Brant, unveiled corncobs in what appears to have been a ritual deposit from the 1760s.[64] Because of the Johnson family's close connections with the Iroquoian Nations, the use of maize here may have been derived from Iroquoian practices.

While it appears more likely that the corncobs at one of the Lott home garret spaces were forming a star, some of them may also have been placed in the shape of an X, a powerful symbol in many cultures. Scholars of the African diaspora have pointed out that the X held spiritual meaning in West Central Africa, and the Kingdom of Kongo in particular, where many of North America's African captives originated. According to Robert Farris Thompson, the X-shaped cross originated from the *dikenga*, a Bakongo cosmogram that represents the connection between the world of the living and that of the dead. In its most pure form, the X would be circled, but noncircled varieties can be found as well, especially in the diaspora. In the Americas, the *dikenga* may have become an important symbol for captive Africans and their descendants because it was a powerful symbol in various pre-Christian African religions as well as in Christianity.[65] Not surprisingly, then, variations of the X have been found across the Americas, including New York, at sites inhabited by enslaved Africans.[66] In her work on what she calls Kongo Christianity, Cécile Fromont contends that the Kongo cross in its various forms held different meanings over time, but she also claims that, in addition to representing power, crosses often served as "trustworthy shields even in matters of life and death."[67] If the enslaved person did indeed place the corncobs at the Lott house in the form of a cross, he or she probably did so in an effort to secure this space.

The artifacts found at the Lott home and elsewhere in New York demonstrate that the enslaved men and women who lived in these Dutch American homes did what they could to escape their enslavers' surveillance and control within these houses, even if only temporarily. They also used the few opportunities available to them to secure these spaces, possibly guarding them from potential harmful sources. The increasing separation of their living and working areas from the main living spaces allowed them to do so more effectively.[68]

The Dual Nature of the Home

When investigating Dutch American homes in early New York, it becomes apparent that enslaved and free inhabitants experienced these domestic spaces very differently from their enslavers. Whereas the main living areas of these houses were usually spacious and often had high ceilings and plenty of windows, the spaces where the enslaved men, women, and children worked and resided were usually small, damp, and largely devoid of natural light. They lived below, above, or behind the primary living spaces in cluttered environments with little to no privacy. Importantly, however, this dual nature of the home extended beyond these physical circumstances. Thus far, this chapter has focused on the physical layout of Dutch American houses; yet, the home fundamentally served as a social and emotional space, a place that symbolized family, domesticity, comfort, and care to the Dutch Americans who inhabited it. To the enslaved men, women, and children who lived in these houses, however, these were spaces of enslavement, forced labor, abuse, and possible separation from family members. To them, these homes represented anything *but* a safe haven.[69]

Ann Stoler's research of Dutch colonial Indonesia reveals this dual nature of the home. She found that whereas Dutch colonists recalled their interactions with their enslaved and servant laborers with great nostalgia and affection, these laborers often remembered these exchanges as moments of exclusion and control.[70] Enslaved and free people in Dutch New York would have experienced their interactions in the home similarly dissimilar, as becomes evident when closely examining the experiences of the enslaved people in these houses.

When investigating interactions in the home, it is important to first consider the ways in which Dutch Americans viewed the enslaved men, women, and children who lived and worked in these spaces. Other than the brief descriptions in family papers and advertisements, we know very little about the racial attitudes of New York's Dutch American population. One document provides a more detailed discussion of such attitudes in the latter part of the eighteenth century: an unsent letter written in 1788 by Dutch Reformed Church minister Peter Lowe in which he lists his congregants' objections to Black men becoming full members in the church. These congregants of Kings County's six congregations claimed that Black people "have no souls" and that "they are accursed by God." The congregants also suggested that African descendants were of a "different species": "Witness their nauseous sweat, complexion, manners."[71] These depictions of Black New Yorkers should not be surprising. Their opposition occurred when slavery peaked in this community, and most Dutch Reformed Church congregants benefited from the labor of enslaved people. At a time that the United States had just passed its Constitution and started building a nation based on the principle of freedom and equality for all, only racist explanations could justify keeping these people in bondage. The same people who lived in their homes, took care of their children, and cooked their meals were considered subhumans and soulless. But these attitudes were not new to these communities, where slavery had already existed for over 150 years.

Even though they held deeply engrained racist thoughts when it concerned Black people, some Dutch Americans nevertheless believed they developed affection for the men, women, and children they held in bondage. For instance, Maria Louw of Kingston, mother of the previously discussed Reverend Peter Lowe, inherited from her father an enslaved man she had known since she was a child. In 1786, the man attempted to flee the Louw household, but he was found and returned to their residency. As punishment, Maria's husband, Benjamin, shackled the man within their home. Maria wrote about these events to her son Petrus Louw, or Peter Lowe, the same Peter Lowe who two years later would face his congregants' resistance to Black membership in a Kings County Dutch Reformed Church. In her letter, she explained that seeing this man in such miserable circumstances greatly distressed her, especially because she had known him since early childhood. Yet, she did not refer to the enslaved man by name, instead calling him *"onse neger"* (our negro).[72] She also did not mention whether or not she opposed her husband when he decided to shackle the man within her home. In fact, her letter emphasized how these events made *her* feel instead of highlighting his suffering. Louw's letter shows how these relationships differed significantly for enslavers and enslaved. Whereas Louw wrote about her affection for the man, he tried to escape the Louw family, and because of his attempt to gain freedom he was now chained, literally, within the house. Surely, the Louw home did not represent comfort or domesticity to him; instead, it was a place of bondage that he wanted to escape. For enslaved New Yorkers like him, the homes of their enslavers served as the most poignant reminders of the power relations necessary to sustain slavery.

Even when contemporaries suggested that Dutch American enslavers supported the family life of the people they held in bondage, research suggests the opposite was true. In her *Memoirs of an American Lady*, Scottish author and poet Anne Grant narrated her experiences living at the Schuyler Flatts estate, north of Albany, as a child in the mid-eighteenth century. She described life and culture in Albany and its surroundings, including slavery and the lives of the enslaved. These depictions often provided an idyllic representation of slavery in these Dutch American communities. For instance, she claimed that enslaved laborers and their children often lived with the same family all their life. She recounted that at the Schuyler Flatts two enslaved women—Maria and Diana—were "the principal roots from whence the many branches, then flourishing, sprung, yet remained. These were two women, who had come originally from Africa while very young; they were most excellent servants, and the mothers or grand-mothers of the whole set."[73] Though some of this depiction may have been true, Grant's discussion does not match the evidence uncovered at the Schuyler Flatts burial ground, where the family's enslaved laborers were laid to rest. When researching several of the remains found at this site, scientists discovered that none of the enslaved people buried there were connected through their mtDNA, which indicates that none of them were related through the matrilineal line.[74] While this does not necessarily mean that Grant misrepresented the family connections of the enslaved families she encountered at the Schuyler Flatts, it does significantly challenge her account. Nevertheless, Grant's description fits common narratives of slavery in North America's Dutch communities as a more genteel form of slavery, thus ignoring the cruel realities of the system.

Like Grant, contemporaries often overstated the opportunities for enslaved people to establish families, but their depictions of slavery in New York's Dutch communities also failed to acknowledge that in addition to living in cramped, cold, and unsanitary spaces, enslaved men, women, and children faced constant threats of abuse and neglect in their enslavers' homes. Correspondence of the Philip Schuyler family suggests that Prince endured extreme neglect before the Schuyler family purchased him, but usually such discussions of neglect and abuse remain undiscussed in the records.[75] The violence committed upon enslaved people becomes especially evident when reading runaway slave advertisements that detailed the scars on the bodies of fugitives.[76] Amos who fled his enslaver in New Paltz, for example, had many scars "on and between his shoulders," which likely resulted from severe whippings on his back.[77] A thirty-year-old man named Tite, who escaped the home of Conrad ten Eyck in Albany County, was, according to the advertisement that announced the search for him, "born with five fingers on each hand, but the small one on each was taken off when he was young." The advertisement did not specify how and why his fingers were "taken off," but one can imagine the abuse he had likely endured.[78] Multiple runaway slave advertisements mentioned fugitives whose toes had been frozen, which suggests that it was not uncommon for enslaved people to lack proper shoes for New York winters. When Harre ran away from Philip Schuyler, for example, he was described as having "large feet, and walks something lame, having had his toes frozen."[79] Just as Prince requested to change enslavers in an effort to escape the abuse he endured, the men, women, and children described in these runaway slave advertisements often fled the houses in which they lived to find some reprieve from violence and neglect.

For enslaved women, it was particularly harrowing to live and work in close proximity to their enslavers, often in intimate spaces where these men could use their control over enslaved women to sexually harass or abuse them. As Catherine Clinton has so poignantly described in her work on sexual coercion, "slavery was not simply a system of labor extraction but a means of sexual and social control as well."[80] Although enslaved men and boys were at times victims of sexual coercion, enslaved women and girls most frequently faced such violence. Very few records mention sexual exploitation of enslaved women in New York, and when they do, they generally leave out the woman's experiences. In 1671, for instance, Jacob Jansz Flodder of Beverwijck (Albany) admitted in court that he could not sell an enslaved child "because the boy was his bastard son."[81] Tellingly, the court records did not mention the enslaved woman who gave birth to his child. She had no control over what happened to her body or the fate of her son.

One of the most famous cases of sexual coercion in Dutch American families occurred in the Schuyler family. According to Grant, one of the Schuyler men, whom she referred to as Colonel Schuyler, fathered a child with one of the family's enslaved women. Grant noted that once the family found out about Colonel Schuyler's relationship with the woman, they never again entrusted

him "with anything of his own, and [he] lived an idle bachelor about the family."
Grant wrote that the Schuyler family took care of the child, whom they referred
to as Chalk, and when he reached maturity they gave him a farm "in the debts
[sic] of the woods," probably as a way to hide the offspring of what they considered a disgraceful relationship.[82] Grant did not say much else about Chalk or the
man who fathered him, but she did not at all describe the boy's mother. We do
not know her name, age, or fate. Again, the woman's experience was omitted
from the records.[83]

While we do not know the specifics of these cases, research of sexual violence enacted upon enslaved women shows how enslavers used their power
to control the movement of enslaved women to place them in physically vulnerable circumstances.[84] Within the home, male predators created situations
in which they would be alone with these women, whether this was in their
office, bedroom, cellar, or any other temporarily private space. Enslaved girls
often became aware of these dangers at a young age; consequently, they
learned how to avoid being alone with their enslaver or male family members,
using their knowledge of the home and grounds to protect themselves from
such sexual violence.[85] They were especially vulnerable if they lived and
worked in close proximity to their enslavers, as was generally the case in New
York, and in the long term they would have struggled to defend themselves
from the men who claimed to own their bodies, especially in an environment
where enslaved women had no protection or legal recourse.[86] In fact, Sharon
Block discovered in her research of rape and sexual coercion that "no historian has recorded a conviction of a white man for the rape of a slave at any
point from 1700 to the Civil War, let alone a conviction of a master raping his
slave."[87] Yet, we know of many cases in which enslaved women were subjected
to sexual violence.[88] To these women, the home certainly did not function as
a safe haven.

For enslaved New Yorkers, these homes also failed to represent family and
domesticity. Instead, enslaved New Yorkers struggled to establish families and
lived with the constant fear that they might be separated from their kin. Grant
suggested that when young children were sold, the action would not be complete "without consulting the mother, who, if expert and sagacious, had a great
deal of say in the family, and would not allow her child to go into any family
with whose domestics she was not acquainted."[89] Her romanticized description of slavery among Albany's Dutch descendants contrasts sharply with Sojourner Truth's account of the sale of her and her siblings by the Hardenbergh
family.[90] In fact, numerous documents show the frequent separation of enslaved families in these Dutch American communities, and not once do they
mention that the child's mother had a say in the decision. In 1738, for exam-

ple, Dutch American painter Gerardus Duyckinck ordered Henry Rensselaer to sell one of his enslaved women with child "if you can get 60, or even 58 pounds in cash for them, or forty eight pounds for her without the child."[91] Not surprisingly, Duyckinck did not direct Rensselaer to consult with the mother before doing so.

Many of these children would have remained in the same county, but there are also plenty of bills of sale that detail transactions in which children were sold to enslavers who lived far from their parents, thus creating long distances between family members. Elizabeth Boelen of New York City, for instance, sold the eleven-year-old Florah to Jacob Van Schaick of Albany in 1752, and in doing so Florah was taken to the upriver settlement far away from her friends and family in New York City.[92] The family of Sare, an enslaved woman in Albany, had been spread out along the Hudson River with her daughter Mace living in Poughkeepsie and her son Bob in New York City.[93] Their separate residencies made the chances that these family members would see each other again highly unlikely.

Dutch American enslavers regularly separated young children from their mothers. According to Anne Grant, enslavers commonly gifted enslaved children to one of their children the first New Year's Day after they had turned three years old. On that day, the child "was solemnly presented to a son or a daughter, or other young relative of the family, who was of the same sex with the child so presented."[94] Several documents confirm such arrangements. Dirck Schepmoes of Kingston left Jenny with "all her children" to his wife Maragrietie Schepmoes of Tappen, but he determined that at the marriage of his daughters Anna and Areyantie they each should be allowed to choose one of Jenny's children: "Anna is to have the first choice of Jenny's children, Areyantie shall have two of Jenny's children."[95] Even infants, as young as one year old, were separated from their mothers. For instance, Jean Hasbrouck of New Paltz stipulated in his 1712 will that the enslaved woman named Molly should go to his daughter Elizabeth, but if Molly were to have a daughter, the child should go to Hasbrouck's son Jacob when she turned one.[96] Johannis Blanshan stated in his will that his wife should inherit the enslaved woman named Beth, but as soon as they no longer required to be nursed, Beth's children were to be divided among his two sons.[97] In another example, Nikus Jans left the eight-year-old boy Jacob to his son John; his son Hendrik would receive Arlin, an enslaved girl of about a year old; and his daughter Leijntie was to get the five-year-old girl named Mat.[98] In these instances, young children, including infants and toddlers, were separated from their mothers, fathers, and siblings.

Due to their limited mobility, enslaved mothers, fathers, and children rarely had opportunities to visit the family members from whom they had

been separated. Many of them would only have memories of the dearly departed ones, and the very little ones who were separated from their families
before their third birthday would eventually lose all memories of the people
who loved them so.

Enslaved fathers and mothers knew that any change in their enslaver's circumstances could result in their family being ripped apart. Sojourner Truth
described how her mother anticipated imminent separation from her children
when Charles Hardenbergh passed away.

> After this event, she was often surprised to find her mother in tears; and
> when, in her simplicity, she inquired, "Mau-mau, what makes you cry?"
> She would answer, "Oh, my child, I am thinking of your brothers and
> sisters that have been sold away from me." And she would proceed to
> detail many circumstances respecting them. But Isabella long since
> concluded that it was the impending fate of her only remaining children,
> which her mother but too well understood, even then, that called upon
> those memories from the past, and made them crucify her heart afresh.

As Truth explained here, her mother understood all too well that soon the last
two children she still had by her side would be taken from her.[99]

Not only did enslaved families daily face the possibility of separation, most
enslaved New Yorkers struggled to even start a family. Throughout the eighteenth century, the male/female ratio of New York's enslaved population was
relatively balanced. In 1755, for example, Ulster County had about four enslaved men for every three enslaved women, and in Kings County there were
around five women for every six men.[100] Nevertheless, most enslaved men and
women found it challenging to find or keep a spouse in communities where
most enslavers held fewer than five people in bondage. Husbands and wives
were often held in bondage by different enslavers and therefore lived in separate homes, separate towns, or even separate counties. Harry, for instance,
lived in Ulster County and had to cross the Hudson River to see his wife in
Dutchess County.[101] These enslaved New Yorkers often relied on brief moments of independence to connect with their partners. They could do so
when they ran errands for their enslavers, at night, or on Sundays if they received some free time. When their enslavers were in bed or in church, they
could try to sneak out unnoticed. Truth's first love, Robert, for instance, frequently visited her even though his enslaver had forbidden him to do so.[102]
These circumstances made unions between enslaved men and women incredibly challenging.

For the enslaved New Yorkers who were bought and sold several times over
the course of their lives, the houses in which they lived became temporary resi-

dencies they shared with enslaved men, women, and children they barely knew. These enslaved men and women would have found it extremely difficult to establish intimate relations. When Harre fled Philip Schuyler, he had already lived in Orange, Dutchess, and Albany County.[103] And at twenty-nine years old, Caesar of Ulster County had been enslaved by three different men in three different towns: Captain Legg of Saugerties, Tjerck Louw of Plattekill, and Stephen Scryver of New Paltz.[104] At a moment's notice these people could be relocated, thus making it especially challenging to build intimate relationships.

Whereas the home symbolized family to its free inhabitants, enslaved New Yorkers often had to flee these homes to reunite with family members. Numerous enslaved New Yorkers responded to the separation from their family and friends by running away in the hope that they could reconnect with lost kin. When in 1764 Lucy, a thirty-year-old woman, ran away, her enslaver believed she would probably travel to "Bucks County, to one Lambert Vandyke's near Shaminy Meeting-house, where she has a daughter."[105] Similarly, Dinah Cesar, a twenty-five-year-old woman from Albany County, was thought to have fled to New York City to find her family.[106] Some enslaved families decided to flee their enslavers together either to avoid being separated or in hopes of finding a place where they could be free. Dan and his wife, Dian, took their seven-month-old baby and two-year-old daughter when they fled their enslaver in Albany County.[107] When Bett and Bill ran away with their children Charles and Jane, they were each held in bondage by different enslavers and lived in different towns.[108] Nancy, described as having "been bred in Dutch families, and talks Dutch pretty freely," fled J. B. Desdoity in 1802 with Richard, also known as Dick Kettle, who, according to the runaway slave advertisement, "talks Dutch, and calls himself her husband."[109] Finally, in 1808, a group of enslaved people ran away from the home of Isaac Cortclyou, one of the largest enslavers in New Utrecht, Kings County. Among them were Dina, her daughter Bett, and her grandson Ben.[110] These men and women attempted to create a family life in ways they would not be able to do in the homes of their enslavers.

Although we rarely know the specifics of their individual cases, close examination of the various surviving records reveals that the homes in which enslaved New Yorkers lived provided little comfort to these inhabitants. The dual nature of these homes proved inescapable to the people who were held in bondage there.

Over the course of the eighteenth century, Dutch Americans took more strategic approaches to housing their enslaved workers. They organized their homes and grounds in an effort to make these people and their labor largely invisible while also being able to surveil and control them most effectively. Ironically, the enslaved inhabitants of these homes were able to take advantage of Dutch Americans' efforts to segregate these labor and living areas by reshaping these spaces into places of resistance whenever possible.

The home also holds important social and emotional meaning. As is evident from the accounts of Sojourner Truth and Anne Grant, the Dutch-American homes of early New York held distinct meanings to their different inhabitants. These women provided vastly different descriptions of the homes they inhabited as children. Whereas Grant remembered a warm and nurturing environment in which the enslaved men, women, and children were treated as family members, Truth details the anxiety and trauma enslaved New Yorkers endured in these homes.

Not surprisingly, the enslaved men, women, and children who lived in the homes of their enslavers never felt comfortable or safe in these spaces. Unlike their enslavers, they would not have associated these homes with safety, comfort, family, and domesticity. More likely, they saw these houses in the same way Frederick Douglass did the building he lived in on a Maryland plantation, which he later described: "Charmless, it was not home to me; on parting from it, I could not feel that I was leaving any thing which I could have enjoyed by staying. . . . I looked for home elsewhere, and was confident of finding none which I could relish less than the one which I was leaving."[111]

CHAPTER 5

Slavery and Social Power in Dutch Reformed Churches

When James Murphy accepted the call of Ulster County's Rochester, Clove, and Wawarsing churches in 1814, he kept a powerful secret (see Figure 5.1). Although he appeared to be a white man, his mother, Jane Cox, was a Black woman who at the time of his birth was held in bondage by David Johnston, patriarch of one of New York's most influential families. As the child of an enslaved woman, Murphy had been enslaved upon birth, but in accordance with Johnston's will he obtained his freedom when Johnston passed away in 1809. Murphy was now twenty-one years old and determined to make the most out of his newly obtained freedom. Within five years, he completed the New Brunswick Theological Seminary and became an ordained minister in the Dutch Reformed Church.[1] When Murphy received a call from the Clove, Wawarsing, and Rochester churches in Ulster County in 1814, he hid his background from the congregation, at one point even claiming that his mother had died when in fact she was still very much alive. He likely did so because he understood that as a freed Black man, he would not be accepted in such a highly respected church position. At the time, the number of Black congregants in Dutch Reformed churches had increased significantly after a century-long period during which very few free and enslaved Black people appeared in New York's Dutch Reformed churches. But these Black congregants were generally seated in a separate section of the church, they often had to wait to receive communion until all white congregants had done so, and Black elders and deacons

James Murphey

ARTOTYPE, E. BIERSTADT, N. Y.

FIGURE 5.1. James Murphy, date unknown. Artotype by E. Bierstadt, NY. Courtesy of the Archives of the Reformed Church of America.

remained nonexistent in the predominantly white Dutch Reformed churches. Black congregants were generally not accepted in church positions of power and certainly not as a minister who literally looked down on his congregation from the elevated pulpit.[2]

Indeed, when congregants discovered that Murphy was a formerly enslaved Black man, it caused great turmoil in his church community. At this point, he had served as their minister for almost ten years. Most of the congregants were willing to accept him regardless of his personal background, possibly because they did not want to draw too much attention to the fact that a freed Black man had been their minister for so long. However, a few of them opposed

Murphy vehemently. Three congregants in particular, Anne Bevier, Dirck Westbrouck, and Rachel Westbrouck (also spelled Westbrook), argued for Murphy's discharge from their congregation. Bevier insinuated that Murphy had lied about his background to hide "the imputation of African mixture in his pedigree." She claimed that the Rochester congregation was willing to forget about his ancestry: "We therefore, as usual, attended his ministry and cheerfully contributed to the promotion of his comfort. His mother was dead—no mutual visits then between mother and son could disturb the public feeling. And in his misfortune we began to forget the mistake he had committed." But doing so became impossible, according to Bevier, when "reports began to circulate that his mother was still alive."[3] Thus, they tried to convince first the consistory and later the classis that Murphy should be terminated from his position. They claimed they were opposed to their pastor because he had lied about the death of his mother.[4] Their testimonies reveal, however, that they were more concerned about the fact that their minister was a formerly enslaved Black man.

At the time that Murphy became an ordained minister in the Dutch Reformed Church, New York was home to a large number of denominations, including the Anglican, Methodist, Baptist, Huguenot, and Lutheran Churches.[5] Even though the Dutch Reformed Church was no longer the only accepted religious institution as it had been during the Dutch colonial period, it still maintained a powerful position throughout the region and especially in the predominantly Dutch American communities. There, the Dutch Reformed Church proved an important social and cultural institution. The church connected congregants to each other as well as to the larger Dutch world, and with Dutch as the predominant language used for sermons and church correspondence throughout most of the eighteenth century, the church continued to stand central at the formation of Dutch American identity.[6] Until the latter part of the eighteenth century, most Dutch Reformed Church ministers received mandatory training in the Netherlands, where many of them were born, and they regularly communicated with the Classis Amsterdam, the governing body that supervised the American congregations until 1772.[7] The church also connected Dutch Reformed communities across the region, and clergy at the various churches often corresponded with each other. Consequently, the church remained a bastion of Dutch culture in North America for several generations.

Not surprisingly, the Dutch Reformed Church's significance extended beyond its religious influence. As was common in other American colonies, the church served as a social and cultural institution, and its buildings functioned as important social and cultural spaces.[8] In New York, Dutch Reformed congregations helped shape and strengthen Dutch communities. But whereas the churches provided a sense of belonging and social standing to their congregants, they also became spaces of exclusion for those who were deemed unworthy.[9] Congregants determined who would be allowed to participate in these spaces, which parts of the spaces they could access, and in what capacity. Thus, Dutch Reformed churches became powerful places of social power, especially in the ways that congregants organized their churches and practiced their religion in these spaces. Although scholars have researched the ways in which social power intersects with church life and architecture in various European and North American Christian denominations, no such study exists of Dutch Reformed churches.[10] When historians research slavery and the Dutch Reformed Church, they often focus on theology, not on the social aspects of church practice or space.[11] This chapter examines the ways in which social power manifested within the church space, focusing in particular on the conditions of free and enslaved Black New Yorkers in these churches. It argues that congregations' practices of selective admission to these spaces, exclusion from these buildings and church yards, and segregation within these spaces reinforced the social and racial hierarchies that supported slavery in their communities.

Spatial analysis of churches has produced a wide array of scholarly works. Some of these studies have examined churches as sacred spaces, a concept central to Mircea Eliade's The Sacred and the Profane, while other research has focused on architecture or church practice within these churches.[12] Similarly important in studies of religion in Early America has been the concept of "lived religion," which originates in David Hall's study of the ways in which religion permeated daily life in New England and proves essential in understanding that people's social and religious life could not be separated.[13] Scholars like Dell Upton, Gretchen Buggeln, Andrew Spicer, Nicholas Beasley, Peter Benes, Louis Nelson, Rhys Isaac, and Jeanne Halgren Kilde have used these concepts to study religion, social power, and space in early modern Europe and early America.[14] Their studies show that in the same way that religion permeated every part of social life, social life shaped religious practice and the organization of religious spaces. Consequently, slavery and racial thought influenced early American churches and religious practice within them, whether these were the Anglican churches of Virginia or the Dutch Reformed churches in New York.[15] As Murphy's experience shows, any challenges within the church to society's social hierarchies threatened slavery and Dutch Americans' social power.

Black Membership

Although a significant number of free and enslaved Africans attended New Amsterdam's Dutch Reformed Church, they became largely absent from church records by the early eighteenth century. Only toward the end of the century, when the Second Great Awakening swept the young nation, did their participation in the church increase again, albeit slowly. Scholars often attribute the apparent decline of Black people's participation in the region's eighteenth-century Dutch Reformed churches to a denomination and clergy that did not welcome enslaved people in large part because they questioned enslaved people's motives for conversion.[16] Examination of Dutch Reformed Church records suggests, however, that the church's governing bodies did not deliberately exclude Black men and women; in fact, a small number of free and enslaved New Yorkers still joined the church. Instead, it is more likely that enslavers prohibited the people they held in bondage from participation and that white church members at times blocked Black New Yorkers from participation and especially membership in the church out of fear that this would challenge the social hierarchy of their slaveholding societies. White congregants could use their power within the church to keep enslaved and free Black New Yorkers from joining.

The church was not just a religious space; in fact, church communities provided powerful social networks. The church, then, was a place of social interaction, and church connections proved invaluable in society at large. Simply being a worshipper in the church could enhance one's social status in New York's Dutch communities. Enslaved Africans in the seventeenth-century Dutch colony likely understood how useful participation in the church could be when they had their children baptized. Although they appeared to improve their societal standing through their participation during the Dutch colonial period, such opportunities became unattainable to enslaved men and women in most eighteenth-century churches.

One of the few remaining sacraments in the Dutch Reformed Church, communion served as a powerful tool of inclusion in and exclusion from the church community. John Calvin had emphasized the significance of communion and encouraged congregations to practice it regularly, but most Dutch Reformed churches held the Lord's Supper a few times a year.[17] Only full members could participate in this sacrament, and not everyone had an opportunity to become a full member in the church, which required a profession of faith after months of regular catechism lessons. Plus, church elders had the power and the obligation to refuse membership to anyone whom they believed was not sincere in his or her profession of faith. According to the Heidelberg

Catechism, one of the church's founding documents, if those unworthy were to be admitted in the church, "the covenant of God would be profaned, and his wrath kindled against the whole congregation." Thus, church elders, responsible for protecting the congregation, were compelled to deny those aspiring members whom they believed to be "infidels" or "ungodly."[18] They also determined whether or not Black men and women could receive access to communion.

Even when someone had been accepted as a full member, that person's right to communion could be taken away.[19] In 1704, for example, the Kingston congregation withdrew Fennetje in 't Veld's right to communion because the congregation believed she had wrongfully accused Johannes Schepmoes of having had sexual relations with her. Her "deception," Schepmoes claimed, was evident after she apparently had given birth to a Black child. The consistory agreed and determined she would no longer be allowed to commune with them until she acknowledged her wrongdoing and repented.[20] Congregants could also put pressure on the consistory to withhold communion from fellow congregants. According to Robert Alexander, who closely studied the Albany church records, Anneke Schaats, daughter of Albany's Domine Schaats, lost her right to communion when some women of the church's congregation found out that the unmarried woman was pregnant. According to Alexander, these women "banded together and declared that they would refuse to take communion from the same table as Anneke Schaats."[21] In these communities, then, allowing access to communion could be used as a mechanism of social control.

Congregants and clergy understood that accepting enslaved men and women as full members could enhance their social standing, and some feared that they might use their full membership to improve their social circumstances or even to obtain their freedom.[22] As early as 1664, Reverend Henricus Selijns expressed his concern that some enslaved men and women wanted their children baptized because this could help them achieve freedom.[23] Such concerns were not completely unwarranted. Several of the men and women enslaved by the Dutch West India Company in New Netherland had used the fact that they were Christians as one of the most successful arguments for manumission.[24] Some eighteenth-century congregations had enslaved people promise during their confession that they would not use their full membership to obtain freedom, as demonstrated in an entry in the Kingston baptismal records, to avoid such challenges to their bondage. When in 1703 an enslaved woman named Rachel received baptism after she made a profession of faith, the baptismal record explicitly stated that she promised the congregation that she would serve her mistress, Catharin Cottyn, "faithfully and diligently until the death of her mistress, and after her mistress's death will serve her master Jan Cottyn another 8 months." Only then would she become free.[25] Even after the New York Council passed a law in 1706 that determined enslaved New Yorkers would not have the right to freedom after they converted to Christianity, enslavers likely continued to worry that the men and women they held in bondage might use their acceptance in the church to obtain their freedom.[26] Regardless of what state law detailed, full membership in the church would improve enslaved New Yorkers' social standing in these communities.

That such social concerns could motivate congregations to keep enslaved people from obtaining full membership in the church is evident from a letter written by Peter Lowe, reverend of the six Kings County congregations. A student of Reverend John Henry Livingston, Peter Lowe—baptized in 1764 as Petrus Louw in the Kingston church—was among the first Dutch Reformed ministers who received their education in North America.[27] He became an ordained pastor at Kings County's six congregations (Brooklyn, Flatlands, Bushwick, New Utrecht, Flatbush, and Gravesend) after he completed his theological studies in October of 1787.[28] Soon after he started this position, a group of Black men requested full membership in one of his churches. In a letter to an unnamed friend, Lowe detailed his congregants' main objections to accepting these Black men as full members in the church. Lowe did not agree with his congregants and believed the men "were Worthy, and had a right to the priveledges [sic] of the Gospel." In fact, he included his own rebuttal to each of the congregants' objections. Their concerns expose a fear that accepting the Black men who had asked to become full members could present serious challenges to the social hierarchy of their slaveholding community, where at the time almost 75 percent of the free, white households included enslaved laborers.[29]

The diverse reasons these congregants presented for exclusion of the Black men exposed the arbitrariness of their arguments, which is particularly evident in the second objection Lowe listed in the letter: "They are descendants of Ham, or of the Treachorous Gibeonites?" While both these biblical accounts were often used to justify slavery, the congregants apparently did not agree which part of the Scripture explained supposed Black people's inferiority or provided a justification for their bondage and exclusion from full membership in the church.[30] Moreover, they suggested that they could not endure these men next to them in church and that they would be ashamed to commune with them because Black people were of a "different species": "witness their nauseous sweat, complexion, manners."[31] Clearly, they considered the church a white space, and they objected to the spatial closeness and intimacy that could occur if Black people were admitted.

The congregants also worried that accepting these men might encourage other Black New Yorkers to request membership, which, according to them, would degrade the value of their congregation: "If those should be admitted who have now applied—the whole county of Blacks will flock to, and what a terrible congrigation [sic] shall we then have." The prospect of Black men becoming church elders or deacons further terrified these congregants, who suggested that granting Black men positions of power would bring chaos and disharmony to the church.[32] "What an awful sight, negro Elders, deacons, Church masters," they exclaimed. Congregants also suggested that their "seeming desire for the privileges of the gospel may leave them; They will then be rotten members, and bring disgrace on the Church." In fact, some congregants suggested that the aspiring church members' "pretended zeal . . . is nothing else than vain parade & ostentation."[33] Thus, these church members suggested that the Black men might not be serious in their request and eventually leave the church.

The objections outlined in Lowe's letter reveal why these Dutch Americans did not want to accept Black men and women as full members in their church, but Lowe also detailed why he disagreed with them, at one point calling the congregants who objected "pharaisaical masters." When the congregants stated that Black people were "a species very different from us" and that they "would be ashamed to commune with them," Lowe suggested that their objections demonstrated that they did not love God. Their claim that Black people "have no souls" provoked another admonition by Lowe: "I pity the Condition of yours, if you have one," he wrote, thus questioning the congregants' humanity. Fears that admitting these men would cause an overwhelming flood of Black people who would want to join the church met Lowe's claim that these church members did not want "success of the Gospel." In response to the assertion that these men were not true Christians because they would gather on Sundays for heathenish celebrations, Lowe declared, "I rejoice that they are a praying People; They do what many of their masters do not."[34] With his rebuttals, Lowe not only expressed his outrage that he could not accept the Black men, he also suggested that these objecting congregants behaved unseemly and lacked religious zeal.

Even though he did not agree with any of the objections listed in the letter, Lowe, a slaveholder himself, did not question the institution of slavery or society's racial hierarchy.[35] When the congregants stated that Black people were descendants of Ham or the Gibeonites, Lowe dared them to prove such a claim. However, he responded to the assertion that African Americans were "accursed by God" by admitting that "servitude is imposed on them," but he then argued that their servitude did not "extend to their spiritual state."[36] In so doing, Lowe suggested that physical slavery did not conflict with spiritual liberation, which was a popular argument among some eighteenth-century Dutch Reformed ministers and theologians. In fact, historian Ryan Hanley argues that this interpretation was typical for Calvinist denominations, which did not consider corporeal freedom necessary to achieve spiritual liberation through conversion to Christianity.[37] In the 1730s and 1740s, the West African Dutch Reformed Church minister and formerly enslaved Jacobus Elisa Johannes Capitein, for instance, argued that slavery did not contradict Christianity; in fact, he defended physical enslavement if accompanied with spiritual liberation.[38] When serving in Suriname in the 1740s, Reverend Lambertus De Ronde, who would later become a minister in New York City, worked tirelessly to convert the enslaved population of this Dutch colony but claimed "it by no means disturbed the bodily condition."[39] Similarly, Lowe suggested that Christianizing slaves did not conflict with their enslavement; indeed, he claimed that "religion will make them good Christians & better servants."[40]

Lowe's assertions as articulated in the letter reflected the church's position. As Lowe suggested, the Dutch Reformed Church never officially objected to Black people's membership; instead, the Classis of Amsterdam generally supported proselytizing among so-called heathens even if they were enslaved. In the eighteenth century, the classis became more active in sending out ordinances to its overseas churches that promoted catechization and eventual baptism of enslaved people. Conversion would not conflict with their status; in fact, it would enhance faithfulness to their enslavers. A 1743 ordinance the classis sent to the Society of Suriname, for instance, informed them that the classis supported active catechization among enslaved Africans.[41] In 1779, the classis sent out a similar ordinance directed to foreign churches, urging enslavers to allow catechization of their enslaved laborers.[42] The classis also proclaimed that in addition to baptism, enslaved people could become full members in the church, which included the rights to receive baptism as well as communion.[43]

Although Lowe could not admit the men, he wrote in his letter that he would raise the question at the next synod in the hope that there, "we shall not be daunted . . . by the opposition made by the ignorant & prejudiced."[44] Maybe not coincidentally, then, the General Synod, the highest authority for the North American churches after they separated from the Classis of Amsterdam, passed its first resolution on this subject in 1788 when it resolved that enslaved people should be accepted in the church, though "overseers of congregations should exercise all proper prudence, by receiving the testimony of masters and mistresses in relation to the subject."[45] When the General Synod met again in 1792, the Reverend Body appended the previous legislation, stating that "slaves or blacks, when admitted to the church possess the same privileges as other members of same standing," and "ministers who deny them any Christian privileges" should be reprimanded.[46]

As evidenced by Lowe's letter, social and economic realities largely motivated exclusion of these Black New Yorkers from full membership. Enslavers could keep their enslaved laborers from attending church or receiving religious instruction, and congregations could keep enslaved and free Black New Yorkers from obtaining full membership in the church. In communities that relied heavily on enslaved labor, enslaved men and women often did not have the necessary support to join these congregations. Because Black New Yorkers in the region's Dutch communities often did not have access to these church communities, they also lacked important opportunities of social advancement.

Black Members and Positions of Power

Because congregants, many of whom slaveholders, controlled access to their churches, the Black presence in Dutch Reformed churches could differ significantly per congregation. Several Dutch Reformed churches had a small number of enslaved and free African Americans and Native Americans who attended church services, received baptism, or had their children baptized. Some of them were accepted as full members. Descendants of the first Africans who joined the Manhattan congregation continued to be members in New York City's churches, although they became more difficult to identify since their names no longer revealed their African ancestry.[47] In addition to these free Black families, at least one enslaved man and one enslaved woman—Willem of Capt. Davidt Provoost, and Anna of Abraham Kip—received baptism in this church in the early eighteenth century.[48] In the 1730s, a relatively large number of enslaved men and women—Jeptha, Abraham, Cobus, Jinny, Elizabeth, Clara, and Jannetje—received baptism in Albany's church after "confession."[49] The Kingston records mentioned only one enslaved woman and two enslaved children who received baptism during the period from 1660 through 1809.[50] Yet, records of the Fonda Church in the frontier town Fonda (previously known as Caughnawaga) listed several enslaved people in the 1770s and 1780s.[51] Although for most of the eighteenth century they did not join the church in large numbers, free and enslaved Black New Yorkers were at times baptized or even accepted as full members.

Though some references to enslaved New Yorkers appeared in these church records, their presence was clearly minimal. Before drawing any conclusions, it is important to acknowledge that the surviving baptismal and membership records may be incomplete. Historian Dirk Mouw suggests that not all people who received baptism were recorded in the church records. While baptism was free, having one's name recorded in the church records generally required a small fee, and coming up with the money to do so was undoubtedly a challenge for enslaved men and women.[52] His research also reveals that some churches held separate records for Black congregants, and these records may not have been preserved with the same care as the records that listed their white counterparts.[53] Even if membership, baptismal, and marriage records do not provide a complete account of their baptism and membership in the church, the above-mentioned church records suggest that Black people's presence in eighteenth-century Dutch Reformed churches remained small for most of the eighteenth century.[54]

By the late eighteenth century, Black baptisms and memberships in North American Dutch Reformed churches increased significantly. Influenced by Enlightenment thought, the American Revolution, and the Second Great Awakening, Dutch Reformed congregations evidently became more accepting of Black women and men in their churches. By the early nineteenth century, the church, its ministry, and some of its members even promoted and celebrated African American inclusion in the church. The Acts and Proceedings of the General Synod of 1816 mentioned in their "Synodical Reports of the State of the Churches" that in the church in Poughkeepsie "the revival has been powerful, and extended its happy influence to the souls of not a few blacks."[55] By 1819, the New Brunswick Sunday school educated at least forty-three Black men, and in 1826 the Particular Synod of New York praised the Classis of Philadelphia because "considerable attention is paid to the instruction of the blacks, small and great."[56] Even the Kings County churches, where Lowe had faced such strong opposition in the 1780s, now accepted Black members.

As their participation increased, free and enslaved Black New Yorkers became more visible in these churches. An increasing number of them achieved full membership, and some of them even moved to positions of power within the church. When they did, they frequently faced opposition from white members. For white congregants, the thought of having to share full membership with the men and women they enslaved was often unbearable. Not only did their full membership suggest that Black congregants were considered worthy, white congregants would also have to share the Lord's Supper with their Black brethren.[57] During communion, full members, regardless of status or skin color, were to gather around the table for the Lord's Supper.[58]

Some congregations may have practiced such an inclusive communion, although to my knowledge no such descriptions have survived. More commonly, however, when congregations included enslaved or free Black communicants,

these men and women were segregated from the white church members during communion. As detailed in Lowe's letter, some of his congregants worried that Black members would "intermix with white People at the Lord's
Table to their great offence," to which Lowe responded that enslaved members would not be seated among their white counterparts: "Are they Phari-
sees to choose the principal Seats.—will not Christian prudence, and humility
dictate to them a place at the last Table—by themselves."[59] Here, Lowe suggested that white and Black congregants could remain separate during communion, and it appears that when enslaved and free Black New Yorkers were
accepted in communion, they rarely shared this sacrament with their white
counterparts. By the early nineteenth century, when the number of black congregants became more substantial, Black members were often seated at a
separate table, or they were made to wait for communion until after their white
peers had finished. While in theory they had access to the same sacrament,
white congregants made sure to spatially and temporally segregate Black members' participation in an effort to avoid physical intimacy and any hints of
equality. Even when Black men and women had access to communion, congregations continued to use this sacrament as a way to delineate rank and assert their supposed superiority over Black women and men.

When congregations welcomed Black women and men in their churches,
they still resisted giving them equal access to positions of power. Kilde explains
how Protestant churches relied on a church governance system that was largely
informed by and reinforced social hierarchies that existed outside of the church.
Elders and deacons, for example, were charged with the monitoring of churchgoers' moral behavior inside and outside of the church.[60] These positions of
power would be reserved for people who had a certain social standing, while
Black men were generally kept "at the fringes of congregational life."[61] This
was not particular to the North American churches. When in 1775 the Classis
of Amsterdam received word from the ministry in St. Croix, it was outraged
to hear that the church there had allowed Black men to become church elders. The church may have allowed Black people to participate, but they were
not expected to receive well-respected church appointments or full equality
within the church.[62]

New York's congregations mostly kept Black men out of powerful church
positions, but doing so proved increasingly challenging when their participation in the church increased. Such efforts likely contributed to the James Murphy controversy. When congregants first discovered that he had misled them,
he had served as their minister for almost a decade, and, as church records indicate, he was well respected in the church community.[63] Even after Murphy
apologized and the consistories of the churches where he served concluded

that "as far we know he has been faithful in the duties of the ministry and we believe that the members of our church unanimously and the Congregation at large are much attached to our minister," Bevier, Rachel, and Dirck Westbrouck continued to discredit him. In fact, Dirck Westbrouck was called upon by the church of Rochester's committee of elders who tried to "convince him of the impropriety of his conduct & open abuse of the minister and Consistory of the Church." They found Westbrouck's behavior at this meeting, which included "treating the consistory with contempt and manifesting the most open insubordination," so reprehensible that they suspended Westbrouck from communion "until he shall give Evidence of Repentance for his conduct and shall show due subordination to the rules of the Church."[64] But Westbrouck did not give up, and the case made it all the way to the General Synod, where in 1823 it was decided that "there is no reasonable ground of grievance."[65] It appeared that Murphy had triumphed over his opponents.

While initially the local churches, the classis, and the synod supported Murphy, his challengers did eventually achieve their objective, as Murphy left the Rochester, Wawarsing, and Clove churches for the Second Church in Glenville, New York. Moreover, in 1824 the particular Synod of Albany directed the Ulster classis to "exercise that discipline upon the Rev. Mr. Murphy, which is prescribed in the constitution towards offending members, and which his case deserves."[66] Murphy managed, however, to remain a relatively well-respected reverend in the church for at least another decade, and in 1840 he presided over North America's General Synod, the first African descendant and formerly enslaved man to do so.[67]

Controversies also complicated Mark Jordan's aspirations of becoming a minister in the church. When Jordan, a long-standing member in New York's Garden Street Church, also known as the South Reformed Church, first revealed in 1822 that he wanted to become a minister in the church, he faced initial scrutiny. After careful examination, the committee that reviewed Jordan's case determined that he did not obtain all the required documents because he had "never passed through a regular course of academical instructions" or studied with a "Professor of Theology." The committee decided, however, that Jordan, "a coloured man" who "desires to labor among the people of colour," could be allowed to serve among Black New Yorkers.[68] Possibly, the classis saw in Jordan an exceptional opportunity to serve a Black congregation. Nevertheless, Jordan's ambitions continued to meet resistance. The Reverend Ezra Cornish objected to Jordan's appointment, suggesting that it would "destroy his moral character."[69] At the request of the New York classis, the consistory of the Garden Street Church investigated these accusations and found Jordan "not guilty." Jordan then became a "student in divinity" under the care of the Classis of New York.[70] Thus, the synod rejected a complaint against the Classis of New York, and in July 1823 the classis licensed Jordan "to preach the gospel."[71] He now led the first Black Reformed Church congregation, which held its services in a public school at Duane Street from 1823 to 1829.[72] The congregation did not survive for very long. According to Graham Hodges, Jordan lost his license in 1828, which also ended the services for this African American congregation.[73]

As Jordan and Murphy's experiences show, Black men struggled to obtain and maintain positions of power within the Dutch Reformed Church. Even when white congregants became more accepting of Black congregants, they often limited their participation and excluded them from the more respected church positions. In a society where church life generally reflected society's social hierarchies, it remained unimaginable that Black people would hold positions of power.

Church Buildings

Churches were places of worship, often considered sacred spaces, but they also reflected and reinforced society's socioeconomic and political dynamics.[74] Even in the Dutch Reformed churches, which appeared more egalitarian than their Catholic or Anglican counterparts, church and social hierarchy were closely intertwined and evident in their buildings. The minister preached from an elevated pulpit, elders and deacons had the most prominent seats close to the pulpit, men often occupied seats in what were considered superior locations, and those who had more money could purchase the most coveted pews. When the number of Black worshippers increased, they were often restricted to certain areas within these churches. Dutch Reformed church buildings mirrored the socioeconomic and political structures of the communities they served, and church seating in particular reflected and reinforced social hierarchy within the church community.[75]

Some of New York's oldest surviving Dutch Reformed churches date back to the eighteenth century. Many of these buildings have imposing porticos, bell towers, organs, galleries, split chancels, and center aisles in between fixed seating. Importantly, most of these churches look nothing like their eighteenth-century counterparts. Church buildings were not static or fixed, and congregations regularly modified these buildings and their interior. Often these modifications reflected cultural and social changes, or they were necessary to accommodate growing congregations. This section will look at some of these changes, and how they mirrored larger American architectural trends. Reconstruction of how these church buildings changed over the course of the eighteenth and early nine-teenth centuries shows that, just like the congregations that worshipped in them, these buildings became increasingly American. As a part of these changes, these buildings would eventually include designated sections for Black worship-pers. Just as these buildings symbolized religion and community to its white congregants, these structures would often become spaces of exclusion for the Black men and women who lived in these communities.

It is important to note that in theory Dutch Reformed church buildings were not considered sacred spaces. According to the teachings of John Cal-vin, there was not one place that was sacred, and thus people could worship anywhere. Holiness depended on the act of worship, not the location of such worship. In this respect, the Dutch Reformed church buildings differed signifi-cantly from the consecrated Catholic and Anglican churches.[76] Because in Calvinist denominations, churches, meetinghouses, or temples were merely places that housed congregations, it was not uncommon for these denomina-tions to worship in spaces that were also used for civic meetings.[77] Several scholars have shown, however, that most churchgoers, including Dutch Re-formed congregants, did likely consider these buildings sacred spaces.[78]

In the seventeenth and early eighteenth centuries, Dutch Reformed churches in the region generally resembled their European counterparts. Some of the church's initial services were held in makeshift spaces, as was the case in New Amsterdam where for a while services were held in the attic of a mill.[79] When congregations raised enough money to build independent churches, these structures often followed European architectural models. Many of these churches had square, hexagonal, or octagonal plans with galleries, turreted roofs, and a belfry in the center (see Figure 5.2).[80] Because the Reformed church focused on the word of God, which was communicated via the minister's ser-mon, the pulpit became the focal point within these buildings. The pulpit was usually elevated, only to be reached through the use of a narrow ladder, and placed in the center of the nave, opposite the entrance. In this location, the minister was not only closer to God, he could also be heard better through-out the church.[81]

Whether it concerned socioeconomic status, race, or gender, seating ar-rangements in the Dutch Reformed churches clearly reflected society's social and political structures. Seventeenth-century churches often did not have fixed seating, thus requiring worshippers to stand or bring their own seats. When churches did have fixed seating, these were often benches on the first floor, along the walls, and in the galleries, *"en manière de theater."*[82] Most of these early churches had galleries; in fact, in her work on Christian architecture, Jeanne Halgren Kilde argues that galleries were an important element of Protestant

A VIEW OF THE LATE PROTESTANT DUTCH CHURCH in the CITY of ALBANY.

FIGURE 5.2. Engraving after Philip Hooker's *A View of the Late Protestant Dutch Church in the City of Albany*, ca. 1810. Yale University Art Gallery.

churches because they brought worshippers closer to the raised pulpit. Kilde also notes that these galleries often became important tools "of delineating social rank."[83] As was the case in the theater, seats along the walls and in the gallery were generally considered more prominent.[84]

When seventeenth- and early eighteenth-century congregations practiced gender-segregated seating, as recommended by John Calvin, men were generally accommodated in the galleries and on benches along the walls.[85] These were considered the best seats in the house, thus reflecting men's superior status within Dutch Reformed religion. These seats also gave them oversight of the center of the church, where women and children were seated. Several New York churches practiced such gender-segregated seating throughout the eighteenth century, and some congregations continued this practice into the nineteenth century.[86] For instance, the first Claverack church building, built in 1727, was a one-room structure with center pews for women and children and pews along the walls that were occupied by the men.[87] Pehr Kalm similarly noted that in the Old Dutch Church in Manhattan the men were seated in the gallery and women on the first floor.[88] Both the first and second church buildings of Albany's congregation had women seated on the main floor and men in the gallery.[89] In the second Albany church, built in 1715, only members of the consistory and the older men who had trouble climbing up to the gallery were seated on the first floor.[90] Some of these churches may even have had separate church entrances for men and women in an effort to keep them completely segregated.[91]

Elders and dignitaries had special seating in these churches. Directed sideways and adjacent to the pulpit, these seats provided these men with a view of both the preacher and the congregation. In 1754, for instance, the Kingston church consistory voted to reserve special seats for several prominent church members.[92] In the eighteenth-century Flatbush church, the elders were seated to the right of the pulpit and the deacons to the left.[93] In his study of Albany's Dutch Reformed Church, Robert Alexander suggests that the elders were seated in the front, close to the minister, so that they could ensure the minister's sermon "properly accorded with scripture."[94] Kilde argues, however, that the elders in congregational churches were regularly seated in these side-oriented, front seats so that they could oversee the congregants. Protestant congregations relied, in part, on surveillance, "as congregation leaders watched worshippers and worshippers watched one another."[95] The community's most respected men were charged with supervising the minister and surveilling the rest of the congregation.

Seventeenth- and eighteenth-century church records generally do not reveal where enslaved churchgoers would have been seated. As "permanent guests" in these churches, they most likely occupied what could be considered *in-between spaces*.[96] It is important to point out that while some enslaved people were able to attend church for religious reasons, most of them undoubtedly were there solely to attend to their enslavers' needs. For example, enslaved women were largely in charge of refilling the charcoal foot stoves that kept their female enslavers warm during service on cold days, and when churches did not have permanent seats, enslaved men or women were likely responsible for bringing seats into the buildings for their enslavers.[97]

While there are few exceptions, the enslaved men and women who attended church usually did not have designated seats. Alexander claims that in the 1715 Albany church, a section of the benches on the east side of the balcony was set aside for Black participants. He also suggests that the 1767 list of pew sales at Albany's church included that part of the benches in the gallery were set aside for Black congregants.[98] Most church plans, however, did not include such designated areas until the early nineteenth century. In fact, records suggest that during most of the eighteenth century, even free Black worshippers did not own pews in these buildings. Instead, Black men and women most commonly would have been occupying the in-between spaces, seated or standing in the aisles close to their enslavers, in the back of the church, or outside the church building.[99] Sextons would be charged with keeping an eye on the Black people who attended. New York City's consistory, for instance, ordered its sexton, Jan de la Montagne, to ensure there would be no "disorderly conduct either by children or by Negroes, neither before, nor during, nor after the sermon."[100] Because there were usually few Black people present in these churches, congregants likely did not feel the urge to restrict them to a specific area of the church.

Over the course of the eighteenth century, church structures were often replaced with larger buildings that could accommodate these communities' growing number of worshippers, but the changes did not stop there. By the latter part of the eighteenth century, newly built churches mostly had a rectangular shape and bell towers instead of turret-mounted belfries. In subsequent changes that generally took place in the late eighteenth and early nineteenth centuries, family pews increasingly replaced church benches. Galleries and the pulpit were lowered, and eventually the pulpit was moved to the narrow side of the church. Benches along the walls were mostly removed. As part of these modifications, the church entrances were moved to the bell tower, across from the pulpit.[101]

These architectural changes were not particular to the Dutch Reformed churches. In fact, they resemble those of the congregational churches in New England, where over the course of the eighteenth century the meetinghouses began to look more like the North American Anglican church buildings.[102] Peter Benes claims that these changes were the result of a more progressive group of churchgoers who wanted a more broadened and modernized church, but Benes and Philip Zimmerman also find that the New England meetinghouses were generally influenced by an increased separation of church and state in the area, which took municipal meetings out of the church buildings.[103] Thus, these buildings became more exclusively spaces of religious worship, which fit their new architectural style.

Similar developments likely influenced the changes in Dutch Reformed churches, and through these changes a typical American church-building style developed across denominations. In fact, by the early nineteenth century, churches across the Atlantic seaboard looked incredibly similar. To some extent Gothic revival but more so Greek revival and Federal styles now influenced church architecture from Charleston to Boston.[104] For instance, by the

1840s many churches included porticos.[105] Albany's First Church, the New Paltz Dutch Reformed Church, and the Shawangunk church buildings still exhibit these imposing entrances (see Figures 5.3 and 5.4).[106] Some changes in worship caused modifications to these structures. Organ music became more prominent in nineteenth-century churches, which required the installation of often large organs in the back of the church, by the bell tower.[107] Thus, influenced by both international and regional cultural trends as well as changes in worship, American church builders had developed their own style by the early nineteenth century.

Seating arrangements in these buildings likewise changed over time, but they continued to reflect and reinforce social hierarchies. By the early nineteenth century, many congregations either had switched or began to switch the seating arrangements to family pews in the nave and in the galleries. At this point, most pulpits and galleries had been lowered, and thus the gallery seats were no longer the most coveted seats in the church. Instead, the cost of these pews depended on their proximity to the pulpit, with pews located closest to the pulpit the most valuable. Thus, socioeconomic status determined which congregants could afford pews closest to the pulpit. Congregants who could not afford a pew often had access to benches on the balcony.[108] Elders and dignitaries were still seated close to the pulpit where they could see both the minister and congregation.

Church plans now more often included reserved seating for Black worshippers, which suggests that as their numbers increased, they more commonly occupied a designated area of the church. Mostly, they were seated on benches in the back of the church by the bell tower, either in the galleries or on the first floor.[109] In those areas, they would have been the farthest removed from the pulpit and least visible from the nave. For instance, Albany's First Church had designated seating for its black congregants in the back of the church, both on the first floor and on the balcony.[110] And when the New Paltz congregation built a new church in 1839 for its growing congregation, a drawing of the pew arrangements included segregated seating for black men and women in the back of the gallery, by the bell tower.[111] Not only were these designated and controlled seating areas of the church—in the back and close to the doors—considered "less desirable," restricting Black worshippers to these seats also allowed for very few interactions between Black and white congregants and caused Black churchgoers to be minimally visible within the churches they often helped build.[112]

Louis Nelson, Dell Upton, and Robert Olwell found similar seating practices in southern churches.[113] Nelson suggests that in South Carolina's Anglican churches it was not until the early nineteenth century that churches actually

FIGURE 5.3. The Reformed Church of Shawangunk, Wallkill, NY. Picture by author.

FIGURE 5.4. Reformed Church of New Paltz, New Paltz, NY. Picture by author.

reserved certain seats for enslaved men and women, and these seats were usually located in the balcony. Before that, their seating may have been more
haphazard, depending on the congregation.[114] Nelson argues that the increased
use of designated seating for enslaved people in South Carolina's Anglican
churches was "an expression of increasing racial anxieties." As more Black
people joined these churches after the American Revolution, they were more
frequently seated in separate and controlled spaces.[115] In his study of Virginia,
Upton proposes that eighteenth-century Anglican churches had no designated
seating for enslaved churchgoers, and that the so-called slave gallery of the
nineteenth century "was a rarity in the eighteenth" when this area of the
church was often reserved for private seating.[116] Jon Sensbach also notices that
among North Carolina's Moravian churches, segregation began in the nineteenth century.[117] In New York's Dutch Reformed churches, white New Yorkers' increased efforts to separate Black people from white spaces in the late
eighteenth and early nineteenth centuries also occurred when a growing number of Black men and women attended Dutch Reformed services. Across denominations, then, gallery seats, especially controlled and subpar areas in the
far back, became the designated section for Black worshippers in these
churches.

Black congregants were not just restricted to the least desirable seats. When
it best suited congregants or the consistory, they had no problem relocating
the church's Black worshippers. The first church of Albany, for example, resolved in 1799 "that the Negro men be placed on the south side of the Gallery
& the Negro Women on the North side."[118] In 1811, the church again reserved
gallery seats for Black churchgoers.[119] When the church needed more income
from pew sales, the consistory decided that "the three Pews heretofore reserved
for the Blacks attending divine service, be sold." The men and women who
had previously used these seats were now redirected to "the three circular Pews
in the South east corner."[120] In some cases, white congregants who objected
to worshipping in close proximity to their Black counterparts used their spending power to keep Black churchgoers from being seated close to their pews.
In 1815, Daniel Winne informed the treasury that he would pay for his pew
"provided the Consistory will remove the Blacks from behind his Pew as was
understood."[121] The consistory then determined that it would sell the pews
on the first floor that were now "occupied by people of colour." Elderly Black
churchgoers had been allotted these seats on the first floor, but now they were
relocated to the gallery. The sexton was told to "direct these people to con-
form themselves accordingly."[122] With churches that relied on pew sales, white
congregants could put monetary pressure on the church if they did not like
where Black churchgoers were seated.

For Black congregants, their unequal treatment in these churches would have been a painful reminder that white congregants controlled these spaces of worship. Their assigned seats in the back of these churches allowed them only limited access to the sermon and clearly symbolized their supposed inferior status within the church and society at large. By the 1820s, when Scotsman James Kent visited New York City, he noted that African Americans in the city's churches of all denominations were "packed up in some back benches in the gallery and not allowed to come near a white mans [sic] person."[123]

While there are no surviving descriptions by Black New Yorkers who attended these Dutch Reformed churches, discussions of Black men who attended white churches elsewhere help reconstruct how these Black worshippers must have felt. Frederick Douglass, for example, explained that he found it a humiliating experience when he attended a New Bedford, Massachusetts, Methodist church where Black congregants were seated in the gallery and allowed to partake in communion only after all white congregants had done so.[124] When Cato Pearce, an enslaved man from Rhode Island who would eventually become an itinerant preacher, attended a New England Presbyterian church, he too had to sit in a section designated for Black worshippers, which was so far from the pulpit that he could barely hear the sermon. He evidently found the experience of being seated in what according to him were commonly called "nigger pews" so traumatizing that he feared he would be sent to such separate pews again when he attended a Baptist church the following Sunday.[125] William J. Brown, a Black man from Providence, claimed in his memoir that many Black Rhode Islanders chose not to attend church altogether because "they were opposed to going to churches and sitting in pigeon holes, as all the churches at that time had some obscure place for the colored people to sit in."[126] He wrote that these circumstances motivated Black Rhode Islanders to establish their own churches.

These descriptions reveal that Black churchgoers often found their experiences in these white-dominated churches humiliating. In fact, many of them would rather not attend church than be submitted to such degradation. Yet, some Black worshippers may have used the fact that they were seated in a separate section as an opportunity to connect with other Black congregants during church service. Since these sections were usually located in the back of these churches, other congregants and even the elders and ministers would have had limited oversight over the people seated there. For some enslaved men and women who had few opportunities to interact with other enslaved people, these few hours in church would have had a valuable social function.

Just as congregations changed over time, so did the buildings that housed them. Dutch Reformed church builders increasingly adopted a more American architecture. Interiors of these churches were also modified by the late eighteenth and early nineteenth centuries. Seating arrangements proved powerful reflections of the communities' social inequalities. White men with significant status and spending power could obtain the most coveted church seats or pews, whereas Black men and women were either left to occupy in-between spaces or restricted to back benches. Both free and enslaved Black New Yorkers were treated as permanent guests in these churches. They had no pews and were quickly forced to move elsewhere in the church when white congregants requested them to do so. Thus, the organization and utilization of these church spaces transmitted a powerful message to all: even when Black men and women had access to the privileges of the gospel, they were never considered equal to their white counterparts in these white-dominated churches.

The Churchyard

The churchyard served as an extension of the church, both as a religious and a social space. Nineteenth-century historian Andrew Mellick provided an especially vivid description of a Bedminster, New Jersey, Dutch Reformed Church when he wrote that "to appreciate what a religious and social factor is Bedminster Church in this well-ordered community, it should be visited on the first day of the week—on a pleasant Sunday morning." He then depicted part of Sunday ritual at this church: "As the hour for service approaches the women have passed inside, but the men gather about the door or under the trees, discussing their horses, the crops and whatever may have been of interest during the past week. This Sunday morning talk is not limited to the one sex, for, on entering, we would find the wives and daughters in animated converse over the backs and partitions of the pews."[127] He later detailed that churchgoers often held picnics in the churchyard at which some enslaved people had "stands on the church-green for the sale of root and malt beer, thick slices of buttered rye bread, sugared olekokes [better known as *oliebollen*, a Dutch version of fried dough], Dutch crullers, and gingerbread."[128] As he portrayed, gathering in the church and churchyard allowed churchgoers to meet and catch up with neighbors, especially in the more rural areas.

The churchyard, then, served as a social space where congregants could catch up on the latest news. In fact, public announcements, which may have included "runaway slave" notifications, were often posted by the church door since that was an especially effective way to reach many in the community.[129] The churchyard also provided a space for displays of social status.[130] The records of the

FIGURE 5.5. Edward Lamson Henry, *Sunday Morning*, 1898. Gilcrease Museum, Tulsa, OK.

Caughnawaga church, for instance, mentioned that "the Visscher brothers always attracted attention because of the fine horses they rode to church, their slaves following them to care for the horses."[131] Edward Lamson Henry's late eighteenth-century painting of the Shawangunk church depicts similar pageantry that became an important part of the Sunday ritual (see Figure 5.5).

While congregants enjoyed these social interactions with their neighbors before or after service, enslaved men and women who escorted their enslavers to church often had opportunities to interact with each other in the churchyard when church was in service. Coachmen would stay in the churchyard so that they could take care of the horses, while some enslaved women may have been required to wait outside and enter the church only when the women who claimed to own them needed their foot stoves refilled. These men and women would have been able to use these brief moments in the churchyard to reconnect with family and friends. And if Mellick's recollections are accurate, some enslaved people who lived close to the church would have been able to sell goods during church picnics.

The church yard also included the cemetery. Calvinist denominations did not consider funerals a sacrament. The Synod of Dordrecht had prohibited burial sermons, and New York churches likely followed these recommendations. The New Amsterdam church, for example, urged congregations to stop holding funeral services because they had been prohibited.[132] Thus, funerals took place outside of the church, even when the deceased were buried in the church cemetery. Nevertheless, these burial grounds became powerful reflections of society's social hierarchies. Churchgoers had to pay a certain fee to be buried in the cemetery, and some areas of the cemetery were more expensive than others. New York City's seventeenth-century church, for example, determined the cost of burial plots per age but also allowed those who wanted to be "buried outside the appointed section," to be able to "do so by paying double."[133] Ministers were often buried beneath or closest to the church. For instance, both Johannes Mauritius Goctschius and Henry Polhelmus were buried in the Shawangunk church.[134] Thus, wealth and social power continued to be displayed in the church cemetery.

Just as these cemeteries became reflections of the church community's social hierarchies, they also served as spaces of exclusion.[135] Enslaved women and men rarely received a burial inside the church cemetery.[136] In fact, Dennis Maika suggests that separate burial grounds for enslaved people probably served as the "most visible example of segregation taking place within the religious communities."[137] According to the African Burial Ground report, between 1727 and 1804 only five Africans were interred by the New York City Dutch Reformed Church, and only one of them, Susannah Rosedale, had been buried in the church cemetery.[138] Janny Venema discovered that Bassie *de neger* had been buried in the Albany church cemetery in 1671, but he is the only Black man known to be interred there.[139] Most often, enslaved and free black New Yorkers would not be buried in the church cemetery.

Because enslaved people were usually not allowed in church cemeteries, they had to bury their dead in separate areas, often on land in the area that was considered of little value. Consequently, enslaved burial grounds can be found across the region. Henry Stiles, for instance, mentioned a "negro burying-ground" in Brooklyn, and Gertrude Vanderbilt suggested that Flatbush had an African burial ground.[140] According to David Steven Cohen, enslaved African Americans who attended the Dutch Reformed Church in the Ramapo Valley were interred outside of the church cemetery.[141] New Paltz and Kingston similarly had separate African American burial grounds. Because these graves and burial grounds were often left unmarked, they frequently disappeared from the public eye as the land was reappropriated.[142] In more recent decades, several of these burial grounds have been rediscovered. Most famously, in 1991 excavations in Lower Manhattan uncovered what is now known as New York City's African Burial Ground, but similar discoveries have taken place in, among others, Colonie, Kingston, New Paltz, Queens, Harlem, and Brooklyn.[143]

As an extension of the church, the churchyard had both a social and a religious function. Similar to the church buildings, the ways in which white congregants utilized this space generally reflected society's social hierarchies. Congregants intermingled in these spaces and they displayed their social status through various forms of pageantry. The cemetery further reinforced social power. Not only could congregants use their economic power to purchase burial plots closest to the church building, they commonly reserved these burial plots for white congregants only.

Black Religious Life

Exclusion from or segregation within Dutch Reformed churches and cemeteries did not prevent Black religious life. In fact, in some cases such practices gave Black New Yorkers opportunities to practice their religions more independently, with less white oversight. Some of them joined churches that did welcome their participation, while others worshipped privately.

When congregations or enslavers prohibited Black New Yorkers from worshipping in a Dutch Reformed church or when Black New Yorkers simply did not feel welcome in these spaces of worship, they sometimes joined other denominations or, after the 1770s, founded Black congregations. As some of the congregants pointed out to Lowe when they were opposed to Black men becoming members in their church, Black people in the area would gather on Sunday evenings for religious celebrations: "They clan together on Sunday evenings, and do what they ought not to do—pray and sing together, not the psalms of David—but hymns & spiritual songs—no one knows how erroneous."[144] In the early nineteenth century, some of these men and women would attend a Methodist church in Brooklyn, which according to one newspaper article caused various frustrations among the town's white population.[145] By the 1780s, New York's Methodist churches had welcomed people from diverse backgrounds, including many African Americans.[146] In fact, historian Richard Boles calculates that by 1790 New York City's Methodist Church counted more Black members than any other denomination.[147] Maybe that is why Lowe's congregants suggested that "it is downright Methodism" to accept Black members to their church.

But Black New Yorkers did not only join Methodist churches. Graham Hodges argues that the Anglican Church "made the strongest institutional effort to convert Africans in the New York region," and indeed hundreds of Black New Yorkers attended Anglican churches during the eighteenth century. Elias Neau was especially successful in reaching New York City's enslaved men and women, many of whom were enslaved in Dutch American households.[148] During the Second Great Awakening, interdenominational camp meetings that were generally more diverse and focused on preaching instead of reading the scripture proved especially appealing to enslaved men and women. Sylvia

Dubois, an enslaved woman in a New Jersey Dutch community, recounted that she would happily walk more than ten miles to attend such camp meetings.[149]

Most enslaved New Yorkers did not have an opportunity to join a church. In many of New York's Dutch communities, the Dutch Reformed Church would be the only denomination in the region. Even if there were other churches in the area that opened their doors to enslaved New Yorkers, these women and men were usually not able to attend the churches without permission from the people who held them in bondage.

Enslaved New Yorkers searched ways to practice their religious beliefs, and especially African religious practices, out of view from their enslavers. Archeological research has helped uncover some of these hidden practices. At the Hendrick I. Lott house in Kings County, for example, archeologists found evidence of religious artifacts under the floorboards of the garret spaces where at least some of the home's enslaved inhabitants lived. A cloth pouch containing an oyster shell and part of a sheep or goat pelvis had been deposited there likely in an effort to safeguard this space.[150] These items resembled cached deposits found across Africa and the diaspora, and the items in these pouches as well as their placement held important religious meaning to the people who created them.[151]

Corncobs that been placed under the same floorboards at the Lott house appear to have formed either a five-pointed star or a cross, which further points to religious practices. The kernels of the cobs were still intact, which indicates that they had been placed there intentionally and possibly ritually. They were found by the entrance of the enslaved people's living quarters, and by the chimney in one of these rooms, suggesting that the people who placed them there did so to safeguard these spaces. The X-shaped cross has been found in various forms in places inhabited by enslaved Africans and on items that belonged to them, revealing that it was a powerful and resilient symbol in the African diaspora. It should be noted, however, that the cross served as an important symbol in many African as well as European cultures, which could explain why it has been so resilient and prevalent in the African diaspora.[152]

Excavations at the outdoor, brick kitchen of the Lott home, the place where some of the family's enslaved and servant laborers likely lived in the late eighteenth and early nineteenth centuries, uncovered an American-made serving bowl with an "X" carved on the bottom.[153] Although at first glance this bowl or the "X" may appear insignificant, archeologists have discovered that the symbol here was likely not just a maker's or owner's mark. While doing fieldwork in South Carolina, anthropologist Leland Ferguson found bowl-shaped pottery known as Colono Ware or Colono-Indian Ware that featured similar

FIGURE 5.6.   Coin amulet, 1736. Brazil. Copper alloy. 32 mm (diameter). A.SSB.1973.58. The cross is visible in the center of the coin. Courtesy of New York State Office of Parks, Recreation and Historic Preservation.

crosses on the bottom, on either the inside or outside.[154] Originally, scholars considered such pottery of Native American making, but further research shows that it was often produced by enslaved Africans. Ferguson argues that these bowls may have been used to cook sacred medicine according to Bakongo tradition, with the cross symbolizing an important connection to the water spirits.[155] If Ferguson is correct, the cross on the bowl at the Lott house tells us not only that this bowl was used and produced by enslaved Africans but also that it was used to make medicine through spiritual ritual.

A perforated ten-réis Portuguese coin, likely used as an amulet, that archeologists discovered during an excavation in Albany also featured the cross (see Figure 5.6). The "X" on the coin stood for ten réis, but it is probable that for the owner the mark held a religious meaning. Archeologists uncovered the coin in the 1970s on State Street at the location where Luycas Wyngaerd and later in the eighteenth century his cousin Volkert S. Veeder lived. Both Wyngaerd and Veeder held people in bondage—among them were Simon, Jeremy

(Jem), and Bet—and the amulet probably belonged to one of them.[156] While it is impossible to find out exactly who owned this amulet, its owner likely originated in West Central Africa or its diaspora. At both an eighteenth-century cemetery in Ngongo Mbata and a burial ground in Luanda, archeologists found similar Portuguese, perforated coins, though of twenty réis. These coins were minted in Portugal in 1697 and 1698. They had two X-marks on one side that represented the twenty-réis value, and a depiction of Saint Anthony welded on the other side, most likely crafted by a Kongolese metalworker. Cécile Fromont deems these pendants perfect examples of Kongo Christianity because they "reformulated central African and imported elements" to form something entirely new.[157] In North America, perforated coins have been found at several African American burial grounds, though these are always American-made coins. The Works Progress Administration (WPA) ex-slave narratives and folkloric studies revealed that in the nineteenth century such amulets were often used as protective charms, especially for small children.[158]

Research shows that enslaved men and women also continued to practice African burial rites in New York's Dutch communities. Some African rituals were uncovered during excavations of New York City's African burial ground. Most of the remains that were found at this site date back to the eighteenth century. These excavations revealed that shells, beads, tobacco pipes, and similar objects had been buried together with their owners, which was a common practice in many precolonial African societies, as discussed by both Olfert Dapper and Willem Bosman.[159] About burial rites in Angola, for example, Dapper said that it was practice to bury the deceased with various goods, including glass beads that were used as jewelry.[160] Maybe not coincidentally, then, one of the burials at New York City's African burial ground contained a woman who was laid to rest with a string of beads and cowrie shells around her hips and "an unused smoking pipe."[161] Moreover, the African Burial Ground report notes that beads found with the body of an infant "were characteristic of West African manufacture."[162] These artifacts show that at least some enslaved New Yorkers incorporated burial practices from their homelands or the lands of their ancestors.

That African descendants maintained part of their traditional burial rites in New York is not at all surprising. These rituals were especially important to people who strongly believed in the continued influence of the ancestors. A proper burial was crucial to let a person go to rest properly and not to offend the ancestors in any way.[163] As such, in many African and African diaspora cultures, burial rites held great significance, and in some cases funeral rites could last for days.[164] The segregation of burial grounds may have given Black New Yorkers more opportunity to continue parts of these burial practices.

Because Dutch Reformed congregations practiced exclusion and segregation, they kept their churches predominantly white. But keeping Black New Yorkers from worshipping in these churches did not keep them from practicing their religious beliefs. When they had the opportunity, many Black New Yorkers joined churches that did accept them or they established their own churches. Much of their religious life, however, took place privately. As archeological research has revealed, they continued religious practices that originated in Africa and its diaspora outside of the established Christian churches.

In his study of the Anglican Church, Robert Olwell found that for most enslaved people "the ceremonies of the established church were rituals of exclusion that served as reminders of their inferior and outsider status."[165] Undoubtedly, enslaved New Yorkers would have felt the same about Dutch Reformed Church rituals. In fact, the churches and churchyards themselves became spaces of exclusion and segregation. When an increasing number of enslaved people were permitted participation in the church by the late eighteenth century, Dutch Reformed congregations often carefully segregated them physically and temporally from their white counterparts. In doing so, white congregants may have worshipped in the same buildings as Black New Yorkers, but they did not actually share their place of worship.

Only when these churches are recognized as social spaces does it become evident that these places of worship became important tools in reinforcing social power. Social hierarchies that were necessary to sustain slavery influenced church communities and buildings. When more enslaved men and women joined Dutch Reformed churches, these communities created spatial methods to assert their superiority over these Black worshippers. Even when theoretically these Black congregants were equal before God, congregations made it clear in their church buildings and practices that Black churchgoers were not equal to their white counterparts.

Considering these circumstances, it is no surprise that James Murphy tried to hide his background, even if that meant he had to pretend his mother was no longer alive. As a minister in the church, he understood all too well how social power influenced congregations and their decisions. Once his background was uncovered, it was only a matter of time before he would lose his position at the Rochester, Clove, and Wawarsing churches. No freed Black man could assume a position of power in churches controlled by enslavers.

Conclusion

A More Benign System of Slavery?

> Our system of slavery was strictly domestic, the negro
> almost invariably living under the same roof with the
> master, or, if his habitation was detached, as certainly
> sometimes happened, it was still near at hand, leaving
> both races as parts of a common family. . . . Among
> the Dutch, in particular, the treatment of the negro
> was of the kindest character, a trusty field-slave often
> having quite as much to say on the subject of the
> tillage and the crops, as the man who owned both the
> land he worked, and himself.
>
> —James Fenimore Cooper, *Satanstoe or The Littlepage
> Manuscripts*

James Fenimore Cooper's words in his 1845 novel
Satanstoe echo a sentiment that has persisted in Dutch American communities
for generations: "Among the Dutch, in particular, the treatment of the negro
was of the kindest character." In those communities, he wrote, enslaved people
were living in the homes of their enslavers "as parts of a common family."
When they worked in the field, they did so at their "master's side."[1] Such descriptions of slavery have been quite common in Dutch New York. Yet, they
completely erase the systems of control, surveillance, and segregation necessary to sustain a system of human bondage in these communities. Frequent
representations of slavery as a benign system in Dutch New York and the misguided notion that enslaved and free people "shared" the home, workplace,
church, and public spaces proved especially powerful in sustaining this myth.

This book has demonstrated that although enslaved New Yorkers often lived
in the same houses as the people who claimed to own them, they were certainly *not* inhabiting the same parts of the home or treated as members of the
family, as Cooper suggested. Through spatial analysis, this book has shown
that even when enslaved people inhabited or frequented the same places as

their enslavers, their experiences within these spaces were inherently different. Enslaved men, women, and children did not live, work, or worship alongside their enslavers. Instead, they were often excluded from worshipping in Dutch Reformed churches, and when they did have access they were commonly relegated to back benches where they could barely hear or see the minister. When enslaved New Yorkers in these communities lived under the same roof as their enslavers, they would be restricted to the back parts of the home. They were forced to sleep in these houses' drafty, small garret spaces or cold, dark cellars. Moreover, they could not walk the streets freely; in fact, they often needed a pass to navigate public spaces where various systems of surveillance were employed to control their activities.

Such systems of control did not yet exist during the earliest years of Dutch colonization, but they became more common in the region as more free New Yorkers began to rely on the labor of enslaved people. During the Dutch colonial period, enslaved men and women in New Amsterdam had been able to use their access to some of these spaces to improve their circumstances. Many of them participated in the Dutch Reformed Church and used the colony's courts to protect their property and wages and to obtain freedom. Over the course of the long eighteenth century, Dutch Americans began to assert their dominance over these spaces and restricted enslaved men and women from accessing them or heavily restricted them within these spaces, a practice that proved integral to sustaining a system of human bondage.

Similarly important, however, is the fact that Cooper's description omitted any references to enslaved New Yorkers' daily acts of resistance. Some enslaved New Yorkers resisted with outright rebellion or by running away, but most resistance took place in often unnoticeable acts. When running errands for their enslavers, for instance, they would often extend the time they had to visit friends or family. At night, when they were not allowed to walk the streets, they used alleyways and backyards to avoid being caught by watchmen. Moreover, they would often practice their religious beliefs in their sleeping quarters, hidden from their enslavers. The chapters in this book have demonstrated that through these actions, enslaved New Yorkers created alternative ways of knowing and navigating the spaces they inhabited and frequented. Regardless of their enslavers' efforts, their movements and activities could not be controlled.

Finally, Cooper suggested that "New York never had slaves on the system of the southern planters, or in gangs of hundreds, to labour in the fields under overseers and who lived apart in cabins of their own." He certainly was not the only one to assert that slavery in the South differed significantly from slavery in New York. Indeed, enslaved New Yorkers did not work on large plantations, and most slaveholders held fewer than five people in bondage. That does not mean, however, that slavery in New York was somehow more humane. There too, men, women, and children had been turned into commodities, or as Cooper detailed, Dutch American farmers owned both the land and the enslaved workers who cultivated it. Whether it was in New York or Virginia, enslaved men, women, and children endured physical and emotional abuse *every single day*. And, as this book has shown, when it concerned enslavers' efforts to control spaces, the system of slavery in Dutch New York much resembled that of southern communities.

Even though Cooper wrote these words in a novel, albeit semiautobiographical, and years after slavery had been abolished in the state, they matter. Frequent repetition of slavery in New York as somehow a more benign system has helped this narrative dominate popular memory.[2] A similar imbalance exists in the archives, where the stories of enslaved men and women are largely told by the people who claimed to own them. That does not mean that the archives do not hold records produced by enslaved New Yorkers, but they are few when compared with the overwhelming amounts of documents produced by their enslavers. Consequently, historians who rely on the archives often struggle to piece together a more complex recounting of the history of slavery. Any study of slavery that relies predominantly on the documents produced by the enslavers runs the risk of perpetuating their power and control over the narrative and its memory. Through research of the spaces of enslavement, this book has presented a more tactile history of slavery that helps show why the narrative of slavery in New York as described by Cooper and others is unequivocally false.

NOTES

Introduction

1. I am aware that the Maison des Esclaves in Senegal has been a site of controversy for decades, with disagreements between scholars about how important this site really was in the transatlantic slave trade. My comments here are not intended to take a position in these debates. Instead, they are merely meant to describe my personal experience when visiting this site.

2. The Slave Dwelling Project blog discusses this and other sleepovers at https://slavedwellingproject.org/there-is-something-special-about-sleepovers/.

3. The archeological work at Royall House as discussed by Alexandra Chan proved especially influential early on in thinking about ways we can use consideration of space to reconstruct the experiences of enslaved people in these spaces. Alexandra Chan, *Slavery in the Age of Reason: Archeology at a New England Farm* (Knoxville: University of Tennessee Press, 2007).

4. Stephanie Camp, *Closer to Freedom: Enslaved Women & Everyday Resistance in the Plantation South* (Chapel Hill: University of North Carolina Press, 2004), 7; Katherine McKittrick, *Demonic Grounds: Black Women and the Cartographies of Struggle* (Minneapolis: University of Minnesota Press, 2006), xviii–xix; Marisa Fuentes, *Dispossessed Lives: Enslaved Women, Violence, and the Archive* (Philadelphia: University of Pennsylvania Press, 2016), 20; Robert Olwell, *Masters, Slaves, and Subjects: The Culture of Power in the South Carolina Low Country, 1740–1790* (Ithaca, NY: Cornell University Press, 1998), 6–7.

5. Stephanie Camp explains that enslaved people created "a rival geography," a term first introduced by Edward Said and used by geographers "to describe resistance to colonial occupation." In her study of southern plantations, the rival geography represents "alternative ways of knowing and using plantation and southern space that conflicted with planters' ideals and demands." Camp, *Closer to Freedom*, 7.

6. Relatively recent studies on slavery in New York include Michael E. Groth, *Slavery and Freedom in the Mid-Hudson Valley* (Albany: State University of New York Press, 2017); Katherine Howlett Hayes, *Slavery before Race: Europeans, Africans, and Indians at Long Island's Sylvester Manor Plantation, 1651–1884* (New York: New York University Press, 2013); Nicole Maskiell, "Bound by Bondage: Slavery among Elites in Colonial Massachusetts and New York" (PhD diss., Cornell University, 2013); Anne-Claire Merlin-Faucquez, "De la Nouvelle-Néerlande à New York: la naissance d'une société esclavagiste (1624–1712)" (PhD diss., Université Paris VIII—Vincennes Saint Denis Ecole Doctorale, 2011); Andrea C. Mosterman, "Sharing Spaces in a New World Environment:

African-Dutch Contributions to North American Culture, 1626–1826" (PhD diss., Boston University, 2012); Jeroen Dewulf, *The Pinkster King and the King of Kongo: The Forgotten History of America's Dutch-Owned Slaves* (Jackson: University Press of Mississippi, 2017); Susanah Shaw Romney, *New Netherland Connections: Intimate Networks and Atlantic Ties in Seventeenth-Century America* (Chapel Hill: University of North Carolina Press, 2014), chap. 4. For earlier studies on slavery in New York, see Craig Steven Wilder, *In the Company of Black Men: The African Influence on African American Culture in New York City* (New York: New York University Press, 2001); Craig Steven Wilder, *A Covenant with Color: Race and Social Power in Brooklyn* (New York: Columbia University Press, 2000); Myra B. Young Armstead, ed., *Mighty Change, Tall Within: Black Identity in the Hudson Valley* (Albany: State University of New York Press, 2003); David N. Gellman, *Emancipating New York: The Politics of Slavery and Freedom, 1777–1827* (Baton Rouge: Louisiana State University Press, 2006); Graham Russell Hodges, *Root & Branch: African Americans in New York & East Jersey* (Chapel Hill: University of North Carolina Press, 1999); Graham Russell Hodges, *Slavery and Freedom in the Rural North: African Americans in Monmouth County, New Jersey, 1665–1865* (Madison, WI: Madison House Publishers, 1997); Patricia Bonomi, "'Swarms of Negroes Comeing about My Door': Black Christianity in Early Dutch and English North America," *Journal of American History* (June 2016): 34–58, https://doi.org/10.1093/jahist/jaw007; Thelma Wills Foote, *Black and White Manhattan: The History of Racial Formation in Colonial New York City* (Oxford: Oxford University Press, 2004); Leslie M. Harris, *In the Shadow of Slavery: African Americans in New York City, 1626–1863* (Chicago: University of Chicago Press, 2003); Vivienne Kruger, "Born to Run: The Slave Family in Early New York, 1626 to 1827" (Ph.D. diss., Columbia University, 1985); Joyce Goodfriend, "Burghers and Blacks: The Evolution of a Slave Society at New Amsterdam," *New York History* (1978): 129–130; Joyce Goodfriend, "Slavery in Colonial New York," *Urban History*, no. 3 (2008): 485–496; Joyce Goodfriend, "Black Families in New Netherland," in *A Beautiful and Fruitful Place*, ed. Nancy McClure Zeller (Albany: New Netherland Project, 1991): 147–156; Joyce Goodfriend, *Before the Melting Pot: Society and Culture in Colonial New York City, 1644–1730* (Princeton, NJ: Princeton University Press, 1992); Ira Berlin and Leslie Harris, eds., *Slavery in New York* (New York: New Press, 2005); A. J. Williams-Myers, *Long Hammering: Essays on the Forging of an African American Presence in the Hudson River Valley to the Early Twentieth Century* (Trenton, NJ: Africa World Press, 1994); Shane White, *Somewhat More Independent: The End of Slavery in New York City, 1770–1810* (Athens: University of Georgia Press, 1991); Oscar Williams, *African Americans and Colonial Legislation in the Middle Colonies* (Milton Park, UK: Routledge, 2014 [repr. ed.]); Edgar J. McManus, *A History of Negro Slavery in New York* (Syracuse, NY: Syracuse University Press, 1966). Recent work on slavery in the North includes Jared Hardesty, *Unfreedom: Slavery and Dependence in Eighteenth-Century Boston* (New York: New York University Press, 2016); Wendy Warren, *New England Bound: Slavery and Colonization in Early America* (New York: Liveright, 2016); Christy Clark-Pujara, *Dark Work: The Business of Slavery in Rhode Island* (New York: New York University Press, 2016); Margaret Ellen Newell, *Brethren by Nature: New England Indians, Colonists, and the Origins of American Slavery* (Ithaca, NY: Cornell University Press, 2015); Harvey Amani Whitfield, *North to Bondage: Loyalist Slavery in the Maritimes* (Vancouver: UBC Press, 2016); and James J. Gigantino II, *The Ragged Road to Abolition:*

Slavery and Freedom in New Jersey, 1775–1865 (Philadelphia: University of Pennsylvania Press, 2014).

7. Cynthia Van Zandt similarly suggests in her study that "enslaved Africans charted the spaces in which they could blunt the oppressive force of slavery . . . , and slavery in the early seventeenth century provided far more such spaces than existed in later periods." Cynthia Van Zandt, *Brothers among Nations: The Pursuit of Intercultural Alliance in Early America, 1580–1660* (Oxford: Oxford University Press, 2008), 9.

8. Hodges, *Root & Branch*, 8.

9. The 1830 Federal Census suggests that slavery had not yet come to its complete demise in New York State. According to this census, seventy-six men, women, and children still lived in bondage in the state. In 1840, New Yorkers reported four enslaved people to the census, three of whom lived in Brooklyn. *Abstract of the Returns of the Fifth Census, showing the number of free people, the number of slaves, the Federal or Representative Number; and the Aggregate of Each County of Each State of the United States. Prepared from the corrected returns of the Secretary of Congress, By the Clerk of the House of Representatives* (Washington, DC: Duff Green, 1832), 9–10; *Compendium of the Enumeration of the Inhabitants and Statistics of the United States, as obtained at the Department of State, from the returns of the sixth census, by counties and principal towns exhibiting the population, wealth, and resources of the country* (Washington, DC: Printed by Thomas Allen, 1841), 22; also see Gellman, *Emancipating New York.*

10. Merlin-Faucquez, "De la Nouvelle-Néerlande à New York," 175–178, 352.

11. Several scholars have written about the ways in which Dutch culture influenced African American ways of life in Dutch American communities. See, for instance, Jeroen Dewulf, "'A Strong Barbaric Accent': America's Dutch-Speaking Black Community from Seventeenth-Century New Netherland to Nineteenth-Century New York and New Jersey," *American Speech* 90, no. 2 (May 2015): 131–153, https://doi.org/10.1215/00031283-3130302; David S. Cohen, *The Ramapo Mountain People* (New Brunswick, NJ: Rutgers University Press, 1986); Linda Heywood and John K. Thornton, "Intercultural Relations between Europeans and Blacks in New Netherland," in *Four Centuries of Dutch-American Relations: 1609–2009*, ed. Hans Krabbendam, Cornelis A. van Minnen, and Giles Scott-Smith (Albany: State University of New York Press, 2009); Mosterman, "Sharing Spaces in a New World Environment."

12. See, for instance, Max Grivno, *Gleanings of Freedom: Free and Slave Labor along the Mason-Dixon Line, 1790–1860* (Urbana: University of Illinois Press, 2011); Hardesty, *Unfreedom*; Jill Lepore, *New York Burning: Liberty, Slavery, and Conspiracy in Eighteenth-Century Manhattan* (New York: Alfred A. Knopf, 2005); Peter Linebaugh and Marcus Rediker, *The Many-Headed Hydra: Sailors, Slaves, Commoners, and the Hidden History of the Revolutionary Atlantic* (Boston: Beacon, 2000); Simon Newman, *A New World of Labor: The Development of Plantation Slavery in the British Atlantic* (Philadelphia: University of Pennsylvania Press, 2013); Seth Rockman, *Scraping By: Wage Labor, Slavery, and Survival in Early Baltimore* (Baltimore: Johns Hopkins University Press, 2009); Christopher Tomlins, *Freedom Bound: Law, Labor, and Civic Identity in Colonizing English America, 1580–1865* (Cambridge: Cambridge University Press, 2010); Serena R. Zabin, *Dangerous Economies: Status and Commerce in Imperial New York* (Philadelphia: University of Pennsylvania Press, 2009).

13. Multiple archival records show that families purchased Dutch books for their children. See, for example, Peter Winne's purchase of *De Trap Der Jeugd* in 1771.

Elmendorph Account Book 1770–1777, December 18, 1771, CV10181: Kingston Collection, box 17, NYSL. Also see Charles T. Gehring, "The Dutch Language in Colonial New York: An Investigation of a Language in Decline and Its Relationship to Social Change" (PhD diss., Indiana University Press, 1973); Gerald F. De Jong, *The Dutch Reformed Church in the American Colonies* (Grand Rapids, MI: Wm. B. Eerdmans, 1978), 86.

14. Ira Berlin, "From Creole to African: Atlantic Creoles and the Origins of African-American Society in Mainland North America," *William and Mary Quarterly*, no. 2 (April 1996): 254, https://doi.org/102307/2947401.

15. Frederick Philipse, Rip Vandam (Van Dam), Anthony Rutgers, Abraham van Horne, Garret Van Horne, John Van Horne, Arnolt Schuyler, Peter Schuyler, Adoniah Schuyler, and John Van Cortland were all listed as slave ship owners. Voyages database, 2013, *Voyages: The Trans-Atlantic Slave Trade Database*, http://www.slavevoyages.org (accessed October 26, 2016).

16. Voyages database, 2013, *Voyages: The Trans-Atlantic Slave Trade Database*, http://www.slavevoyages.org (accessed October 26, 2016); Walter Rucker, *The River Flows On: Black Resistance, Culture, and Identity Formation in Early America* (Baton Rouge: Louisiana State University, 2006), 31. For more about the Philipse family and the Madagascar trade, see Jacob Judd, "Frederick Philipse and the Madagascar Trade," *New York Historical Society Quarterly*, no. 4 (September 1971): 354–374.

17. Voyages database, 2013, *Voyages: The Trans-Atlantic Slave Trade Database*, http://www.slavevoyages.org (accessed October 26, 2016).

18. Rucker, *River Flows On*, 32–33. According to Rucker, a fourth of New York's newly imported slaves came directly from Africa, primarily from the Gold Coast, in the first half of the eighteenth century. British slaves imported from Jamaica, Antigua, and Barbados mainly came from the Bight of Biafra, the Bight of Benin, the Gold Coast, and West Central Africa.

19. Gregory O'Malley has calculated that more than 92 percent of the enslaved people who were traded in the British intercolonial trade had only recently arrived in the Americas from Africa. Gregory E. O'Malley, *Final Passages: The Intercolonial Slave Trade of British America, 1619–1807* (Chapel Hill: University of North Carolina Press, 2014), 21, 202. About 3,350 enslaved Africans arrived in New York from the Caribbean, whereas about 6,089 enslaved Africans came directly from Africa during the period from 1701 through 1775. The number of African captives who arrived in New York by transatlantic slave trade is based on the number of people who survived the journey and disembarked in New York. Many more African captives boarded these ships but never made it to New York. Examination of the eighteenth-century British slave trade reveals that most African captives who arrived in the Americas on board British ships would have come from the Bight of Biafra, the Gold Coast, and West Central Africa. Estimates from Voyages database, 2013, *Voyages: The Trans-Atlantic Slave Trade Database*, http://www.slavevoyages.org (accessed November 16, 2016).

20. E. B. O'Callaghan and Berthold Fernow, trans and ed., *Documents Relative to the Colonial History of the State of New-York: Documents relating to the history and settlements of the towns along the Hudson and Mohawk Rivers (with the exception of Albany), from 1630 to 1684* (Albany: Weed & Parsons, 1881), 2:537. Also see Maskiell, "Bound by Bondage," 108; Ansel Judd Northrup, *Slavery in New York: A Historical Sketch* (Albany: University of the State of New York, 1900), 305; Charles Zebina Lincoln, William H. Johnson,

and Ansel Judd Northrup, eds., *The Colonial Laws of New York from the Year 1664 to the Revolution, Including the Charters to the Duke of York, the Commission and Instructions to Colonial Governors, the Dukes Laws, the Laws of the Donagan and Leisler Assemblies, the Charters of Albany and New York and the Acts of the Colonial Legislature from 1691 to 1775* (Minneapolis: J. B. Lyon, State Printer, 1894), 1:598; 3:1060.

21. Camp, *Closer to Freedom*, 7.

22. His speech was later published: Michel Foucault, "Of Other Spaces," *Diacritics* 16 (1986): 22–27, https://doi.org/10.2307/464648.

23. Robert T. Tally, *Spatiality* (New York: Routledge, 2012), 11–12.

24. Tally, 4.

25. Henri Lefebvre, *The Production of Space*, trans. Donald Nicholson-Smith (Oxford: Blackwell, 1991. First published in French in 1974), 12.

26. Michel de Certeau, *The Practice of Everyday Life*, trans. Steven Rendall (Berkeley: University of California Press, 1984), 117.

27. Edward Soja, *Postmodern Geographies: The Reassertion of Space in Critical Theory* (London: Verso, 1989), 19.

28. Lefebvre, *Production of Space*, 12.

29. Michel Foucault, *Discipline and Punish: The Birth of the Prison*, trans. Alan Sheridan (New York: Vintage Books, 1995), 195–230.

30. Lepore, *New York Burning*; Vincent Brown, "Slave Revolt in Jamaica, 1760–1761: A Cartographic Narrative," http://revolt.axismaps.com/project.html; also see Vincent Brown, *Tacky's Revolt: The Story of an Atlantic Slave War* (Cambridge, MA: Belknap Press, 2020).

31. Rashauna Johnson, *Slavery's Metropolis: Unfree Labor in New Orleans during the Age of Revolutions* (Cambridge: Cambridge University Press, 2016).

32. James A. Delle, *An Archeology of Social Space: Analyzing Coffee Plantations in Jamaica's Blue Mountains* (New York: Plenum, 1998); Terrence W. Epperson, "Race and the Disciplines of the Plantation," *Historical Archeology* 24, no. 4 (1990): 29–36; Theresa A. Singleton, "Slavery and Spatial Dialectics on Cuban Coffee Plantations," *World Archeology* 33, no. 1 (2001): 98–114; Theresa A. Singleton, ed., *The Archeology of Slavery and Plantation Life* (San Diego: Academic Press, 1985); Theresa A. Singleton, "The Archeology of Slavery in North America," *Annual Review of Anthropology* 24 (1995): 119–140; Terrence W. Epperson, "Panopticon Plantations: The Garden Sights of Thomas Jefferson and George Mason," in *Lines that Divide: Historical Archaeologies of Race, Class, and Gender*, ed. James A. Delle, Stephen Mrozowski, and Robert Paynter (Knoxville: University of Tennessee Press, 2000), 58–77.

33. Camp, *Closer to Freedom*; McKittrick, *Demonic Grounds*; Fuentes, *Dispossessed Lives*.

34. Elizabeth Maddock Dillon, "A Sea of Texts: The Atlantic World, Spatial Mapping, and Equiano's *Narrative*," in *Religion, Space, and the Atlantic World*, ed. John Corrigan (Columbia: University of South Carolina Press, 2017), 38–39.

35. Ann Laura Stoler, *Carnal Knowledge and Imperial Power: Race and the Intimate in Colonial Rule* (Berkeley: University of California Press, 2010 [repr. ed.]), 183.

36. Many thanks to art historian Anna Mecugni for her help analyzing this painting.

37. Camp, *Closer to Freedom*, 7. James Delle has termed these "spatialities of movement," the ways in which enslaved people "expressed control over the spatiality of

movement, at least for a brief time." Delle, *Archeology of Social Space*, 165. Also see Rebecca Ginsberg and Clifton Ellis, eds., *Slavery in the City: Architecture and Landscapes of Urban Slavery in North America* (Charlottesville: University of Virginia Press, 2017), 2–3; Aisha Finch, *Rethinking Slave Rebellion in Cuba: La Escalera and the Insurgency of 1841–1844* (Chapel Hill: University of North Carolina Press, 2015), 53; Robert Ross, *Status and Respectability in the Cape Colony, 1750–1870: A Tragedy of Manners* (Cambridge: Cambridge University Press, 1999), 131–132.

38. A growing number of scholars are paying attention to these silences in the archives. See, among others, Fuentes, *Dispossessed Lives*; Saidiya Hartman, *Lose Your Mother: A Journey Along the Atlantic Slave Route* (New York: Farrar, Straus and Giroux, 2007); Saidiya Hartman, "Venus in Two Acts," *Small Axe* 26 (June 2008): 1–14; Michel-Rolph Trouillot, *Silencing the Past: Power and the Production of History* (Boston: Beacon, 1995); Stephanie Smallwood, "The Politics of the Archive and History's Accountability to the Enslaved," *History of the Present: A Journal of Critical History* 6, no. 2 (Fall 2016): 117–132, https://doi.org/10.5406/historypresent.6.2.0117.

1. Enslaved Labor and the Settling of New Netherland

1. In the historical records, Groot Manuel is also referred to as Groote Manuel or Manuel de Groote. For clarity, I will continue to use Groot Manuel. Some scholars confuse Groot Manuel and Manuel de Gerrit de Reus, but these are clearly two different men. Robert Swan details how Manuel de Gerrit de Reus likely got his name. Robert J. Swan, "Slaves and Slaveholding in Dutch New York," *Journal of the Afro-American Historical and Genealogical Society* 17, no. 1 (1998): 56.

2. Court Proceedings, January 17, 1641, NYCM, IV, 83, NYSA; Sentence of Manuel de Gerrit de Reus, January 24, 1641, NYCM, IV, 84, NYSA; Council Minutes, January 24, 1641, NYCM, IV, 85, NYSA. Many scholars have discussed these events. See, for example, Romney, *New Netherland Connections*, 220–221; Van Zandt, *Brothers among Nations*, 158; Cynthia Jean Van Zandt, "Negotiating Settlement: Colonialism, Cultural Exchange, and Conflict in Early Colonial Atlantic North America, 1580–1660" (PhD diss., University of Connecticut, 1998), 142–186; Jaap Jacobs, "Van Angola naar Manhattan. Slavernij in Nieuw-Nederland in de seventiende eeuw," in *Slaven en schepen. Enkele reis, bestemming onbekend*, ed. Remmelt Daalder, Andrea Kieskamp, and Dirk J. Tang (Leiden: Primavera Pers, 2001), 69–75; Christopher Moore, "A World of Possibilities: Slavery and Freedom in Dutch New Amsterdam," in *Slavery in New York*, ed. Ira Berlin and Leslie Harris (New York: New Press, 2005), 39; Peter Christoph, "The Freedmen of New Amsterdam," in *A Beautiful and Fruitful Place: Selected Rensselaerswijck Seminar Papers*, ed. N. A. McClure Zeller (n.p., 1991), 158.

3. Minutes, February 25, 1644, NYCM, IV, 183, NYSA; A. J. F. van Laer, *Council Minutes, 1638–1649* (New York Historical Manuscripts: Dutch. Baltimore, Genealogical Publishing Co., 1974), 4:213.

4. When discussing slavery in Batavia, Niemeijer writes, "Deze zwarte Indiers, hetzij vrij of slaaf, kwamen soms met een christelijke identiteit in Batavia of zouden er weldra een krijgen. Het doel was om in Batavia een betrouwbare, 'christelijk-inlandse' burgerij te vormen." Hendrik E. Niemeijer, *Batavia: Een koloniale samenleving in de zeventiende eeuw* (Amsterdam: Uitgeverij Balans, 2005), 42.

5. Cynthia Van Zandt also argues in her book *Brothers among Nations* that the company may have spared their lives because they were too valuable to the company. Van Zandt, *Brothers among Nations*, 149–156.

6. See, for example, P. C. Emmer, *De Nederlandse Slavenhandel, 1500–1850* (Amsterdam: Uitgeverij De Arbeidspers, 2000), 56–57; Willem Frijhoff and Jaap Jacobs, "The Dutch, New Netherland, and Thereafter (1609–1780s)," in *Four Centuries of Dutch-American Relations, 1609–2009*, ed. Hans Krabbendam, Cornelis A. van Minnen, and Giles Scott-Smith (Albany: State University of New York Press, 2009), 46; Jaap Jacobs, *New Netherland: A Dutch Colony in Seventeenth-Century America* (Leiden: Brill, 2015). For more about the Dutch West India Company's efforts to colonize the region, see, among others, Susanah Shaw Romney, "'With & alongside his housewife': Claiming Ground in New Netherland and the Early Modern Dutch Empire," *William and Mary Quarterly* 73, no. 2 (April 2016): 187–224, https://doi.org/10.5309/willmaryquar.73.2.0187.

7. At least one document uses the term *half-free* to refer to such conditional freedom. This document declares that a group of men would become "half free" (*datse half-vrij sullen sijn*). This document later details when "this half freedom" (*dese halve vrijdom*) will go into effect. Council Minutes, December 8, 1663, NYCM, X, 429, NYSA. A December certificate of freedom also included the term *half-freedom*. Council Minutes, December 11/21, NYCM, X, 327, NYSA. On September 4, 1664, the council minutes includes a petition from men who had obtained such half-freedom in which they requested to be released from "half-slavery" (*halve slavernije*). Council Minutes, September 4, 1664, X, 317, NYSA.

8. Indeed, as Cátia Antunes explains, "perpetuating a binary narrative (VOC/WIC, East/West) when analysing the Early Modern Dutch maritime expansion overseas obscures and neglects the importance of the features of empires actually encapsulated by this expansion." Cátia Antunes, "From Binary Narratives to Diversified Tales: Changing the Paradigm in the Study of Dutch Colonial Participation," *TVGESCH* 131, no. 3 (2018): 387, https://doi.org/110.5117/TVGESCH2018.3.001.ANTU. Also consider connections between the families involved in the WIC and VOC as discussed in Julia Adams, *The Familial State: Ruling Families and Merchant Capitalism in Early Modern Europe* (Ithaca, NY: Cornell University Press, 2005).

9. Antunes, "From Binary Narratives," 393, 401.

10. Gerrit Knaap, "Kasteel, stad en land: Het begin van het Nederlandse Imperium in de Oost," *Leidschrift* 21, no. 2 (September 2006): 19. Also see Matthias van Rossum, "Labouring Transformations of Amphibious Monsters: Exploring Early Modern Globalization, Diversity, and Shifting Clusters of Labour Relations in the Context of the Dutch East India Company (1600–1800)," *IRSH* 64 (2019): 20–21, https://doi.org/10.1017/S0020859019000014.

11. Benjamin Schmidt, "The Dutch Atlantic: From Provincialism to Globalism," in *Atlantic History: A Critical Appraisal*, ed. Jack P. Greene and Philip D. Morgan (Oxford: Oxford University Press, 2009), 170.

12. Erin Kramer, "New York's Unrighteous Beginnings," Gotham Center Blog, https://www.gothamcenter.org/blog/new-yorks-unrighteous-beginnings, August 5, 2020. For more on early Munsee-Dutch encounters, see Donna Merwick, *The Shame and the Sorrow: Dutch-Amerindian Encounters in New Netherland* (Philadelphia: University of Pennsylvania Press, 2006); Andrew Lipman, *The Saltwater Frontier: Indians and the*

Contest for the American Coast (New Haven, CT: Yale University Press, 2015). Also see Adam Clulow, "The Art of Claiming: Possession and Resistance in Early Modern Asia," *American Historical Review* 121, no. 1 (February 2016): 19, https://doi.org/10.1093/ahr/121.1.17. Although Dutch officials claimed legal ownership of such territory, indigenous populations frequently challenge these legal claims. See, for instance, Saliha Belmessous, ed., *Native Claims: Indigenous Law against Empire, 1500–1920* (Oxford: Oxford University Press, 2012); William Cronon, *Changes in the Land: Colonists and the Ecology of New England* (New York: Hill & Wang, 1983); Lisa Brooks, *The Common Pot: The Recovery of Native Space in the Northeast* (Minneapolis: University of Minnesota Press, 2008).

13. Nigel Worden, "Space and Identity in VOC Cape Town," *Kronos* 25 (1998–99): 76–77.

14. Marsely L. Kehoe, "Dutch Batavia: Exposing the Hierarchy of the Dutch Colonial City," *Journal of Historians of Netherlandish Art* 7, no. 1 (Winter 2015): 8, 14, 16–17, https://doi.org/10.5092/jhna.2015.7.1.3.

15. Edmund B. O'Callaghan, *History of New Netherland; or, New York Under the Dutch,* (New York: D. Appleton, 1846), 1:400. Also see Wim Klooster, *The Dutch Moment: War Trade, and Settlement in the Seventeenth-Century Atlantic World* (Ithaca, NY: Cornell University Press, 2016), 198; Henk den Heijer, "The Dutch West India Company, 1621–1791," in *Riches from the Atlantic Commerce: Dutch Transatlantic Trade and Shipping, 1585–1817,* ed. Johannes Postma and Victor Enthoven (Leiden: Brill, 2003), 85. For a detailed discussion of the West India Company, see Henk den Heijer, *De geschiedenis van de WIC* (Zutphen: Walburg Pers, 2002).

16. Knaap, "Kasteel, stad en land," 24; Markus Vink, "'The World's Oldest Trade': Dutch Slavery and Slave Trade in the Indian Ocean in the Seventeenth Century," *Journal of World History* 14, no. 2 (June 2003): 164, https://doi.org/10.1353/jwh.2003.0026; Clulow, "Art of Claiming," 19.

17. For initial Dutch portrayals of Native Americans as possible allies against the Spanish, see Benjamin Schmidt, "Exotic Allies: The Dutch-Chilean Encounter and the Failed Conquest of America," *Renaissance Quarterly* 52, no. 2 (Summer 1999): 440–473, https://doi.org/10.2307/2902060; Benjamin Schmidt, *Innocence Abroad: The Dutch Imagination and the New World, 1570–1670* (New York: Cambridge University Press, 2001); Arthur Weststeijn, "Republican Empire: Colonialism, Commerce and Corruption in the Dutch Golden Age," *Renaissance Studies* 26, no. 2 (September 2012): 496–497; Pepijn Brandon and Karwan Fatah-Black, "'For the Reputation and Respectability of the State': Trade, The Imperial State, Unfree Labor, and Empire in the Dutch Atlantic," in *Building the Atlantic Empires: Unfree Labor and Imperial States in the Political Economy of Capitalism, ca. 1500–1914,* ed. John Donoghue and Evelyn Jennings (Leiden: Brill, 2016), 90. For Hugo Grotius and just war in Dutch colonial expansion, see Martine Julia van Ittersum, "The Long Goodbye: Hugo Grotius' Justification of Dutch Expansion Overseas, 1615–1645," *History of European Ideas* 36 (2010): 386–411, https://doi.org/10.1016/j.histeuroideas.2010.05.003.

18. In fact, Susanah Shaw Romney suggests that "Dutch intellectuals thought settlement and trade inseparable within a republican empire." Romney, "'With & alongside his housewife,'" 190.

19. Brandon and Fatah-Black, "'For the Reputation,'" 85.

20. Deborah Hamer, "Marriage and the Construction of Colonial Order: Jurisdiction, Gender, and Class in Seventeenth Century Dutch Batavia," *Gender & History* 29, no. 3 (November 2017): 633–634, https://doi.org/10.1111/1468-0424.12316; Leonard Blussé, "Batavia: 1619–1740: The Rise and Fall of a Chinese Colonial Town," *Journal of Southeast Asian Studies* 12, no. 1 (March 1981): 167.

21. Alison Games, "Cohabitation, Suriname-Style: English Inhabitants in Dutch Suriname after 1667," *William and Mary Quarterly*, 3d ser., 72, no. 2 (April 2015): 241, https://doi.org/10.5309/Willmaryquar.72.2.0195.

22. See, for example, Jean Gelman Taylor, *The Social World of Batavia: Europeans and Eurasians in Colonial Indonesia* (Madison: University of Wisconsin Press, 2009); Gijs Kruijtzer, "European Migration in the Dutch Sphere," in *Dutch Colonialism, Migration and Cultural Heritage*, ed. Gert Oostindie (Leiden: KITLV, 2008), 97–154.

23. Romney, "'With & alongside his housewife,'" 210.

24. Blussé, "Batavia," 167; Remco Raben, "Facing the Crowd: The Urban Ethnic Policy of the Dutch East India Company, 1600–1800," in *Mariners, Merchants, and Oceans: Studies in Maritime History*, ed. Skaria Mathew Kuzhippallil (New Delhi: Manohar, 1995), 216.

25. Tonio Andrade, "The Rise and Fall of Dutch Taiwan, 1624–1662: Cooperative Colonization and the Statist Model of European Expansion," *Journal of World History* 17, no. 4 (December 2006): 430, https://doi.org/10.1353/jwh.2006.0052. Also see Tonio Andrade, *How Taiwan Became Chinese: Dutch, Spanish, and Han Colonization in the Seventeenth Century* (New York: Columbia University Press, 2008 [Gutenberg-e]).

26. Brandon and Fatah-Black, "'For the Reputation,'" 90. Similarly, Rik van Welie writes, "All overseas possessions of the Dutch depended to varying degrees on the labour of slaves who were imported from diverse and often remote areas." Rik van Welie, "Patterns of Slave Trading and Slavery in the Dutch Colonial World, 1596–1863," in *Dutch Colonialism, Migration and Cultural Heritage*, ed. Gert Oostindie (Leiden: KITLV, 2008), 155.

27. As quoted in Adam Clulow, *Amboina, 1623: Fear and Conspiracy on the Edge of Empire* (New York: Columbia University Press, 2019), 50.

28. Vink, "'World's Oldest Trade,'" 152; Clulow, *Amboina, 1623*, 51, 56.

29. Clulow, "Art of Claiming," 19; Vink, "'World's Oldest Trade,'" 161.

30. Raben, "Facing the Crowd," 452.

31. Remco Raben, "Cities and the Slave Trade in Early-Modern Southeast Asia," in *Linking Destinies: Trade, Towns and Kin in Asian Histories*, ed. Peter Boomgaard, Dick Kooiman, and Henk Schulte Nordholt (Leiden: KITLV, 2008), 125. Hendrik Niemeijer points out that by the late seventeenth century more than half of Batavia's population was enslaved. Niemeijer, *Batavia*, 51. For more on the Dutch slave trade in the Indian Ocean, see Clulow, *Amboina, 1623*; Linda Mbeki and Matthias van Rossum, "Private Slave Trade in the Dutch Indian Ocean World: A Study into the Networks and Backgrounds of the Slavers and the Enslaved in South Asia and South Africa," *Slavery & Abolition* 38, no. 1 (2017), 95–116; Rik van Welie, "Slave Trading and Slavery in the Dutch Colonial Empire: A Global Comparison," *New West Indian Guide/Nieuwe West-Indische Gids* 82, no. 1 & 2 (2008): 73; Richard B. Allen, "Satisfying the 'Want for Labouring People': European Slave Trading in the Indian Ocean, 1500–1850," *Journal of World History* 21, no. 1 (2010): 45–73, https://doi.org/10.1353/jwh.0.0100; Vink, "'World's Oldest Trade.'"

32. Nicolaes van Wassenaer, "Historisch Verhael," in *Narratives of New Netherland, 1609–1664*, ed. J. Franklin Jameson (New York: Charles Scribner's Sons, 1909), 89. Also see Nicolaes Wassenaer, *Historisch verhael aldaer ghedenck-weerdichste geschiedenisse, die vanden beginner des jaers 1621 (tot 1632) voorgevallens syn* (Amsterdam, 1622–1635), International Institute of Social History, Amsterdam. See Jaap Jacobs for additional Dutch descriptions of New Netherland. Jacobs, *New Netherland*, chap. 1.

33. Jaap Jacobs, for instance, claims that the Dutch had "little incentive to go overseas." Jaap Jacobs, "Migration, Population, and Government in New Netherland," in *Four Centuries of Dutch-American Relations, 1609–2009*, ed. Hans Krabbendam, Cornelis A. Van Minnen, and Giles Scott-Smith (Albany: State University of New York Press, 2009), 87. In his book *New Netherland*, Jacobs provides great detail on migration to the colony and the various strategies of the company to promote or force migration. In this chapter, he does not discuss enslaved people. Jacobs, *New Netherland*, chap. 2. A later version of the book includes a one-page description of enslaved people in a chapter on the colony's population. Jaap Jacobs, *The Colony of New Netherland: A Dutch Settlement in Seventeenth-Century America* (Ithaca, NY: Cornell University Press, 2009), 55–56. Wim Klooster provides a similar discussion about migration in the Dutch Atlantic, including New Netherland. Klooster, *Dutch Moment*, chap. 6.

34. Jeroen Dewulf, "Emulating a Portuguese Model: The Slave Policy of the West India Company and the Dutch Reformed Church in Dutch Brazil (1630–1654) and New Netherland (1614–1664) in Comparative Perspective," *Journal of Early American History* 4 (2014): 7, https://doi.org/10.1163/18770703-00401006; Klooster, *Dutch Moment*, 19; José Antônio Gonsales de Mello, *Nederlanders in Brazilië, (1624–1654): de invloed van de Hollandse besetting op het leven en de cultuur in Noord-Brazilië*, trans. G. N. Visser (Zutphen: Walburg, 2001 [repr. ed.]), 190; Clulow, *Amboina, 1623*, 57–58.

35. Vrijheden privilegien ende Exemtien, SG 1.01.03, inv. no. 5753, Nat. Arch. Also see Hugh Hastings et al., eds., *Ecclesiastical Records, State of New York* (Albany: J. B. Lyon, state printer, 1901), 1:78–79; Charles T. Gehring, "New Netherland: The Formative Years, 1609–1632," in *Four Centuries of Dutch-American Relations, 1609–2009* (Albany: State University of New York Press, 2009), 83. Mark Meuwese discusses the debates within the Amsterdam chamber of the WIC that led to the creation of patroonships. Mark Meuwese, *Brothers in Arms, Partners in Trade: Dutch-Indigenous Alliances in the Atlantic World, 1595–1674* (Leiden: Brill, 2012), 48–49. Also see Jaap Jacobs, "Dutch Proprietary Manors in America: The Patroonships in New Netherland," in *Constructing Early Modern Empires: Proprietary Ventures in the Atlantic World*, ed. Lou Roper (Leiden: Brill, 2007), 301–326.

36. Ernst van den Boogaart, "The Servant Migration to New Netherland, 1624–1664," in *Colonialism and Migration; Indentured Labour before and after Slavery*, ed. P. C. Emmer (Dordrecht: Martinus Nijhoff, 1986), 57. According to Isaac Jogues, already in 1646 there were "four or five hundred men of different sects and nations" on Manhattan Island, and only about a hundred people in Rensselaerswijck. Isaac Jogues, "Novum Belgium," in *Narratives of New Netherland, 1609–1664*, ed. J. Franklin Jameson (New York: Charles Scribner's Sons, 1909), 262. Jaap Jacobs also discusses the early challenges to attract settlers. Jacobs, *New Netherland*, 45–46.

37. Rapport & advijs over de gelegentheijt van nieu nederlant, December 15, 1644, SG 1.01.07, inv. no. 12564.30A, Nat. Arch.

38. Wim Klooster points out that many Dutch migrants returned to the Dutch Republic. Wim Klooster, "The Dutch in the Atlantic," in *Four Centuries of Dutch-American Relations, 1609–2009*, ed. Hans Krabbendam, Cornelis A. van Minnen, and Giles Scott-Smith (Albany: State University of New York Press, 2009), 70.

39. Arnold J. F. van Laer, ed. and trans., *Minutes of the Court of Rensselaerswyck, 1648–1652* (Albany: University of the State of New York, 1922), 163.

40. Johannes Winckelman contra Abraham Pietersen, March 13, 1642, NYCM, IV, 115, NYSA; Van Laer, *Council Minutes 1638–1649*, 135.

41. Resolution, December 5, 1647, NYCM, IV, 353, NYSA; Van Laer, *Council Minutes 1638–1649*, 470–472.

42. Minutes, August 9, 1640, NYCM, IV, 73, NYSA; Ordinance, October 1648, NYCM, XVI, 17, NYSA.

43. Jacobs, *New Netherland*, 47.

44. Klooster, *Dutch Moment*, 91; Jacobs, *New Netherland*, 373.

45. Van den Boogaart, "Servant Migration," 57.

46. Jacobs, *New Netherland*, 47.

47. Letter from the Directors to Stuyvesant, November 23, 1654, NYCM, XII, 17, NYSA; Directors in Amsterdam to Stuyvesant, January 20, 1660, NYCM, XV, 97, NYSA; Letter to the Staten Generaal, n.d., SG 1.01.07, inv. no. 12564.30A, 10–11, Nat. Arch. In 1645, the States General instructed the WIC to bring slaves to New Netherland. Instructions by the West India Company for the Council and Director General of New Netherland, July 8, 1645, SG 1.01.07, inv. no. 12564.30A, Nat. Arch. For more on the slave trade with New Netherland, see P. C. Emmer, "De Slavenhandel van en naar Nieuw-Nederland," *Economisch-Historisch Jaarboek* 35 (1972), 94–148; Albert van Dantzig, *Het Nederlandse aandeel in de slavenhandel* (Bussum: Fibula-van Dishoeck, 1968); Joyce Goodfriend, "Burghers and Blacks," *New York History* 49 (1978), 125–144; E. B. O'Callaghan, ed. and trans., *Voyages of the slavers St. John and Arms of Amsterdam, 1659, 1663: together with additional papers illustrative of the slave trade under the Dutch* (Albany: J. Munsell, 1867). For more on the seventeenth-century Dutch Atlantic slave trade, see, among others, Johannes Postma, *The Dutch in the Atlantic Slave Trade, 1600–1815* (Cambridge: Cambridge University Press, 1990); Klaas Ratelband, *Nederlanders in West-Afrika 1600–1650* (Zutphen: Uitgeverijmaatshappij Walburg Pers, 2000), 91–120; Filipa Ribeiro da Silva, *Dutch and Portuguese in Western Africa: Empires, Merchants and the Atlantic System, 1580–1674* (Leiden: Brill, 2011), 213–270; Jelmer Vos, David Eltis, and David Richardson, "The Dutch in the Atlantic World: New Perspectives from the Slave Trade with Particular Reference to the African Origins of the Traffic," in *Extending the Frontiers: Essays on the New Transatlantic Slave Trade Database*, ed. David Eltis and David Richardson (New Haven, CT: Yale University Press, 2008); Johannes Postma, "A Reassessment of the Dutch Atlantic Slave Trade," in *Riches from Atlantic Commerce: Dutch Transatlantic Trade and shipping, 1585–1817*, ed. Johannes Postma and Victor Enthoven (Leiden: Brill, 2003), 115–138; Ernst van den Boogaart, "The Trade between Western Africa and the Atlantic World, 1600–90: Estimates of Trends in Composition and Value," *Journal of African History* 33, no. 2 (November 1992): 369–385; Pieter Emmer and Ernst van den Boogaart, *The Dutch in the Atlantic Economy, 1580–1880: Trade, Slavery and Emancipation* (Aldershot: Ashgate, 1998); Johannes Postma, "The Dimensions of the Dutch Slave Trade from Western Africa," *Journal of African History* 13, no. 2 (1972): 237–248; H. den Heijer, "Goud, ivoor en slaven.

Scheepvaart en handel van de Tweede Westindische Compagnie of Afrika, 1674–1740" (PhD diss., Universiteit van Leiden, 1997); Christian Koot, "Anglo-Dutch Trade in the Chesapeake and the British Caribbean, 1621–1733," in *Dutch Atlantic Connections, 1680–1800: Linking Empires, Bridging Borders*, ed. Gert Oostindie and Jessica V. Roitman (Leiden: Brill, 2014): 72–99; Ernst van den Boogaart and Pieter Emmer, *The Dutch Participation in the Atlantic Slave Trade* (Leiden: Centre for the History of European Expansion, 1979).

48. Vrijheden privilegien ende Exemtien, SG 1.01.03, inv. No. 5753, Nat. Arch.

49. Willem Frijhoff, *Wegen van Evert Willemsz: Een Hollands weeskind op zoek naar zichzelf, 1607–1647* (Nijmegen: SUN, 1995), 768; Janny Venema, *Beverwijck: A Dutch Village on the American Frontier, 1652–1664* (Albany: State University of New York Press, 2003), 114–115; Goodfriend, "Burghers and Blacks," 127.

50. Report on New Netherland, December 15, 1644, SG 1.01.07, inv. no. 12564.30A, Nat. Arch.

51. O'Callaghan, *Voyages of the slavers*, 198–200.

52. Charles T. Gehring, ed. and trans., *Correspondence, 1647–1653* (Syracuse, NY: Syracuse University Press, 2000), 222–223.

53. Directors in Amsterdam to Stuyvesant, March 9, 1659, NYCM, VIII, 74, NYSA.

54. Directors in Amsterdam to Stuyvesant, January 20, 1660, NYCM, XV, 97, NYSA.

55. November 15, 1663, NYCM, XV, 77, NYSA; Directors to Stuyvesant, January 20, 1664, NYCM, XV, 97, NYSA; Contract, 1664, NYCM, XV, 98, NYSA; Stuyvesant to Beck, May 7, 1664, NYCM, XV, 123, NYSA; New Netherland Council to Directors at Amsterdam, August 17, 1664, NYCM, XV, 139, NYSA; O'Callaghan, *Voyages of the slavers*, 200–201. Also see Emmer, "De Slavenhandel van en naar Nieuw-Nederland," 124–126; Dennis J. Maika, "To 'Experiment with a Parcel of Negros': Incentive, Collaboration, and Competition in New Amsterdam's Slave Trade," *Journal of Early American History* 10, no. 1 (2020): 33–69. For more about the colony on the Delaware, see G. Murray Bakker, "Iets over de stichters van Nieuw-Nederland en hunne afstammelingen," *Eigen Haard*, no. 32 (1888): 384; Simon Hart, "The City-Colony of New Amstel on the Delaware: II," *de Halve Maen: Journal of The Holland Society of New York* 40, no. 1 (April 1965): 5–6, 13–14; C. A. Weslager, "The City of Amsterdam's Colony on the Delaware, 1656–1664," *Delaware History* 20 (1982): 1–25, 73–97; Mark L. Thompson, *The Contest for the Delaware Valley: Allegiance, Identity, and Empire in the Seventeenth Century* (Baton Rouge: Louisiana State University Press, 2013). For more about the *Gideon* and the city colony New Amstel, see Andrea C. Mosterman, "Een slavenschip voor Nieuwer-Amstel, stadskolonie aan de Delaware," in *Amsterdam en de Slavernij in Oost en West*, ed. Pepijn Brandon, Guno Jones, Nancy Jouwe, and Matthias van Rossum (Amsterdam: Uitgeverij Het Spectrum, 2020), 164–171.

56. See O'Malley, *Final Passages*. For the ships that arrived in New Netherland via intra-American trade, see the Intra-American Slave Trade Database at slavevoyages.org.

57. Request, October 20, 1657 [Received April 26, 1658], SG 1.01.07, inv. no. 12564.46, Nat. Arch; Court Proceedings, September 30, 1652, NYCM, V, 65, NYSA. Also see Goodfriend, "Burghers and Blacks," 129; Romney, *New Netherland Connections*, 199–200. Romney spells his name as Geert Tÿssen.

58. Johannes de Laet [Ioannes de Laet], "Kort Verhael uit de voorgaende Boecken getrocken," in Johannes de Laet, *Historie ofte Iaerlijck Verhael van de Verrichtinghen der*

Geoctroyeerde West-Indische Compagnie, Zedert haer Begin/ tot het eynde van 't jaer sesthien-hondert ses-en-dertich (Leiden: Bonaventuer ende Abraham Elsevier, 1644), 21. Also see O'Callaghan, *Voyages of the slavers*, xii; Morton Wagman, "Corporate Slavery in New Netherland," *Journal of Negro History* 65, no. 1 (Winter 1980): 34, https://doi.org/10.2307/3031546.

59. O'Callaghan, *Voyages of the slavers*, 108–110; Letter to the States General, no date, SG 1.01.07, inv. no. 12564.30A, 10–11, Nat. Arch. A 1653 description of New Netherland notes that the WIC allowed some independent merchants to travel to Africa to purchase African captives and sell them in the Caribbean and New Netherland. Description of New Netherland, July 24, 1653, NYCM, XI, 86, NYSA.

60. Court Minutes, March 6, 1656, Original Dutch Records of New Amsterdam, I, December 1655–August 1656, 525, NYCMA; E. B. O'Callaghan, trans., Berthold Fernow, ed., *The Records of New Amsterdam from 1653 to 1674 Anno Domini* (New York: Knickerbocker, 1897), 2:54.

61. List of Purchasers, May 29, 1664, NYCM, X, 28, NYSA; O'Callaghan, *Voyages of the slavers*, 203–206.

62. Jameson, *Narratives of New Netherland, 1609–1664*, 330; Extract of Council and Director General of New Netherland Resolution, May 31, 1664, SG 1.01.07, inv. no. 12564.57, Nat. Arch.

63. Letter from Stuyvesant to Vice-Director Curaçao, July 30, 1664, NYCM, XV, 137, NYSA.

64. Jonathan Pearson, trans., A. J. F. van Laer, ed., *Early Records of the City and County of Albany and Colony of Rensselaerswyck* (Albany: University of the State of New York, 1919), 4:112; Venema, *Beverwijck*, 116. According to Venema, this is the only recorded public slave sale in Beverwijck.

65. For trade between New Amsterdam and the Chesapeake, see April Hatfield, "Dutch and New Netherland Merchants in the Seventeenth-Century English Chesapeake," in *The Atlantic Economy during the Seventeenth and Eighteenth Centuries: Organization, Operation, Practice, and Personnel*, ed. Peter A. Coclanis (Columbia: University of South Carolina Press, 2005), 212.

66. See, among others, Linda M. Heywood and John K. Thornton, *Central Africans, Atlantic Creoles, and the Foundation of the Americas, 1585–1660* (Cambridge: Cambridge University Press, 2007); Meuwese, *Brothers in Arms*; John K. Thornton and Andrea C. Mosterman, "A Re-Interpretation of the Kongo-Portuguese War of 1622 According to New Documentary Evidence," *Journal of African History* 51 (2010): 235–248.

67. According to Jan de Vries, the Dutch transported 31,533 slaves to Brazil from 1630 to 1650. Jan de Vries, "The Dutch Atlantic Economies," in *The Atlantic Economy during the Seventeenth and Eighteenth Centuries: Organization, Operation, Practice, and Personnel*, ed. Peter A. Coclanis (Columbia: University of South Carolina Press, 2005), 4.

68. Estimates database, 2013, *Voyages: The Trans-Atlantic Slave Trade Database*, http://www.slavevoyages.org (accessed October 18, 2016).

69. The Dutch slaver *St. Jan*, for example, shipwrecked on the Reef of the Caribbean island of Rocus in 1659. Initially, the crew fled the sinking ship, leaving the enslaved men, women, and children to drown. When they returned to the ship to fetch those enslaved people who were still alive, they could not prevent a privateer from capturing eighty-four of the surviving enslaved Africans. But even before the ship

stranded on the reef, 110 of the African captives who boarded *St. Jan* in Africa had already died. Among them were four children who died due to the poor conditions on the ship, and an enslaved man who jumped overboard. Journal kept by Adriaen Blaes van der Veer, March 4, 1659—November 4, 1659, NYCM, VIII, 43a, NYSA; List of Slaves who died aboard the slaver *St. Jan*, June 30—October 29, 1659, NYCM, VIII, 43b, NYSA; Depositions relating to the seizure by pirates of slaves aboard the wrecked slaver *St. Jan*, November 27, 1659, NYCM, VIII, 52, NYSA. Charles T. Gehring, trans. and ed., *Curaçao Papers 1640–1665* (Albany: New Netherland Research Center and the New Netherland Institute, 2011), 135–140.

70. Testimony, March 22, 1639, NYCM, I, 112–113, NYSA.

71. Court Proceedings, September 8, 1644, NYCM, IV, 202, NYSA; Robert Swan points out that they did not carry the same weapons as the company soldiers. Swan, "Slaves and Slaveholding," 55; Jacobs, *New Netherland*, 382. Also see De Mello on the company's use of enslaved and indigenous people to defend Brazil. De Mello, *Nederlanders in Brazilië (1624–1654)*, 184; Meuwese, *Brothers in Arms*, 147–158.

72. A. J. F. van Laer, trans., and ed., *Register of the Provincial Secretary, 1642–1647* (New York Historical Manuscripts: Dutch, Baltimore: Genealogical Publishing Co., 1974), 2:187–188 [NYCM, II, 93e]. Also see Jacobs, *New Netherland*, 382. For more on Kieft's War, see, among others, Meuwese, *Brothers in Arms*, 241–249; Paul Otto, *The Dutch-Munsee Encounter in America* (New York: Berghahn Books, 2006), 110–132; Merwick, *Shame and the Sorrow*, 133–179.

73. For example, enslaved laborers functioned as executioners, a task deemed fit for people of low status. Van Zandt, *Brothers among Nations*, 152; Pieter Spierenburg, *The Spectacle of Suffering: Executions and the Evolution of Repression: From a Preindustrial Metropolis to the European Experience* (Cambridge: Cambridge University Press, 2008), 13–24.

74. Directors in Amsterdam to Petrus Stuyvesant, April 7, 1657, A1810 Correspondence, 56, NYSA; Jacobs, *New Netherland*, 382; Goodfriend, "Burghers and Blacks," 131.

75. Stuyvesant to Vice Director of Curaçao, October 28, 1659, NYCM, XIII, 49, NYSA.

76. Minutes, February 3, 1639, NYCM, I, 31, NYSA.

77. July 11, 1642, NYCM, IV, 129, NYSA; Van Laer, *Council Minutes 1638–1649*, 151, 174. The Van Laer transcription of the July 11, 1642, ordinance says "mette negros te arbeyden inde kettingh sonder ymant te verschoonen." For use of the term *in de ketting gaan*, see, among others, Jan Janszoon Struys, *Drie aanmerkelijke en seer rampspoedige Reysen door Italien, Griekenlandt, Lijslandt, Mascovien, Tartarijen, Meden, Persien, Oost-Indien, Japan, en verscheyden andere Gewesten* (Amsterdam: Jacob van Meurs, 1676), 235.

78. Minutes, April 15, 1658, NYCM, VIII, 831, NYSA; Gehring, *Council Minutes, 1652–1654*, 185.

79. Sentence, April 12, 1658, NYCM, VIII, 829, NYSA; Minutes, April 15, 1658, NYCM, VIII, 831, NYSA; Sentence, July 13, 1658, NYCM, VIII, 922, NYSA.

80. Clulow, *Amboina, 1623*, 65–67; F. de Haan, *Oud Batavia* (Batavia: G. Kolff, 1922), 1:354–355. Also see A. Reid, "'Closed' and 'Open' Slave Systems in Pre-Colonial Asia," in *Slavery, Bondage, & Dependency in Southeast Asia*, ed. Anthony Reid (New York: St. Martin's, 1983); J. Fox, "'For Good and Sufficient Reasons': An Examination of Early Dutch East India Company Ordinances on Slaves and Slavery," in *Slavery, Bondage, & Dependency in Southeast Asia*, ed. Anthony Reid (New York: St. Martin's, 1983).

81. Minutes, April 8, 1654, NYCM, V, 242, NYSA.

82. Petition, n.d., NYCM, VIII, 933–934, NYSA; Venema, *Beverwijck*, 122.

83. Minutes, January 24, 1641, NYCM, IV, 85, NYSA; A. J. F. van Laer, "Introduction," in *Minutes of the Court of Rensselaerswyck*, ed. and trans. A. J. F. van Laer (Albany: University of the State of New York Press, 1922), 12; Dennis Sullivan, *The Punishment of Crime in Colonial New York* (New York: Peter Land, 1997), 71; Van Zandt, *Brothers among Nations*, 152; Spierenburg, *Spectacle of Suffering*, 13–24. These enslaved men were often compensated for these services. In 1662, for instance, Pieter requested payment for "executing the sentence on one Mesaack Martens and Marten van Weert." Court Minutes, January 31, 1662, Original Dutch Records of New Amsterdam, III, November 1661–August 1662, 428, NYCMA; O'Callaghan and Fernow, *Records of New Amsterdam from 1653 to 1674*, 4:24.

84. Directors in Amsterdam to Petrus Stuyvesant, March 26, 1663, NYCM, XV, 7, NYSA.

85. Deed from the Directors of the WIC to Petrus Stuyvesant, March 12, 1651, NYCM, III, 87b [copy], NYSA; Gehring, *Correspondence, 1647–1653*, 122.

86. Indenture, May 25, 1644, NYCM, II, 111b, NYSA.

87. Minutes, November 7, 1661, NYCM, IX, 915, NYSA; Minutes, December 8, 1661, NYCM, IX, 917, NYSA; Wagman, "Corporate Slavery in New Netherland," 37.

88. Charles T. Gehring, trans. and ed., *Correspondence 1654–1658* (Syracuse, NY: Syracuse University Press, 2003), 106.

89. Letter Secretary van Ruyven to Jacques Corteljou, June 14, 1658, NYCM, VIII, 894, NYSA; Permit, July 2, 1658, NYCM, VIII, 900, NYSA; Order, November 28, 1658, NYCM, VIII, 1046, NYSA. Also see Jacobs, *New Netherland*, 383.

90. Wagman, "Corporate Slavery," 34; Merlin-Faucquez, "De la Nouvelle-Néerlande à New York," 136; Jacobs, *New Netherland*, 381–382. For an analysis of individual enslavers in New Amsterdam and their ethnicity and socioeconomic status, see Goodfriend, "Burghers and Blacks," 142–143.

91. Minutes, May 1, 1657, NYCM, VIII, 547, NYSA; Gehring, *Council Minutes, 1655–1656*, 203, also see pp. 199–201; Arnold J. F. van Laer ed. and trans., *Correspondence of Jeremias Van Rensselaer 1651–1674* (Albany: University of the State of New York Press, 1932), 220.

92. Court Minutes, September 16, 1664, Original Dutch Records of New Amsterdam, IV, May 1664–April 1665, 448, NYCMA; O'Callaghan and Fernow, *Records of New Amsterdam from 1653 to 1674*, 5:111–112.

93. Court Minutes, September 9, 1659, Original Dutch Records of New Amsterdam, II, August 1659–June 1660, 348, NYCMA; O'Callaghan and Fernow, *Records of New Amsterdam from 1653 to 1674*, 3:40.

94. Van Laer, *Correspondence of Jeremias Van Rensselaer*, 136, 152–153, 196.

95. Van Laer, 159.

96. Van Laer, 167.

97. Jean Barbot, *Barbot on Guinea: The Writings of Jean Barbot on West Africa, 1678–1712*, ed. P. E. H. Hair, Adam Jones, and Robin Law (London: Hakluyt Society, 1992), 1:84, 90, 100; Olfert Dapper, *Naukeurige Beschrijvinge der Afrikaensche Gewesten* (Amsterdam: Jacob van Meurs, 1668), 353. Also see John K. Thornton, *Africa and Africans in the Making of the Atlantic World, 1400–1800* (Cambridge: Cambridge University Press, 1998), 293–294; Barton C. Hacker, "Firearms, Horses, and Slave Soldiers: The Military

History of African Slavery," *Icon* 14 (2008), 62–83; Robin Law, "Horses, Firearms, and Political Power in Pre-Colonial West Africa," *Past and Present Society*, no. 72 (August 1976), 119–120; John K. Thornton, *Warfare in Atlantic Africa* (London: Routledge, 2000). Jeremias had bought Andries for his brother in 1657 from Catharina Roelofs, the widow of Lucas Roodenburg, who was the former vice director at Curaçao. In the early seventeenth century, several slave ships from the Senegambia traveled to the Spanish Americas. Certainly, some enslaved Senegambians would have ended up in Curaçao during Roodenburg's tenure, and several of them would have been brought to New Netherland. For more on the Senegambian presence in Curaçao, see Bart Jacobs, "The Upper Guinea Origins of Papiamentu: Linguistic and Historical Evidence," *Diachronica* 26, no. 3 (2009): 319–379, https://doi.org/10.1075/dia.26.3.02jac.

98. Minutes, February 25, 1644, NYCM, IV, 183, NYSA; Van Laer, *Council Minutes 1638–1649*, 213. A case in 1663 confirms that children who were born after the resolution would remain *lijff eijgenen* or serfs of the company. The records appear to use the terms *lijff eijgenen* and *slaven* interchangeably. Minutes, December 6, 1663, NYCM, X, 417, NYSA.

99. Van Laer, *Council Minutes 1638–1649*, 212–213.

100. Patricia Bonomi, among others, discusses these similarities. She suggests that thus these men were technically free. Bonomi, "'Swarms of Negroes,'" 41–42.

101. Petition, December 28, 1662, NYCM, X, 296, NYSA; Minutes, December 8, 1663, NYCM, X, 429, NYSA.

102. Minutes, February 17, 1649, NYCM, III, 30b, NYSA; Van Laer, *Council Minutes 1638–1649*, 342. According to Christoph, the annual wage of a farm laborer was 150 guilders. Christoph, "Freedman of New Amsterdam," 159.

103. Kruger, "Born to Run," 49; Berlin, "From Creole to African," 270; Jaap Jacobs suggests that Kieft and the council's motivations may have been financial in nature. Jacobs, *New Netherland*, 384.

104. José Antônio Gonsales de Mello argues that the Dutch treated enslaved Africans according to the "indisputably humane" Portuguese example. In his article on the Dutch slave trade with New Netherland, Dutch historian Pieter Emmer contends that racial slavery never developed in New Netherland. Boogaart, "Servant Migration," 69–70; Wagman, "Corporate Slavery," 40; De Mello, *Nederlanders in Brazilië*, 190; Emmer, "De Slavenhandel van en naar Nieuw-Nederland," 129.

105. Charles Gehring, trans. and ed., *Council Minutes, 1652–1654* (Baltimore: Genealogical Pub. Co., 1983), 70.

106. Their children's continued bondage proved a topic of interest among Dutch authorities. In 1649, Jacob van Couwenhoven, Jan Evertsen Bout, and Adriaen van der Donck traveled to *patria* to voice their complaints about New Netherland's leadership. When they presented a list of grievances to the States General, they claimed that keeping the children of these freed men and women enslaved went against "all people's rights." Kort begrijp van d'excessen en hoochschaedelijck versuijm, in en over nieuw-nederlandt gepleeght, January 27, 1650, SG 1.01.07, inv. no. 12564.30A, unpaginated, Nat. Arch. For more on the conflict with the colony's leadership, see J. Jacobs, *New Netherland*, 144–152. The company defended the practice, however, by explaining that only three of the children actually remained in bondage: one of them lived at Director General Petrus Stuyvesant's house, another stayed at *Huys de Hoop* (Hope House, a Dutch trading post and fort in present-day Connecticut), and a third child served set-

tler Marten Cregier. Antwoort van Bewint hebberen op de remonstrantie uijt N.Nederlant, January 3, 1650, SG 1.01.07, inv. no. 12564.30A, 43, Nat. Arch.; Cort bericht ofte antwoorde op eenige poncten, begrepen inde schrifte deductie van Adriaen vander Donck cum socijs aen ho: mo: heeren Staten Generael overgelevert, November 24, 1650, SG 1.01.07, inv. no. 12564.30A, unpaginated, Nat. Arch.

107. Henrik Mouritsen, *The Freedman in the Roman World* (Cambridge: Cambridge University Press, 2015); Rachel Zelnick-Abramovitz, *Not Wholly Free: The Concept of Manumission and the Status of Manumitted Slaves in the Ancient Greek World* (Boston: Brill, 2005); Cam Grey, "Slavery in the Late Roman World," in *The Cambridge World History of Slavery: The Ancient Mediterranean World*, ed. Keith Bradley and Paul Cartledge (Cambridge: Cambridge University Press, 2011), 1:505.

108. William D. Phillips, Jr., "Manumission in Metropolitan Spain and the Canaries," in *Paths to Freedom: Manumission in the Atlantic World*, ed. Rosemary Brana-Shute and Randy J. Sparks (Columbia: University of South Carolina Press, 2009), 45. Similar conditional freedoms existed throughout the Americas and elsewhere. See, for example, Uma Kothari, "Geographies and Histories of Unfreedom: Indentured Labourers and Contract Workers in Mauritius," *Journal of Development Studies* 49, no. 8 (2013): 1042–1057, https://doi.org/10.1080/00220388.2013.780039.

109. De Haan, *Oud Batavia*, 1:457–458. Rik van Welie suggests that some enslaved people in the East and in New Netherland were "cases of manumission as a strategy toward cost-effectiveness among Dutch colonists." Rik van Welie, "Slave Trading and Slavery in the Dutch Colonial Empire: A Global Comparison," *New West Indian Guide/Nieuwe West-Indische Gids* 82, no. 1 and 2 (2008): 84, https://doi.org/10.1163/13822373-90002465.

110. See, for instance, Dewulf, "Emulating a Portuguese Model," 10–11.

111. Though various forms of Roman-Dutch law had been used in the sixteenth century, the Dutch legal scholar Hugo Grotius provided a clear basis for this law in his *Introduction of Jurisprudence (Inleiding tot de Hollandsche Rechtsgeleerdheid)* in 1631. Another Dutch legal text that influenced the judicial systems of both the Dutch Republic and New Netherland was Joost Damhouder, *Practycke in Civile Saecken, seer nut/profijtelijck ende nodigh allen Schouten, Borghemeesteren Magistraten ende andere Rechteren* ('s Gravenhage: Ordinaris Druckers vande Ho.Mo. Heeren Staten Generael, 1626). Also see Sullivan, *Punishment of Crime*, 29–30; Venema, *Beverwijck*, 121.

112. Cornelis Ch. Goslinga, *The Dutch in the Caribbean and on the Wild Coast, 1680–1791* (Maastricht/Assen: Van Gorcum, 1985 [repr. ed.]), 529; Adriana van Zwieten, "The Orphan Chamber of New Amsterdam," *William and Mary Quarterly* 53, no. 2 (April 1996): 325, https://doi.org/10.2307/2947403. Also see Jaap Jacobs's discussion on the status of their children. Jacobs, *New Netherland*, 384–385. Several scholars note that the Dutch often followed the Portuguese model. Dewulf, "Emulating a Portuguese Model," 7; Klooster, *Dutch Moment*, 19; De Mello, *Nederlanders in Brazilië*, 190; Clulow, *Amboina, 1623*, 57–58.

113. Jaap Jacobs points out that Black people in New Netherland, free or enslaved, "were at the bottom of the social ladder" and they "had little chance of improving their circumstances." J. Jacobs, *New Netherland*, 387–388.

114. When De Reus petitioned for his freedom in 1644, the petition noted that he and his fellow petitioners had been company slaves for eighteen or nineteen years. Consequently, scholars have generally concluded that these enslaved men were among

the first African slaves in the colony in 1625 or 1626. Susanah Shaw Romney has rightly pointed out that there is no evidence to prove that they were in the colony this early, since they could have been company property elsewhere in the Atlantic. Nevertheless, they likely were among the first African captives in the colony. Romney, *New Netherland Connections*, 191–244.

115. Paulo Angola, Groot Manuel, Sijmon Congo, Antonij Portugies, Gracia, Cleijn Antonij, and Jan Fort Orange all obtained conditional freedom after they admitted to killing Jan Premero. Van Laer, *Register of the Provincial Secretary, 1638–1642*, 123 [NYCM, I, 91]; Minutes, February 25, 1644, NYCM, IV, 183, NYSA; Van Laer, *Council Minutes 1638–1649*, 213; Francis J. Sypher, ed. and trans., *Liber A of the Collegiate Churches of New York*, pt. 2 (Grand Rapids: William B. Eerdmans, 2015); Romney, *New Netherland Connections*, 215–216.

2. The Geography of Enslaved Life in New Netherland

1. Minutes, April 19, 1663, NYCM, X, 71, NYSA. According to Heywood and Thornton, she was "the earliest named African in New Netherland." Heywood and Thornton, "Intercultural Relations," 19.

2. Minutes, April 19, 1663, NYCM, X, 71, NYSA; Petition, December 28, 1662, NYCM, X, 296, NYSA; Certificate of Manumission, April 17, 1664, NYCM, X, 170, NYSA.

3. Minutes, April 19, 1663, NYCM, X, 71, NYSA.

4. See, for instance, McManus, *History of Negro Slavery*, 11; Christoph, "Freedmen of New Amsterdam," 166; A. Judd Northrup, "Slavery in New York: A Historical Sketch," *State Library Bulletin History* no. 4 (Albany, 1900): 254; Wagman, "Corporate Slavery in New Netherland," 40.

5. Heywood, Thornton, Jeroen DeWulf, and Ira Berlin emphasize the significance of their African and Atlantic backgrounds. Heywood and Thornton, *Central Africans*; Dewulf, *Pinkster King*; Ira Berlin, *Many Thousands Gone: The First Two Centuries of Slavery in North America* (Cambridge, MA: Belknap Press, 1998); Berlin, "From Creole to African." Willem Frijhoff attributes their active participation largely to their Christian background. Frijhoff, *Wegen van Evert Willemsz.*, 773–775. Susanah Shaw Romney and Cynthia Van Zandt both show how crucial their close connections to each other proved in achieving certain legal successes. Romney, *New Netherland Connections*, 212–224; Van Zandt, *Brothers among Nations*, 137.

6. In the church records, Jan Premero is regularly referred to as Jan Premier. Sypher, *Liber A of the Collegiate Churches of New York, part 2*, 472. Sentence of Manuel Gerrit, January 24, 1641, NYCM, IV, 84, NYSA. A document from 1639 refers to the "swarte huijsen," which may have referred to the slave quarters. Court Proceeding, September 22, 1639, NYCM, IV, 50, NYSA.

7. I. N. Phelps Stokes, *The Iconography of Manhattan Island, 1498–1909* (New York: Robert H. Dodd, 1916), 2:207.

8. Patent to Evert Duyckingh, June 22, 1643, Land Papers, GG, 67, NYSA; Patent to Touchyn Briel, July 6, 1643, Land Papers, GG, 77, NYSA.

9. Patent to Adriaen Dircksen Coen, June 19, 1654, Land Papers, HH, 11, NYSA.

10. Stokes, *Iconography of Manhattan Island*, 2:297; Goodfriend, "Burghers and Blacks," 130.

11. Patent to Adriaen Dircksen Coen, June 19, 1654, Land Papers, HH, 11, NYSA; Stokes, *Iconography of Manhattan Island*, 2:297. In comparison, Thomas Hall contracted builders to build him a house of 32 by 18 feet, or 576 square feet in 1639. Philip Gerardy contracted Juriaen from Osenbruch to build him a home of 25 by 18 feet, or 450 square feet. Two English carpenters were to build a dwelling home for Isaac de Forest of 30 by 18 feet, or 540 square feet. Van Laer, *Register of the Provincial Secretary, 1638–1642*, 217–218, 336–337, 338.

12. Documents do not provide conclusive information on how many enslaved people belonged to the company. In the early 1640s, there must have been at least thirty people enslaved by the company in New Amsterdam and its immediate surroundings, but this number would have decreased significantly after many of them obtained conditional freedom in 1644. A source from the 1650s suggests that at that time the total number of workers enslaved by the company in New Amsterdam who were capable of doing strenuous physical labor ranged from eleven to sixteen. A source from 1663 indicates that at that time there were only seven or eight enslaved company laborers left. On August 23, 1664, the city of New Amsterdam requested twenty-five slaves from the company, but this request came only eight days after the ship *Gideon* arrived in the harbor with 291 enslaved men, women, and children on board. Councilor Johan de Deckere to Petrus Stuyvesant, August 26, 1658, NYCM, VIII, 955–957; Directors in Amsterdam to Petrus Stuyvesant, March 26, 1663, NYCM, XV, 7, NYSA; Court Records, August 23, 1664, Original Dutch Documents, IV, May 1664–April 1665, 439, NYCMA; O'Callaghan and Fernow, *Records of New Amsterdam from 1653 to 1674*, 5:104.

13. Directors in Amsterdam to Petrus Stuyvesant, March 26, 1663, NYCM, XV, 7, NYSA.

14. Van Laer, *Register of the Provincial Secretary, 1638–1642*, 380–381; Deed, March 12, 1651, NYCM, III, 87b [copy], NYSA; Arnold J. F. Van Laer, trans. and ed., *Register of the Provincial Secretary, 1648–1660* (New York Historical Manuscripts. Baltimore: Genealogical Publishing Co., 1974), 3:216. Also see Goodfriend, "Burghers and Blacks," 132–133.

15. Court Minutes, March 21, 1662, Original Dutch Documents, III, November 1661–August 1662, 465, NYCMA; O'Callaghan and Fernow, *Records of New Amsterdam from 1653 to 1674*, 4:53.

16. Patent to Evert Duyckingh, June 22, 1643, Land Papers, GG, 67, NYSA.

17. Stokes, *Iconography of Manhattan Island*, 2:294.

18. Patent to Domingo Antony, July 13, 1643, Land Papers, GG, 80, NYSA; Patent to Catelina Antony, July 13, 1643, Land Papers, GG, 81, NYSA.

19. Certificate, April 20/30, 1665, NYCM, X, 329, NYSA.

20. Stokes, *Iconography of Manhattan Island*, 2:302.

21. Stokes, 2:294.

22. Court Minutes, March 7, 1662, Original Dutch Records, III, November 1661–August 1662, 455–456, NYCMA; O'Callaghan and Fernow, *Records of New Amsterdam from 1653 to 1674*, 4:45–46.

23. Ordinance, April 29, 1648, NYCM, IV, 382, NYSA; Hugh Hastings et al., eds., *Ecclesiastical Records, State of New York* (Albany: James B. Lyon, State Printer, 1901), 1:512.

24. Court Minutes, March 7, 1662, Original Dutch Records, III, November 1661–August 1662, 455–456, NYCMA; O'Callaghan and Fernow, *Records of New Amsterdam*, 4:45–46.

25. Court Minutes, February 28, 1662, Original Dutch Records, III, November 1661–August 1662, 449, NYCMA; O'Callaghan and Fernow, *Records of New Amsterdam*, 4:42.

26. Swan Loange (or Swaen van Luane) later obtained his freedom and became a farmer on Long Island. See, among others, Henry Hoff, "Swan Janse Van Luane: A Free Black in 17th Century Kings County," *New York Genealogical and Biographical Record* 125 (April 1994): 74–77; Robert Swan, "The Black Presence in Seventeenth-Century Brooklyn," *de Halve Maen: Magazine of the Dutch Colonial Period in America* 63, no. 4 (December 1990): 3–5; Rogier van Kooten, "'Like a Child in Their Debt, and Consequently Their Slave'? Power Structures in the Commercial Circuits of a Colonial Agro-system near New York around 1675" (MA thesis, University of Antwerp, 2016), 51; Dennis Maika, "Slavery, Race, and Culture in Early New York," *de Halve Maen: Magazine of the Dutch Colonial Period in America* 73 (Summer 2000): 30; Romney, *New Netherland Connections*, 211.

27. Minutes, June 6, 1644, NYCM, IV, 189–190, NYSA.

28. Court Minutes, March 6, 1656, Original Dutch Records of New Amsterdam, vol. 1, December 1655–August 1656, 526, NYCMA; Court Minutes, April 8, 1656, Original Dutch Records of New Amsterdam, vol. 1, December 1655–August 1656, 556, NYCMA; O'Callaghan and Fernow, *Records of New Amsterdam*, 2:54, 84–85.

29. Van Zwieten, "Orphan Chamber," 332.

30. O'Callaghan, *Voyages of the slavers*, 196–198.

31. Frijhoff, *Wegen van Evert Willemsz.*, 765–779; Dewulf, "Emulating a Portuguese Model"; Heywood and Thornton, *Central Africans*; Berlin, "From Creole to African"; Bonomi, "'Swarms of Negroes'"; Gerald De Jong, "The Dutch Reformed Church and Negro Slavery in Colonial America," *Church History* 4, no. 4 (1971); Hodges, *Root & Branch*; Foote, *Black and White Manhattan*; Goodfriend, "Slavery in Colonial New York"; Leendert Jan Joosse, *Geloof in de Nieuwe Wereld: Ontmoeting met Afrikanen en Indianen* (1600–1700) (Kampen: Kok, 2008); Dennis Maika, "Encounters: Slavery and the Philipse Family: 1680–1751," in *Dutch New York: The Roots of Hudson Valley Culture*, ed. Roger Panetta (New York: Fordham University Press, 2009), 35–72.

32. Anthonie van Angola and Lúcie d'Angool entered their intentions to marry on May 5, 1641. At the time, Anthonie was the widower of Catalina van Angola and Lúcie had been married to Laurens van Angola. Sypher, *Liber A of the Collegiate Churches of New York, part 2*, 472.

33. Sypher, 471–475.

34. Sypher, 472–596.

35. Sypher, 4–7. Jan Fort-Oragnien is in this document referred to as Jan van 't fort Orangien.

36. Sypher, 3–37.

37. Most Black children received baptism when Everardus Bogardus was the reverend of the church. Except for the baptism of Jan de Vries's son Jan, born to an enslaved Black mother, all baptisms of Black children took place before Bogardus departed in August of 1647. After his departure, the percentage of African baptisms dropped from about 11 percent in 1647 to 4 percent in 1648 when only one, possibly two Black children were baptized in the church. Johannes Backerus was in charge of New Amsterdam's congregation from Bogardus's departure until Johannes Megapolensis's arrival in July of 1649. During these years, it appears that only one Black child was baptized: Emanuel

Swager van Angola's son Dominicus received baptism on February 16, 1648. That this dramatic decline in baptisms of Black children might have had something to do with Backerus becomes especially evident when considering that after Megapolensis arrived in July of 1649 several Africans had their children baptized. In fact, on August 22 and 29, five African men presented their children for baptism. Sypher, *Liber A of the Collegiate Churches of New York, part 2*; also see Swan, "Slaves and Slaveholding," 60.

38. Frijhoff, *Wegen van Evert Willemsz.*, 589.

39. Frijhoff, 706.

40. Sypher, *Liber A of the Collegiate Churches of New York, part 2*, xxiv–xxx, 473–475. Sypher explains that the Dutch Reformed marriage records listed the marriage intentions, not the actual dates of the marriage. Later marriage records include both the date of the intention and the wedding, which usually took place a few weeks later. For more on the marriage intentions in the Dutch Republic and marriage law in general, see L. J. van Apeldoorn, *Geschiedenis van het Nederlandsche Huwelijksrecht voor de invoering van de Fransche wetgeving* (Amsterdam: Uitgeversmaatschappij Holland, 1925), 47–54, and 84–89 in particular on marriage intentions.

41. Sypher, *Liber A of the Collegiate Churches of New York, part 2*, 3–5.

42. C. G. A. Oldendorp and Gudrun Meier, eds., *Historie Der Caribischen Inseln Sanct Thomas, Sanct Crux Und Sanct Jan: Insbesondere Der Dasigen Neger Und Der Mission Der Evangelischen Brüder Unter Denselben* (Berlin: VWB, Verlag für Wissenschaft und Bildung, 2000), 742 (III: §120); Berlin, "From Creole to African," 278; Romney, *New Netherland Connections*, 212–219.

43. Sypher, *Liber A of the Collegiate Churches of New York, part 2*, 18, 488; Petition, March 21, 1661, NYCM, IX, 557, NYSA.

44. Romney, *New Netherland Connections*, 215–216.

45. Sypher, *Liber A of the Collegiate Churches of New York, part 2*, 3.

46. Sypher, 24. Swan states that "in twenty-two occurrences, it is assumed that a white witness to a Black baptism owned the parents. Few examples, such as Teunis Craey and Jan de Vries, can be substantiated." Swan, "Slaves and Slaveholding," 61.

47. Sypher, *Liber A of the Collegiate Churches of New York, part 2*, 22, 45.

48. John K. Thornton, "Religious and Ceremonial Life in the Kongo and Mbundu Areas, 1500–1700," in *Central Africans and Cultural Transformations in the American Diaspora*, ed. Linda Heywood (Cambridge: Cambridge University Press, 2002), 83; Georges Balandier, *Daily Life in the Kingdom of the Kongo: From the Sixteenth to the Eighteenth Century* (New York: Pantheon Books, 1968), 45; John K. Thornton, "Afro-Christian Syncretism in the Kingdom of Kongo," *Journal of African History* 54, no. 1 (2013); Heywood and Thornton, *Central Africans*, 49–108; Cécile Fromont, *The Art of Conversion: Christian Visual Culture in the Kingdom of Kongo* (Chapel Hill: University of North Carolina Press, 2014); Frijhoff, *Wegen van Evert Willemsz.*, 772–773; Dewulf, *Pinkster King*. Even though several scholars have pointed to the Central African majority among New Netherland's enslaved population, some historians still question whether the enslaved African population was really that homogenous or if West Central Africans could be considered Christians before they reached the North American shores. See, for instance, Susanah Shaw Romney's discussion on the African origins of New Netherland's African population. Evan Haefeli argues that most enslaved Africans in New Netherland were not Christian, and that they most likely attended the church to obtain freedom. Romney, *New Netherland Connections*, 198; Evan Haefeli,

New Netherland and the Dutch Origins of American Religious Liberty (Philadelphia: University of Pennsylvania Press, 2012), 126–129.

49. Ferdinand van Capelle to the Directors, March 1642, OWIC 46, unpaginated, 5th folio, Nat. Arch.

50. Dionigi de Carli and R.R.F.F. Michele Angelo de Guattini, "A Curious and Exact Account of a Voyage to Congo, in the years 1666 and 1667," in *A General Collection of the Best and Most Interesting Voyages and Travels in All Parts of the World; Many of which are now first translated into English*, ed. John Pinkerton (London: Longman, 1814), 16: 168.

51. Heywood and Thornton, *Central Africans*, 98–108.

52. Minutes, February 25, 1644, NYCM, IV, 183, NYSA; Van Laer, *Council Minutes 1638–1649*, 213.

53. Minutes, February 25, 1644, NYCM, IV, 183, NYSA; Van Laer, *Council Minutes 1638–1649*, 213.

54. Minutes, March 21, 1661, NYCM, IX, 557, NYSA; E. B. O'Callaghan, trans., K. Scott, and K. Stryker-Rodda, eds., *The Register of Salomon Lachaire, Notary Public of New Amsterdam, 1661–1662. Translated from the original Dutch Manuscript in the Office of the Clerk of the Common Council of New York* (New York Historical Manuscripts: Dutch) (Baltimore, 1978), 22–23; Minutes, December 6, 1663, NYCM, X, 416, NYSA; Order by P. Stuyvesant and Nicasius de Sille, December 6, 1663, NYCM, X, 417, NYSA; Christoph, "Freedmen of New Amsterdam," 161; Goodfriend, "Black Families in New Netherland," 151.

55. Minutes, March 21, 1661, NYCM, IX, 557, NYSA; O'Callaghan, Scott, and Stryker-Rodda, *Register of Salomon Lachaire*, 22–23.

56. Order by P. Stuyvesant and Nicasius de Sille, December 6, 1663, NYCM, X, 417, NYSA; Christoph, "Freedmen of New Amsterdam," 161; Goodfriend, "Black Families in New Netherland," 149.

57. Petition, December 6, 1663, NYCM, X, 416, NYSA; Order on the above petition, December 6, 1663, NYCM, X, 417, NYSA; Note, September 16, 1664, NYCM, X, 417, NYSA; O'Callaghan and Fernow, *Records of New Amsterdam from 1653 to 1674*, 4:42; Sypher, *Liber A of the Collegiate Churches of New York, part 2*, 511; Christoph, "Freedmen of New Amsterdam," 161; Goodfriend, "Black Families in New Netherland," 151. This is the same Swan who previously had been interrogated for drinking on the Sabbath. Christina Emanuels and Swan van Loange married in February of 1664.

58. Council Minutes, April 15, 1638, NYCM, IV, 3, NYSA [A. J. F. Van Laer transcription]; E. B. O'Callaghan, trans. and ed., *Laws and Ordinances of New Netherland, 1638–1674* (Albany: Weed, Parsons and Company, printers and stereotypers, 1868), 12; Van Laer, *Council Minutes 1638–1649*, 4.

59. See, among others, Hodges, *Root & Branch*, 12; Heywood and Thornton, *Central Africans*, 289. A. Leon Higginbotham also points out that this ordinance did not prohibit interracial relations. Leon A. Higginbotham, *In the Matter of Color: The Colonial Period* (Oxford: Oxford University Press, 1978), 110.

60. Instructions for Jacob Pietersen Tolck, Director of Curaçao, August 15, 1640, NYCM, XVII, 1, NYSA.

61. Hans de Mol, "Het Huwelyck is goddelyck van aart, wanneer men tsaam uyt reine liefde paart," in *Kent, en Versint eer datje Mint: Vrijen en trouwen 1500–1800*, ed.

Petra van Boheemen et al. (Zwolle: Waanders Uitgeverij, 1989), 106. For more on marriage in the Dutch Atlantic, see Deborah Hamer, "Creating an Orderly Society: The Regulation of Marriage and Sex in the Dutch Atlantic World, 1621–1674" (PhD diss., Columbia University, 2014). While a marriage between people of different faiths would not be denied, church and state did strongly discourage and complicate such unions. De Mello, *Nederlanders in Brazilië*, 193.

62. Sypher, *Liber A of the Collegiate Churches of New York, part 2*, 483.

63. All these names signify Van Salee's exceptional background. Genealogical research indicates that Van Salee was the son of the Dutch sailor turned pirate Jan Jansz. van Haarlem, after his conversion to Islam in 1618 also known as Murad Reis, and his second wife, whom he married in either Morocco or Spain. His son Anthony Jansen van Salee's Dutch marriage record notes Cartagena as his birthplace. Both Anthony and his brother Abraham were often identified as mulatto. Their mother may have been a descendant of West Africans who had been taken to North Africa and Southern Europe in the trans-Saharan slave trade, or she may have been part of the Afro-Iberian community that largely originated in Central Africa. For more about Van Salee, see Leo Herskowitz, "The Troublesome Turk: An Illustration of Judicial Process in New Amsterdam," *New York History* 46, no. 4 (1965): 299–310; Swan, "Black Presence," 2–3; Nicolaes Wassenaer, *Historisch verhael aldaer ghedenck-weerdichste geschiedenisse, die vanden beginner des jaers 1621 (tot 1632) voorgevallens syn*, 3 (Amsterdam, 1623), 53; Arne Zuidhoek, *Zeerovers van de Gouden Eeuw* (Bussum: De Boer, 1977), 65–76; Henry B. Hoff, "A Colonial Black Family in New York and New Jersey: Pieter Santomee and His Descendants," *Journal of the Afro-American Historical and Genealogical Society* 9 (1988): 101–134.

64. Van Laer, *Register of the Provincial Secretary, 1638–1642*, 11.

65. Council Minutes, April 7, 1639, NYCM, IV, 38, NYSA [Van Laer transcription]; Van Laer, *Council Minutes, 1638–1649*, 46–47; Van Laer, *Register of the Provincial Secretary, 1638–1642*, 66–67, 69.

66. Council Minutes, April 7, 1639, NYCM, IV, 38, NYSA [Van Laer transcription]; Van Laer, *Council Minutes, 1638–1649*, 46–47.

67. Van Salee continued to have disputes with almost everyone, even with his son in law, Thomas Southart, who was married to Van Salee's daughter Annica, and for many years Van Salee and the magistrates of Gravesend argued over the borders of Van Salee's land. Council Minutes, April 12, 1656, NYCM, VI, 364, NYSA; Council Minutes, July 19, 1656, NYCM, VI, 73, NYSA; Council Minutes, July 20, 1656, NYCM, VI, 73, NYSA; Council Minutes, August 18, 1656, NYCM, VI, 140, NYSA; Council Minutes, April 20, 1648, NYCM, IV, 38, NYSA [Van Laer transcription]; Van Laer, *Council Minutes, 1638–1649*, 513.

68. Historian Willem Frijhoff argues that Bogardus used his charges against Van Salee and his wife, neither of whom attended the Dutch Reformed Church, to emphasize the public honor code of Christian piety that should be upheld in New Netherland's society. Frijhoff, *Wegen Van Evert Willemsz.*, 712.

69. Sypher, *Liber A of the Collegiate Churches of New York, part 2*, 36. On August 25, 1647, they had their son Jan baptized in New Amsterdam's Dutch Reformed Church. While she was named Swartinne in the baptismal records, she was likely Elaria Crioole, who inherited some of De Vries's land after his death. Deed, March 31, 1651, NYCM, III, 75a, NYSA; Van Laer, *Register of the Provincial Secretary, 1648–1660*, 228–229. For more on slavery and sexual coercion, see, among others, Sharon Block, "Lines of Color,

Sex, and Service: Comparative Sexual Coercion in Early America," in *Sex, Love, Race: Crossing Boundaries in North American History* (New York: New York University Press, 1999): 141–163; Catherine Clinton, "'Southern Dishonor': Flesh, Blood, Race, and Bondage," in *In Joy and In Sorrow: Women, Family, and Marriage in the Victorian South, 1830–1900*, ed. Carol Bleser (Oxford: Oxford University Press, 1991), 52–68; Brenda Stevenson, "What's Love Got to Do with It? Concubinage and Enslaved Women and Girls in the Antebellum South," in *Sexuality & Slavery: Reclaiming Intimate Histories in the America*, ed. Daina Ramey Berry and Leslie M. Harris (Athens: University of Georgia Press, 2018), 159–188; Kirsten Fischer and Jennifer Morgan, "Sex, Race, and the Colonial Project," *William and Mary Quarterly* 60, no. 1 (January 2003): 197–198, https://doi.org/10.2307/3491504; Sharon Block and Kathleen M. Brown, "Clio in Search of Eros: Redefining Sexualities in Early America," *William and Mary Quarterly* 60, no. 1 (January 2003): 5–12, https://doi.org/10.2307/3491493; Jennifer Morgan, *Laboring Women: Reproduction and Gender in New World Slavery* (Philadelphia: University of Pennsylvania Press, 2004). Also see chap. 4 for a discussion on this subject in Dutch New York.

70. Court Proceedings, February 11, 1648, NYCM, IV, 361, NYSA; Van Laer, *Council Minutes, 1638–1649*, 480–481.

71. Court Minutes, March 27, 1656, Original Dutch Records of New Amsterdam, I, December 1655–August 1656, 547, NYCMA; Court Minutes, April 3, 1656, Original Dutch Records of New Amsterdam, I, December 1655–August 1656, 553, NYCMA; April 24, 1656, Original Dutch Records of New Amsterdam, I, December 1655–August 1656, 560, NYCMA; O'Callaghan and Fernow, *Records of New Amsterdam from 1653 to 1674*, 2:76, 82. Thanks to Deborah Hamer and Jaap Jacobs for helping to translate the original Dutch document.

72. Certificate, December 8, 1663, NYCM, X, 429, NYSA.

73. Minutes, September 4, 1664, NYCM, XII, 317, NYSA.

74. For more on slavery, race, and Dutch jurisprudence, see Van Zandt, *Brothers among Nations*, 144; J. Jacobs, *New Netherland*, 380; Romney, *New Netherland Connections*, 191–244; Christoph, "Freedmen of New Amsterdam"; Heywood and Thornton, *Central Africans*; Berlin, "From Creole to African"; Wagman, "Corporate Slavery in New Netherland," 38.

75. Articulen ende Conditien door de Camer van Amsterdam, 1635, SG 1.01.03, inv. no. 5755, unpaginated, Nat. Arch.; Venema, *Beverwijck*, 118. Because the court of Rensselaerswijck, which handled its first case in 1632, was not under the control of the West India Company, it had the authority to handle all local civil and criminal matters. Also see Martha Shattuck, "Dutch Jurisprudence in New Netherland and New York," in *Four Centuries of Dutch-American Relations, 1609–2009*, ed. Hans Krabbendam, Cornelis A. van Minnen, and Giles Scott-Smith (Albany: State University of New York Press, 2009), 143–153; Martha Shattuck, "A Civil Society: Court and Community in Beverwijck, New Netherland, 1652–1664" (PhD diss., Boston University, 1993); Goslinga, *Dutch in the Caribbean and on the Wild Coast*, 529–531; Van Zwieten, "Orphan Chamber." For scholarship on seventeenth-century Dutch jurisprudence, see Florike Egmond, "Fragmentatie, rechtverscheidenheid en rechtsongelijkheid in de Noordelijke Nederlanden tijdens de zeventiende en acttiende eeuw," in *Nieuw Licht op Oude Justitie: Misdaad en straf ten tijde van de republiek*, ed. Sjoerd Faber (Muiderberg: Dick Coutinhio, 1989), 9–23; Florike Egmond, *Underworlds: Organized Crime in the*

Netherlands, 1650–1800 (Cambridge: Polity Press, 1993); Pieter Spierenburg, "Judicial Violence in the Dutch Republic: Corporal Punishment, Executions and Torture in Amsterdam, 1650–1750" (PhD diss., University of Amsterdam, 1978); Spierenburg, *Spectacle of Suffering.*

76. Gehring, *Council Minutes,* xiv.

77. De Vries, "Dutch Atlantic Economies," 14; J. Jacobs, *New Netherland,* 144.

78. Jaap Jacobs, "'To Favor This New and Growing City of New Amsterdam with a Court of Justice': The Relations between Rulers and Ruled in New Amsterdam," *Amsterdam–New York: Transatlantic Relations and Urban Identities Since 1653,* ed. George Harinck and Hans Krabbendam (Amsterdam: VU Uitgeverij, 2005), 23.

79. Shattuck, "Civil Society," 201.

80. James Homer Williams, "Dutch Attitudes towards Indians, Africans, and Other Europeans in New Netherland, 1624–1664," in *Connecting Cultures: The Netherlands in Five Centuries of Transatlantic Exchange,* ed. Rosemarijn Hoefte and Johanna Kardux (Amsterdam: VU Press, 1994), 43.

81. Court Proceedings, December 9, 1638, NYCM, IV, 29, NYSA; Court Proceedings, December 16, 1638, NYCM, IV, 29, NYSA. Van Zandt explains that since Antonij Portugies was termed a company slave during the 1641 Premero murder case, he must have been enslaved during his 1638 court case. Van Zandt, *Brothers among Nations,* 224n29.

82. Van Laer, *Register of the Provincial Secretary, 1638–1642,* 123.

83. Minutes, November 19, 1643, NYCM, IV, 180, NYSA; Van Laer, *Council Minutes, 1638–1649,* 208–209. In some documents, Celes's name was spelled as Selis.

84. Minutes, November 26, 1643, NYCM, IV, 180, NYSA; Van Laer, *Council Minutes, 1638–1649,* 208–209.

85. See, for example, Kathryn Joy McKnight and Leo Garofalo, eds., *Afro-Latino Voices: Narratives from the Early Modern Ibero-Atlantic World, 1550–1812* (Indianapolis: Hackett, 2009); Heywood and Thornton, *Central Africans;* Berlin, *Many Thousands Gone;* Jane Landers, "Traditions of African American Freedom and Community in Spanish Colonial Florida," in *The African American Heritage in Florida,* ed. David R. Colburn and Jane L. Landers (Gainesville: University Press of Florida, 1995), 17–41; Gwendolyn Midlo Hall, *Africans in Colonial Louisiana: The Development of Afro-Creole Culture in the Eighteenth Century* (Baton Rouge: Louisiana State University Press, 1995). When enslaved people had access to the court, not only did they participate in the legal system, but in fact they often shaped legislation. For more on enslaved people using the courts, see, among others, Alejandro de la Fuente, "Slaves and the Creation of Legal Rights in Cuba: *Coartacion* and Papel," *Hispanic American Historical Review* 87, no. 4 (2007): 659–692, https://doi.org/10.1215/00182168; Camillia Cowling, "Gendered Geographies: Motherhood, Slavery, Law, and Space in Mid-nineteenth-century Cuba," *Women's History Review* 27, no. 6 (2018): 939–953, https://doi.org/10.1080/09612025.2017.1336845; Camillia Cowling, *Conceiving Freedom: Women of Color, Gender, and the Abolition of Slavery in Havana and Rio de Janeiro* (Chapel Hill: University of North Carolina Press, 2013); Michelle A. McKinley, *Fractional Freedoms: Slavery, Intimacy, and Legal Mobilization in Colonial Lima* (Cambridge: Cambridge University Press, 2016); Lauren Benton, *Law and Colonial Cultures: Legal Regimes in World History, 1400–1900* (Cambridge: Cambridge University Press, 2001); Lauren Benton and Richard Ross, eds., *Legal Pluralism and Empires, 1500–1850* (New York: New York University Press,

2013); Kimberly M. Welch, *Black Litigants in the Antebellum South* (Chapel Hill: University of North Carolina Press, 2018); Anne Twitty, *Before Dred Scott: Slavery and Legal Culture in the American Confluence, 1787–1857* (Cambridge: Cambridge University Press, 2018); Jane Landers, *Black Society in Spanish Florida* (Urbana: University of Illinois Press, 1999); Berlin, "From Creole to African"; Lea Vandervelde, *Redemption Songs: Suing for Freedom before Dred Scott* (Oxford: Oxford University Press, 2014); Kelly Kennington, *In the Shadow of Dred Scott: St. Louis Freedom Suits and the Legal Culture of Slavery in Antebellum America* (Athens: University of Georgia Press, 2017); Martha Jones, *Birthright Citizens: A History of Race and Rights in Antebellum America* (Cambridge: Cambridge University Press, 2018).

86. Berlin, "From Creole to African," 254.

87. In the Portuguese Kingdom of Angola, for example, the courts implemented Angolan adaptations of Portuguese law. Linda Heywood, "Queen Njinga Mbandi Ana De Sousa of Ndongo/Matamba: African Leadership, Diplomacy, and Ideology, 1620s–1650s," in *Afro-Latino Voices: Narratives from the Early Modern Ibero-Atlantic World, 1550–1812*, ed. Kathryn McKnight and Leo Garofalo (Indianapolis: Hackett, 2009), 38; Giovanni Antonio Cavazzi, "Missione evagelica nel Regno de Congo," trans. John K. Thornton, http://centralafricanhistory.blogspot.com/2008/08/book-i-chapter-3.html (accessed on November 3, 2016), bk. 1, chap. 3; Joseph Miller, *Kings and Kinsmen: Early Mbundu States in Angola* (Oxford: Clarendon, 1976), 232–235; Heywood and Thornton, "Intercultural Relations," 20. Since both the Portuguese and Dutch legal systems were based on Roman law, Portuguese influences caused important similarities between Angola's and New Netherland's legal system. The Kingdom of Kongo had a well-organized judicial system that predated European contact. Heywood and Thornton, *Central Africans*, 61; John Thornton, *The Kingdom of Kongo: Civil War and Transition, 1641–1718* (Madison: University of Wisconsin Press, 1983), 45; Anne Hilton, *The Kingdom of Kongo* (Oxford: Clarendon, 1985), 85; Linda Heywood and John Thornton, "The Treason of Dom Pedro Nkanga a Mvemba against Dom Diogo, King of Kongo, 1550," in *Afro-Latino Voices: Narratives from the Early Modern Ibero-Atlantic World, 1550–1812*, ed. Kathryn McKnight and Leo Garofalo (Indianapolis: Hackett, 2009). In West Central Africa and other parts of the diaspora, Africans had a long history of petitioning local authorities. Their frequent petitioning to the Spanish and Portuguese courts, among others, demonstrates that Africans in the diaspora had successfully utilized this technique. Leo Garofalo, "Afro-Iberian Subjects: Petitioning the Crown at Home, Serving the Crown Abroad, 1590s–1630s," in *Afro-Latino Voices: Narratives from the Early Modern Ibero-Atlantic World, 1550–1812*, ed. Kathryn McKnight and Leo Garofalo (Indianapolis: Hackett, 2009), 52–54.

88. Venema writes that in 1652 there were "only few Africans in the upper Hudson area." Venema, *Beverwijck*, 114. Also see Wagman, "Corporate Slavery in New Netherland," 36.

89. Van Laer, *Minutes of the Court of Rensselaerswyck 1648–1652*, 192.

90. Staten Generaal to Petrus Stuyvesant and Council, September 6, 1656, Staten Generaal 1.01.07, 12564.46, unpaginated, Nat. Arch. For more about the slave trade, see chap. 1. As Susanah Shaw Romney has pointed out, many of the captives who had been brought into the colony by Geurt Tijsen had been changed to different enslavers at least once over a four-year period. Romney, *New Netherland Connections*, 206. Also see Goodfriend, "Burghers and Blacks," 132.

91. Fred van Lieburg, "The Dutch and Their Religion," in *Four Centuries of Dutch-American Relations, 1609–2009*, 155.

92. Hastings, *Ecclesiastical Records*, 1:488; Joyce Goodfriend, "The Souls of African American Children: New Amsterdam," *Common-Place* 3, no. 4 (July 2003), http://www.common-place-archives.org/vol-03/no-04/new-york/.

93. People who lived in this area of Manhattan also attended church here. Hastings, *Ecclesiastical Records*, 1:488–490; Stokes, *Iconography of Manhattan Island*, 2:80; Sypher, *Liber A of the Collegiate Churches of New York, part 2*, 524–572; Bonomi, "'Swarms of Negroes,'" 43.

94. Although inferior or local courts were founded across the region, many settlements were not considered large enough to have their own court. In the 1650s, there were seven courts in Long Island, one in Manhattan, and two in the Upper Hudson region. Gehring, *Council Minutes 1655–1656*, xiv; J. Jacobs, *Colony of New Netherland*, 87–89.

3. Control and Resistance in the Public Space

1. Court Minutes, March 7, 1671, Original Dutch Records, VI, October 1670–October 1671, 36, NYCMA; O'Callaghan and Fernow, *Records of New Amsterdam*, 6:286; Minutes, December 6, 1663, NYCM, X, 416, NYSA; Petition, December 28, 1662, NYCM, X, 296, NYSA; Minutes, April 19, 1663, NYCM, X, 71, NYSA; Minutes, April 17, 1664, NYCM, X, 170.

2. Petition, December 6, 1663, NYCM, X, 416, NYSA; Order, December 6, 1663, NYCM, X, 417, NYSA; Christoph, "Freedmen of New Amsterdam," 161; Goodfriend, "Black Families in New Netherland," 151.

3. See A. J. Williams-Myers for an in-depth discussion of the types of labor enslaved people in NY performed. Williams-Myers, *Long Hammering*, chap. 2.

4. *Heads of Families at the First Census of the United States taken in the Year 1790: New York*, Washington, DC: Government Printing Office, 1908, 9.

5. Berlin, *Many Thousands Gone*, 188. Also see Hardesty, *Unfreedom*, 5.

6. Elijah Anderson discusses "the white space" in the post–Civil Rights era. Similar to what we see in enslaving communities like New York, "black people [in modern America] are required to navigate the white space as a condition of their existence." He points out that "while operating in the white space, they can be subject to social, if not physical, jeopardy." Elijah Anderson, "The White Space," *Sociology of Race and Ethnicity* 1, no. 1 (2015): 11–12, https://doi.org/10.1177/2332649214561306.

7. Anderson, "White Space," 10–21. Also see Elijah Anderson, "Cosmopolitan Canopy," *Annals of the American Academy of Political and Social Science* 595 (September 2004): 14–31, https://doi.org/10.1177/0002716204266833.

8. The area of this free Black community most closely resembled the neighborhoods that Anderson defined as "black space." Anderson, "White Space," 11.

9. Stephanie Camp explains that enslaved people created "a rival geography," a term first introduced by Edward Said and used by geographers "to describe resistance to colonial occupation." Camp, *Closer to Freedom*, 7. Similar challenges to their enslavers' control can be seen in other regions. As noted by Rebecca Ginsberg and Clifton Ellis, the way enslaved men, women, and children "expressed their autonomy, restored their dignity, and even achieved their freedom was through manipulation of the very landscapes designed to restrict them." Ginsberg and Ellis, *Slavery in the City*, 3. Finch notes

that "black mobility was one of the most important but difficult for slaveowners to police." Finch, *Rethinking Slave Rebellion in Cuba*, 53. James Delle has termed these "spatialities of movement," the ways in which enslaved people "expressed control over the spatiality of movement, at least for a brief time." Delle, *Archeology of Social Space*, 165. Also see Ross's discussion of similar dynamics in South Africa. Ross, *Status and Respectability*, 131–132.

10. For more on slave societies, see Berlin, *Many Thousands Gone*, 8–9; Ira Berlin, *Generations of Captivity: A History of African-American Slaves* (Cambridge, MA: Belknap Press, 2003), 8–11.

11. "Kings County, NY 1698 Census," in *Documentary History of the State of New York*, ed. E. B. O'Callaghan (Albany: Weed, Parsons, 1850), 3:87–89; *Heads of Families at the First Census of the United States taken in the Year 1790: New York*, 9.

12. Dingman Versteeg, trans., Peter R. Christoph, Kenneth Scott, and Kenn Stryker-Rodda, eds., *Kingston Papers: Kingston Court Records, 1668–1675 and Secretary's Papers, 1664–1675* (Baltimore: Genealogical Publishing Co., 1976), 2:213–214, 650.

13. Thomas L. Purvis, *Colonial America to 1763*, ed. Richard Balkin (New York: Infobase, 2014), 148; O'Callaghan, *Documentary History*, 1:693, 696. By 1756, they reached 1,500 out of a total population of 8,105, or just below 19 percent. And although their total population increased significantly over the next few decades, up to 2,906 in 1790, they now made up a smaller part of the total population.

14. Bureau of Census, F. S. Crum, "A Century of Population Growth, 1790–1900 (1909)," *Publications of the American Statistical Association* 12, no. 92 (1910), 181; Purvis, *Colonial America to 1763*, 149; O'Callaghan, *Documentary History*, 1:693. For more on Albany's enslaved population, see Oscar Williams, "Slavery in Albany, New York, 1624–1827," *Afro-Americans in New York Life and History* 34, no. 2 (July 2010): 154–168.

15. Merlin-Faucquez, "De la Nouvelle-Néerlande à New York," 175–178, 352. In New York City, English cultural and political influence spread most quickly and successfully after the region came under English control. That did not mean, however, that the city and its population completely lost their Dutch character. Goodfriend, *Before the Melting Pot*; Joyce Goodfriend, *Who Should Rule at Home? Confronting the Elite in British New York City* (Ithaca, NY: Cornell University Press, 2017).

16. *Heads of Families at the First Census of the United States taken in the Year 1790: New York*, 96–98.

17. *Heads of Families at the First Census of the United States taken in the Year 1790: New York*, 36, 52, 55.

18. Thomas Humphrey argues that by the 1770s, "the Hudson River Valley had emerged as one of the foremost grain-producing regions in the North American colonies." Thomas J. Humphrey, "Agrarian Rioting in Albany County, New York: Tenants, Markets and Revolution in the Hudson Valley, 1751–1801" (PhD diss., Northern Illinois University, 1997), 2; Joyce Goodfriend, "Why New Netherland Matters," in *Explorers, Fortunes, & Love Letters*, ed. Martha Dickinson Shattuck (New York: New Netherland Institute and Mount Ida Press, 2009), 153.

19. Various primary sources reveal the tasks completed by enslaved laborers and special skills they had. See the following runaway slave advertisement, *New York Evening Post*, October 8, 1808. Also see, Indictment, 1722, the Ulster County Tomlins Collection, 1670–1729, item 21, N-YHS; Slave Bill of Sale, October 14, 1728, ArMs 1974.106 William P. Hulst Papers, f.14, BHS; Abraham Van Gaasbak to Gerret Elmen-

dorf, January 8, 1762, Elmendorph, Garret—Accounts, Bills and Receipts, 1737–1774, box 1, folder 28, SC23070 Dumond-Elmendorph-Smith Family Papers, 1727–1914, NYSL; Susan Stessin-Cohn and Ashley Hurlburt-Biagini, eds., *In Defiance: Runaways from Slavery in New York's Hudson River Valley, 1735–1831* (Delmar, NY: Black Dome Press, 2016), 55, 110, 122, 166; Jacob Van Schaick, Vrooman, and Degraff to Jacob Gordon, June 12, 1786, SC10837 Van Schaick Family Papers, box 1, folder 7, NYSL; Crooke-Elmendorph Account Book, 1770–1777, CV10181 Kingston Collection, box 17, NYSL. Also see Williams-Myers, *Long Hammering*, 13–42; White, *Somewhat More Independent*, 10–11, 21–22; Hodges, *Root & Branch*, 40–47.

20. Alexander Coventry, *Memoirs of an Emigrant: The Journal of Alexander Coventry, M.D.; in Scotland, the United States and Canada during the Period 1783–1831* (Albany: Albany Institute of History and Art and the New York State Library, 1978), 145.

21. William Strickland, *Journal of a Tour in the United States of America, 1794–1795* (New York: New-York Historical Society, 1971), 163. Also see David S. Cohen, *The Dutch-American Farm* (New York: New York University Press, 1993), 144–145.

22. Lincoln, Johnson, and Northrup, *Colonial Laws of New York*, 1:761–763, 922–923.

23. *Heads of Families at the First Census of the United States taken in the Year 1790: New York*, 9; Federal Census, 1800, ArMs 1977.351 Helen Zunser Wortis Collection, 351 B #33, BHS.

24. "An Act for the Gradual Abolition of Slavery, 1799," March 29, 1799, Dept. of State, Bureau of Miscellaneous Records, Enrolled Acts of the State Legislature, Series 13036–78, Laws of 1799, chap. 62, NYSA.

25. Kings, NY, 1810 U.S. Census, transcribed by Jeri Shangle, USGenWeb Archives; *Abstract of the Returns of the Fifth Census*, 9–10; *Compendium of the Enumeration of the Inhabitants and Statistics of the United States, as obtained at the Department of State, from the returns of the sixth census*, 22.

26. Franklin to Schuyler, May 27, 1776, given to Schuyler Mansion by Louisa Lee Schuyler and Georgina Schuyler on October 13, 1921, Schuyler Mansion, Albany.

27. Fiske discusses similar dynamics in present-day society. John Fiske, "Surveilling the City: Whiteness, the Black Man and Democratic Totalitarianism," *Theory, Culture & Society* 15, no. 2: 72, 86, https://doi.org/10.1177/026327698015002003.

28. In what now were New York City, Staten Island, and Westchester County, these laws came into effect as early as 1665. Kingston (formerly Esopus) began to use the Duke's laws in 1669, while in Albany (Beverwijck) significant changes in the judicial system did not take place until late 1674. Sullivan, *Punishment of Crime*, 210–211; Shattuck, "Civil Society," 18; Lincoln, Johnson, and Northrup, *Colonial Laws of New York*, 1:18; Hodges, *Slavery and Freedom*, 2.

29. *Proceedings of the General Court of Assizes held in the City of New York, October 6, 1680, to October 6, 1682* (New York: New-York Historical Society, 1913), 37–38; Higginbotham, *In the Matter of Color*, 116–117.

30. Lincoln, Johnson, and Northrup, *Colonial Laws of New York*, 1:519–520; Higginbotham, *In the Matter of Color*, 119.

31. Lincoln, Johnson, and Northrup, *Colonial Laws of New York*, 1:597–598.

32. This ban was repeated in, among others, 1710 and 1713. Lincoln, Johnson, and Northrup, 1:666, 708, 788.

33. Lincoln, Johnson, and Northrup, 1:762.

34. Herbert L. Osgood et al., eds., *Minutes of the Common Council of the City of New York, 1675–1776* (New York: Dodd, Mead, 1905), 2:323, 327.

35. Osgood et al., 2:242–243.

36. Osgood et al., 3:28.

37. J. Munsell, *Collections on the history of Albany: from its discovery to the present time; with notices of its public institutions, and biographical sketches of citizens deceased* (Albany: J. Munsell, 1865–81), 2:268; Scott, "Ulster County, New York, Court Records, 1693–1775," 277.

38. For similar efforts in Dutch communities elsewhere, see Worden, "Space and Identity," 76–77; Kehoe, "Dutch Batavia," 8, 14, 16–17.

39. Fuentes, *Dispossessed Lives*, 37.

40. Barry Higman, *Slave Populations of the British Caribbean* (Mona, Jamaica: University of West Indies Press, 1995), 243.

41. Osgood et al., *Minutes of the Common Council*, 4:497–98; 5:85–86, 158. According to Douglas Greenburg, "prosecutions for theft were almost twice as frequent among blacks as in the population at large." Douglas Greenburg, "Patterns of Criminal Prosecution in Eighteenth Century New York," in *Courts and Law in Early New York: Selected Essays*, ed. Leo Hershkowitz and Milton M. Klein (Port Washington, NY: Kennikat, 1978), 67.

42. Ordinary Sessions, August 12, 1676, Kingston Papers, bk 2:446, Ulster County Clerk, Archives Division.

43. Scott, "Ulster County, New York, Court Records, 1693–1775," 278.

44. Oscar Newman, *Defensible Space: Crime Prevention through Urban Design* (New York: Macmillan, 1972), 3.

45. Newman, 18.

46. Newman, 7; Munsell, *Collections on the history of Albany*, 2:419–420.

47. Foucault, *Discipline and Punish*, 201. Foucault built his theory on Jeremy Bentham's work on the panopticon.

48. May 21, 1796, 11155: Society for Apprending slaves, 1796, NYSL.

49. In Munsell's history of Albany, Munsell notes that Albany's bell ringer would go to the Dutch Reformed Church every night at 8 P.M. "to ring the suppaan bell. This was the signal for all to eat their suppaan, or hasty-pudding, and prepare for bed. It was equivalent to the English curfew bell." Munsell, *Collections on the history of Albany*, 2:27–28. Louis P. Nelson discusses similar curfews in eighteenth-century Charleston. Louis P. Nelson, *The Beauty of Holiness: Anglicanism & Architecture in Colonial South Carolina* (Chapel Hill: University of North Carolina Press, 2008), 298.

50. In New York City, a *ratelwacht*, or rattle guard, had been formed as early as 1658. In Beverwijck, a rattle guard was established in 1659. Bellmen and watchmen were usually tasked with watching for fires and helping to fight criminal behavior such as burglaries and escapes from the city's gaol, which apparently occurred regularly. These bellmen were to go "Every hour in the Night through the several Streets of this City and publishing the time of the Night and Apprehending all disturbers of the peace Felons Negro and Indian Slaves and Other persons and also take care that No damage be done in this City by fire or Other Casualties." Osgood et al., *Minutes of the Common Council*, 2:33, 209–210, 242–243, 291, 313, 425, 432; 3:61, 94, 362–363, 405–406, 451; 4:122–128, 127–128, 238–239, 266–267, 268, 299, 322, 360–361, 392, 449, 480; 5:7, 43–44, 78–80, 319. The examination of Bet a Negro Female Slave of Philip S. Van Rensse-

laer Esquire taken the 28th day of November 1793, NYSL; A Law Establishing a Night Watch, November 27, 1793, S.A.R.A. City Records, Common Council 1765–1840, box 1, 88-02947, nos. 75 & 188, Albany County Hall of Records. Also see Foote, *Black and White Manhattan*, 199; Jill Lepore, "The Tightening Vise: Slavery and Freedom in British New York," in *Slavery in New York*, ed. Ira Berlin and Leslie Harris (New York: New Press, 2005), 78; J. Jacobs, *New Netherland*, 370.

51. Run-Away Slave Advertisement, *Daily Advertiser*, June 9, 1798; Permission, February 25, 1800, Slavery Collection, N-YHS; For Sale, *Mercantile Advertiser*, June 19, 1802; Stessin-Cohn and Hurlburt-Biagini, *In Defiance*, 203, 277.

52. Sylvia Dubois and C. W. Larison, *Sylvia Dubois, a Biography of the Slav Who Whipt Her Mistres and Gand Her Freedom* (Oxford: Oxford University Press, 1988), 70–71.

53. Osgood et al., *Minutes of the Common Council*, 3:30–31.

54. Osgood et al., 3:402. For more on slave patrols, see Sally E. Hadden, *Slave Patrols: Law and Violence in Virginia and the Carolinas* (Cambridge, MA: Harvard University Press, 2001), 3–4.

55. Lincoln, Johnson, and Northrup, *Colonial Laws of New York*, 2:656.

56. White, *Somewhat More Independent*, 119.

57. Jonathan Prude, "To Look upon the 'Lower Sort': Runaway Ads and the Appearance of Unfree Laborers in America, 1750–1800," *Journal of American History* 78, no. 1 (June 1991): 127, https://doi.org/10.2307/2078091; David Waldstreicher, "Reading the Runaways: Self-Fashioning, Print Culture, and Confidence in Slavery in the Eighteenth-Century Mid-Atlantic," *William and Mary Quarterly* 56, no. 2 (April 1999): 247, https://doi.org/10.2307/2674119; Lorenzo J. Greene, "The New England Negro as Seen in Advertisements for Runaway Slaves," *Journal of Negro History* 29, no. 2 (April, 1944): 125–146, https://doi.org/10.2307/2715307.

58. Stessin-Cohn and Hurlburt-Biagini, *In Defiance*, 42.

59. Stessin-Cohn and Hurlburt-Biagini, 44.

60. Stessin-Cohn and Hurlburt-Biagini, 76; *Albany Gazette* (Albany, NY), June 3, 1815.

61. Hillitje DeWitt to Peter DeWitt, May 17, 1804, LK15161 DeWitt Family Papers, box 5, folder 7, NYSL.

62. *Albany Register*, November 18, 1793; *Albany Register*, November 25, 1793; Elizabeth Covart, "Collision on the Hudson: Identity, Migration, and the Improvement of Albany, New York, 1750–1830" (PhD dissertation, University of California, Davis, 2011), 178–179.

63. Bet and Dean were convicted and executed on Friday, March 14, 1794. *Albany Register*, March 17, 1794. Pompey was executed almost a month later, on April 11, 1794. Edwin Olson, "The Slave Code in Colonial New York," *Journal of Negro History* 29, no. 2 (1944): 160–161, https://doi.org/10.2307/2715308.

64. Elizabeth Covart points out that several fires occurred in the city after Bet, Dean, and Pompey had been arrested. In the aftermath of the fire, the city established a citizen's nightwatch. Covart, "Collision on the Hudson," 179. Also see "A Law, establishing a Night-Watch of the Citizens," *Albany Register*, December 2, 1793. It also prohibited enslaved people from wandering the streets after 9 P.M. Don R. Gerlach, "Black Arson in Albany, New York: November 1793," *Journal of Black Studies* 7, no. 3 (March 1977): 307; Bradford Verter, "Interracial Festivity and Power in Antebellum New

York: The Case of Pinkster," *Journal of Urban History* 28, no. 4 (2002): 409, https://doi.org/10.1177/0096144202028004002.

65. The examination of Bet a Negro Female Slave of Philip S. Van Rensselaer Esquire taken the 28th day of November 1793, 3–4, NYSL.

66. Osgood et al., *Minutes of the Common Council*, 4:497–98.

67. Bernard L. Herman, "Slave and Servant Housing in Charleston, 1770–1820," *Historical Archeology* 33, no. 3 (1999): 90.

68. Aisha Finch discusses such circulation of people, goods, and ideas in Cuba. Finch, *Rethinking Slave Rebellion in Cuba*, 54–55.

69. Strickland, *Journal of a Tour*, 163. Also see Cohen, *Dutch-American Farm*, 144–145.

70. As Sally Hadden notes about Barbados, just because slave codes existed, that did not mean they were strictly enforced. In fact, regular reenactment of the various laws suggests that enslaved people found ways to circumvent or break these laws. Hadden, *Slave Patrols*, 12.

71. Court Minutes, May 3, 1710, The Court of General Sessions, 1683–1847, New York City, 179, microfilm.

72. William Livingston to unknown, November 21, 1774, GLC 04842.10, Gilder Lehrman Collection.

73. Petition, January 24, 1792, no. 88, 10970 Ulster County Residents Signed Petition [copy], NYSL.

74. Court Minutes, August 28, 1696, New York County Clerk Court of General & Quarter Sessions of the Peace, 1683–1742, microfilm, reel 1, 15.

75. Court Minutes, August 2, 1710, New York County Clerk Court of General & Quarter Sessions of the Peace, 1683–1742, microfilm, reel 1, 188.

76. Court Minutes, November 10, 1738, New York County Clerk Court of General & Quarter Sessions of the Peace, 1683–1742, microfilm, reel 1, 257–258.

77. Scott, "Ulster County, New York, Court Records, 1693–1775," 278.

78. Scott, 283.

79. Lincoln, Johnson, and Northrup, *Colonial Laws of New York*, 2:679–680.

80. Petition, January 24, 1792, 10970: Ulster County Residents Signed Petition, NYSL.

81. See, for instance, Lepore, *New York Burning*; Linebaugh and Rediker, *Many-Headed Hydra*, 174–210.

82. Hardesty, *Unfreedom*, 94.

83. Jacob Van Schaick to Jacob Gordon, June 12, 1786, SC10837: Van Schaick Family Papers, box 1, folder 7, NYSL.

84. Lincoln, Johnson, and Northrup, *Colonial Laws of New York*, 1:582–584.

85. Graham Russell Hodges, ed., *"Pretends to Be Free": Runaway Slave Advertisements from Colonial and Revolutionary New York and New Jersey* (New York: Garland, 1994), xxxiii. Others have also pointed out that attempts to escape enslavement increased during the Revolution, including White, *Somewhat More Independent*, 141; Henry Reed Stiles, *A History of the City of Brooklyn* (Brooklyn, 1869), 303; Gertrude Lefferts Vanderbilt, *The Social History of Flatbush: And Manners and Customs of the Dutch Settlers in Kings County* (New York: D. Appleton, 1881), 325.

86. Stessin-Cohn and Hurlburt-Biagini, *In Defiance*, 127.

87. Run-Away Slave Advertisement, *Daily Advertiser*, June 9, 1798.

88. Stessin-Cohn and Hurlburt-Biagini, *In Defiance*, 203.

89. *Albany Register*, June 2, 1815.

90. *Daily Advertiser*, June 29, 1803.

91. White, *Somewhat More Independent*, 99; Shane White, "Pinkster: Afro-Dutch Syncretization in New York City and the Hudson Valley," *Journal of American Folklore* 102, no. 403 (January–March 1989): 70, https://doi.org/10.2307/540082.

92. Hodges, *Root & Branch*, 87.

93. For more about Negro Election Day and General Training, see, among others, William D. Piersen, *Black Yankees: The Development of an Afro-American Subculture in Eighteenth-Century New England* (Amherst: University of Massachusetts Press, 1988), 117–128; Joseph P. Reidy, "'Negro Election Day' & Black Community Life in New England, 1750–1860," *Marxist Perspectives* 1, no. 3 (Fall 1978), 106; Shane White, "'It Was a Proud Day': African Americans, Festivals, and Parades in the North," *Journal of American History* 81, no. 1 (June 1994): 24, https://doi.org/10.2307/2080992; James Oliver Horton and Lois E. Horton, *In Hope of Liberty: Culture, Community, and Protest among Northern Free Blacks, 1700–1860* (New York: Oxford University Press, 1997); Camp, *Closer to Freedom*, 65; Nicholas Beasley, *Christian Ritual and the Creation of British Slave Societies* (Athens: University of Georgia Press, 2009), 45; Rashauna Johnson, *Slavery's Metropolis: Unfree Labor in New Orleans during the Age of Revolutions* (Cambridge: Cambridge University Press, 2016), 88–89; David Steven Cohen, "In Search of Carolus Africanus Rex: Afro-Dutch Folklore in New York and New Jersey," *Journal of Afro-American Historical and Genealogical Society* 5 (Fall & Winter 1984): 154; A. J. Williams-Myers, "Pinkster Carnival: Africanisms in the Hudson River Valley," *Afro-Americans in New York Life and History* 9, no. 1 (1985): 7–17.

94. White, "'It was a Proud Day,'" 29; Hardesty, *Unfreedom*, 99.

95. A. Th. van Deursen, *Mensen van Klein Vermogen: Het Kopergeld van de Gouden Eeuw* (Amsterdam: Prometheus, 1999), 130; Jan ter Gouw, *De Volksvermaken* (Haarlem: Erven F. Bohn, 1871), 3:226–227.

96. Ordinance, December 31, 1655, A1875: Ordinances, 62, NYSA; Court Minutes, December 31, 1655, Original Dutch Documents, I, December 1655–August 1656, 464–465, NYCMA; Fernow and O'Callaghan, *Records of New Amsterdam*, 1:172, 420; Van Laer, *Minutes of the Court of Rensselaerswijck*, 138; Gehring, *Council Minutes, 1652 1654*, 118–119. Also see Venema, *Beverwijck*, 112; J. Jacobs, *New Netherland*, 433–434, 464–471.

97. Marc Wingens, "De Pinksterkroon is Weer in 'T Land, Hoezee! Het Pinksterkroon Feest in Deventer," *Volkscultuur* 6, no. 2 (1989): 7–8.

98. Jasper Danckaerts, *Journal of Jasper Danckaerts, 1679–1680* (New York: C. Scribner's Sons, 1913), 239.

99. Gabriel Furman, *Antiquities of Long Island* (New York: J. W. Bouton, 1875), 264–269.

100. Coventry, *Memoirs of an Emigrant*, 215.

101. William Dunlap, *Diary of William Dunlap, 1766–1839: the Memoirs of a Dramatist, Theatrical Manager, Painter, Critic, Novelist, and Historian*, ed. Dorothy C. Barck (New York: C. Scribner's Sons, 1913), 65.

102. Camp, *Closer to Freedom*, 65.

103. Saidiya V. Hartman, *Scenes of Subjection: Terror, Slavery, and Self-Making in Nineteenth-Century America* (Oxford: Oxford University Press, 1997), 44–45.

104. James Fenimore Cooper, *Satanstoe; Or, the Family of Littlepage: A Tale of the Colony* (New York: Burgess, Stringer, 1845), 72–73.

105. White, "Pinkster," 70.

106. White, 70.

107. "Albany Fifty Years Ago," *Harper's Magazine* (March 1857), 451–463.

108. Cooper, *Satanstoe*, 77.

109. *Albany Centinel* (Albany, NY), June 17, 1803; *Daily Advertiser*, June 29, 1803.

110. Geraldine R. Pleat and Agnes N. Underwood, "Pinkster Ode, Albany, 1803," *New York Folklore Quarterly* 8, no. 1 (Spring 1952): 37. For more about the likely author of the ode, see Verter, "Interracial Festivity," 413.

111. Natalie Zemon Davis, *Society and Culture in Early Modern France* (Stanford, CA: Stanford University Press, 1975), 130.

112. Daniel Miller, *Unwrapping Christmas* (Oxford: Oxford University Press, 1993), 9.

113. Evan M. Zuesse, "Perseverance and Transmutation in African Traditional Religions," in *African Traditional Religions in Contemporary Society*, ed. Jacob K. Olupona (New York: Paragon House, 1991), 176.

114. Wingens, "De Pinksterkroon is Weer in 'T Land, Hoezee!," 13–14; K. ter Laan, *Folkloristisch Woordenboek Van Nederland En Vlaams België* ('s Gravenhage: GB van Goor Zonen, 1949), 300. For more about Pinkster celebrations in the Netherlands, see S. J. van der Molen, *Levend Volksleven: Een Eigentijdse Volkskunde Van Nederland* (Van Gorcum: HJ Prakke & HMG Prakke, 1961), 84; Ter Gouw, *De Volksvermaken*, 3:224. My mother, who grew up in Drenthe in the 1940s and 1950s, remembered similar Pinkster celebrations took place there.

115. Wingens, "De Pinksterkroon is weer in 't land, hoezee!," 13–14. See also Charlotte Wilcoxen, *Seventeenth Century Albany: A Dutch Profile* (Albany: Education Dept., Albany Institute of History and Art, 1984), 119–120.

116. *Albany Centinel*, June 17, 1803; *Daily Advertiser*, June 29, 1803.

117. Pleat and Underwood, "Pinkster Ode," 35.

118. *Albany Centinel* (Albany, NY), June 17, 1803; *Daily Advertiser*, June 29, 1803. For more on complaints about the increased participation of white Albanians, see Verter, "Interracial Festivity," 412. For more on Albany's changing demographics in the late eighteenth century, see, among others, Covart, "Collision on the Hudson"; David G. Hackett, *The Rude Hand of Innovation: Religion and Social Order in Albany, New York, 1652–1836* (Oxford: Oxford University Press, 1991).

119. *Albany Centinel* (Albany, NY), June 17, 1803; *Daily Advertiser*, June 29, 1803.

120. A Law to Regulate the Amusements of the Negroes during the Whitsuntide Holidays, July 17, 1804, S.A.R.A., box 1, 88-02947, no. 131, Albany County Hall of Records. Also see Verter, "Interracial Festivity," 412.

121. White, "'It was a Proud Day,'" 30; Verter, "Interracial Festivity," 400.

122. Reidy, "'Negro Election Day,'" 106.

123. Prude, "To Look," 130–133; Peter Burke, *Popular Culture in Early Modern Europe* (New York: New York University Press, 1978), 3.

124. Horton and Horton, *In Hope of Liberty*, 30.

125. "Death of Capt. Shawk," *Albany Centinel* (Albany, NY), July 13, 1804.

126. Stiles, *History*, 2: 40; White, "'It was a Proud Day,'" 28.

127. Ross, *Status and Respectability*, 125–127.

128. Johnson, *Slavery's Metropolis*, 117.

129. Sojourner Truth, *Narrative of Sojourner Truth* (Mineola, NY: Dover, 1999), 35.

130. Sonjah Stanley Niaah, "Mapping Black Atlantic Performance Geographies: From Slave Ship to Ghetto," in *Black Geographies and the Politics of Place*, ed. Katherine McKittrick and Clyde Woods (Boston: South End, 2007), 194.

131. Truth, *Narrative of Sojourner Truth*, 35.

132. Description by Ferdinand van Capelle, OWIC 46, March 1642, unpaginated, 5th folio, NA. Also see chap. 2.

133. Hilton, *Kingdom of Kongo*, 96.

134. Thornton, *Africa and Africans*, 244; John K. Thornton, "Religious and Ceremonial Life in the Kongo and Mbundu Areas, 1500–1700," in *Central Africans and Cultural Transformations in the American Diaspora*, ed. Linda M. Heywood (Cambridge: Cambridge University Press, 2002), 85.

135. Hilton, *Kingdom of Kongo*, 96.

136. Both *Harper's New Monthly* and the "Pinkster Ode" suggest that Albany's Pinkster celebration was located close to a burial ground. Pleat and Underwood, "Pinkster Ode," 42; "A Glimpse of an Old Dutch Town," *Harper's New Monthly Magazine* 62 (March 1881): 525–526. Jeroen Dewulf argues that the Pinkster Ode here refers to Dean, the enslaved girl who had been executed in 1794 for the Albany fire and who, according to Dewulf, was buried close to the Pinkster Hill. He does not provide any evidence to support this claim. Dewulf, *Pinkster King*, 162.

137. John K. Thornton, *The Kongolese Saint Anthony: Dona Beatriz Kimpa Vita and the Antonian Movement, 1684–1706* (Cambridge: Cambridge University Press, 1998), 31–33. Also see David Birmingham, *Trade and Conflict in Angola: The Mbundu and Their Neighbours under the Influence of the Portuguese, 1483–1790* (Oxford: Clarendon, 1966), 97.

138. Thornton, "Religious and Ceremonial Life," 85; Hilton, *Kingdom of Kongo*, 96–97.

139. Fromont, *Art of Conversion*, 268. Jeroen Dewulf's book argues that the Pinkster festival is rooted in these Kongolese celebrations. Dewulf, *Pinkster King*.

140. Willem Bosman, *Nauwkeurige Beschryving Van De Guinese Goud-Tand-En Slave-Kust* (Utrecht: Anthony Schouten, 1704), 2:159.

141. Barbot, *Barbot on Guinea*, 2:395–396.

142. Melvin Wade, "'Shining in Borrowed Plumage': Affirmation of Community in the Black Coronation Festivals of New England (c. 1750–c. 1850)," *Western Folklore* 40, no. 3 (July 1981): 219, https://doi.org/10.2307/1499693.

143. Reidy, "'Negro Election Day,'" 108.

144. *Daily Advertiser*, June 29, 1803. Also see "Pinkster Festivities in Albany Sixty Years Ago," in Munsell, *Collections on the history of Albany*, 2:323–327.

145. "The Albany Theatre," in Munsell, *Collections on the history of Albany*, 2:56.

146. Pleat and Underwood, "Pinkster Ode," 34.

147. Several scholars have examined the close link between music and religion in precolonial African societies. Joseph M. Murphy, for instance, found that music and dance played an important role in religious ceremony since they served as way to connect with the otherworld. Joseph Murphy, *Working the Spirit: Ceremonies of the African Diaspora* (Boston: Beacon, 1994), 5–6.

148. De Carli and Guattini, "Curious and Exact Account," 165.

149. De Carli and Guattini, 160.

150. Pleat and Underwood, "Pinkster Ode," 36.

151. Sterling Stuckey, *Slave Culture: Nationalist Theory and the Foundations of Black America* (New York: Oxford University Press, 1987), 11.

152. African Americans in western Long Island still celebrated Pinkster in 1874. Goodfriend, "Why New Netherland Matters," 155; Cohen, *Dutch-American Farm*, 163; Furman, *Antiquities of Long Island*, 264–269.

4. Enslavement and the Dual Nature of the Home

1. Truth, *Narrative of Sojourner Truth*, 2. For more about Truth's life and legacy, see, among others, Margaret Washington, *Sojourner Truth's America* (Champaign: University of Illinois Press, 2009); Nell Irvin Painter, *Sojourner Truth: A Life, A Symbol* (New York: W. W. Norton, 1996); Carleton Mabee, *Sojourner Truth: Slave, Prophet, Legend* (New York: New York University Press, 1995); Larry G. Murphy, *Sojourner Truth: A Biography* (Santa Barbara, CA: Greenwood, 2011); Margaret Washington, "'From Motives of Delicacy': Sexuality and Morality in the Narratives of Sojourner Truth and Harriet Jacobs," *Journal of African American History* 92, no. 1 (Winter 2007): 57–73.

2. Truth, *Narrative of Sojourner Truth*, 13.

3. *Heads of Families at the First Census of the United States taken in the Year 1790: New York*, 96–97; White, *Somewhat More Independent*, 18.

4. *Heads of Families at the First Census of the United States taken in the Year 1790: New York*, 12–55.

5. A few scholars have looked at this history in early New York, including Thomas J. Davis, "These Enemies within Their Own Household: Slaves in 18th Century New York," in *A Beautiful and Fruitful Place*, ed. Nancy McClure Zeller (Albany: New Netherland Project, 1991); Maskiell, "Bound by Bondage"; H. Arthur Bankoff and Frederick A. Winter, "The Archeology of Slavery at the Van Cortlandt Plantation in the Bronx, New York," *International Journal of Historical Archeology* 9, no. 4 (December 2005): 291–318, https://doi.org/10.1007/s10761-005-9302-5; Kruger, "Born to Run"; Goodfriend, "Black Families in New Netherland," 147–156.

6. Camp, *Closer to Freedom*, 7.

7. Sean E. Sawyer, "Constructing the Tradition of Dutch American Architecture, 1609–2009," in *Dutch New York: The Roots of Hudson Valley Culture*, ed. Roger Panetta (New York: Fordham University Press, 2009), 98; Roderic H. Blackburn and Ruth Piwonka, *Remembrance of Patria: Dutch Arts and Culture in Colonial America, 1609–1776* (Albany: Albany Institute of History and Art, 1988), 117–118.

8. Joseph Manca, "Erasing the Dutch: The Critical Reception of Hudson Valley Dutch Architecture, 1670–1840," in *Going Dutch: The Dutch Presence in America, 1609–2009*, ed. Joyce D. Goodfriend, Benjamin Schmidt, and Annette Stott (Leiden: Brill, 2008), 60; Blackburn and Piwonka, *Remembrance of Patria*, 92–116.

9. "Schuyler Mansion: A Historic Structure Report" (Division for Historic Preservation Bureau of Historic Sites, 1977), 12; Sawyer, "Constructing the Tradition," 103–104.

10. Today, Bartel Engelbertszen Loth is more commonly known as Engelbart Lott.

11. E. B. O'Callaghan, *Census of Slaves, 1755* (New York, 1850). This census did not provide any information on the number of children under the age of fourteen.

12. Johannes Lott Probate Record, June 11, 1803, Robert Billard Collection (private).

13. Dell Upton claims one- or two-room homes were popular in early eighteenth-century Virginia, even among more well-to-do families. Dell Upton, "Vernacular Domestic Architecture in Eighteenth-Century Virginia," in *Common Places: Readings in American Vernacular Architecture*, ed. Dell Upton and John Michael Vlach (Athens: University of Georgia Press, 1986), 316–317.

14. Robert K. Fitts discusses the constant "alien status" of enslaved New Yorkers, which became especially evident when slaveholders segregated certain activities. He explains that even though free and enslaved New Yorkers shared the most intimate spheres, white families would never eat with the people they enslaved, share their pews with them, or bury them in the same graveyards as their families. Robert K. Fitts, "The Landscapes of Northern Bondage," *Historical Archeology* 30, no. 2 (1996): 54–73, https://doi.org/10.1007/BF03373588.

15. Christopher Gerard Ricciardi, "Changing through the Century: Life at the Lott Family Farm in the Nineteenth Century Town of Flatlands, Kings County, New York" (PhD diss., Syracuse University, 2004), 84. Such two-room structures were not uncommon in the colonies. See Gabrielle M. Lanier, *Everyday Architecture of the Mid-Atlantic: Looking at Buildings and Landscapes* (Baltimore: Johns Hopkins University Press, 1997), 20–21; James Deetz, *In Small Things Forgotten: An Archeology of Early American Life* (New York: Doubleday Dell, 1996), 130.

16. H. Arthur Bankoff, Christopher Ricciardi, and Alyssa Loorya, "Remembering Africa under the Eaves," *Archeology* 54, no. 3 (May–June 2001): 38.

17. Bankoff, Ricciardi, and Loorya, 38.

18. Excavations of the brick kitchen's location uncovered very few kitchen utensils but did unearth various personal items, including buttons, toys, and hairpins, with manufacturing dates that ranged from 1790 to 1842. The quality of these items, such as the buttons made of bone and shell, suggest that they belonged to servants or enslaved inhabitants who likely lived there. Ricciardi, "Changing through the Century," 136–137, 185–186.

19. According to Ricciardi, the Lott family freed all but one of the family's enslaved laborers in the early nineteenth century and then hired them to work on the farm as paid laborers. Ricciardi, 49.

20. Sawyer, "Constructing the Tradition," 98–99.

21. Truth, *Narrative of Sojourner Truth*, 2. Archeologist Joe Diamond has worked on the Abraham Hasbrouck home in New Paltz, where he has found evidence that enslaved people lived in the basement of the home. Phone conversation, January 13, 2017.

22. Anne MacVicar Grant, *Memoirs of an American Lady, With Sketches of Manners and Scenery in America* (New York: D. Appleton, 1846), 38.

23. According to Abbott Lowell Cummings, some homes in Boston contained cellar kitchens due to a lack of lateral space in the city. Abbott Lowell Cummings, *The Framed Houses of Massachusetts Bay, 1625–1725* (Cambridge, MA: Belknap Press of Harvard University Press, 1979), 39. Many thanks to Christa Beranek for bringing this to my attention. Robert Blair St. George and Marla Miller show that lean-to additions to southern New England homes of the area's well-to-do families became the main places for domestic tasks such as food preparation. Robert Blair St. George, "'Set Thine House in Order': The Domestication of the Yeomanry in Seventeenth-Century New England," in *Common Places: Readings in American Vernacular Architecture*, ed. Dell Upton

and John Michael Vlach (Athens: University of Georgia Press, 1986), 355; Marla Miller, "Labor and Liberty in the Age of Refinement: Gender, Class, and the Built Environment," *Perspectives in Vernacular Architecture* 10 (2005): 15–31. Comparable architectural changes had also occurred in Europe. Some families in Amsterdam moved their kitchen to the back of the home or the basement as early as the sixteenth century to free the home from the "heat, bad smells, and smoke" that came from the kitchen. Ir. R. Meischke, H. J. Zantkuijl, W. Raue, and P.T.E.E. Rosenberg, *Huizen in Nederland: Amsterdam. Archtitectuurhistorische verkenningen aan de hand van het bezit van de Vereniging Hendrick de Keyser* (Zwolle: Waanders Uitgevers, 1995), 1:23. In the late seventeenth and early eighteenth centuries, well-to-do Amsterdam families often moved the kitchen to the basements of these homes to create more space in the main living areas, and eventually these basements and summer kitchens became the predominant areas of domestic labor. Meischke, Zantkuijl, and Rosenberg, *Huizen in Nederland: Amsterdam*, 1:72–73; Ir. R. Meischke, *Het Nederlandse Woonhuis van 1300–1800: Vijftig jaar Vereniging Hendrick de Keyser* (Haarlem: H. D. Tjeenk Willink & Soon N.V., 1969), 97. A similar shift took place in many seventeenth-century English homes where elite families began to relegate service activities to basements. By 1750, cooking and food preparations had been moved out of most of these homes' central halls to specialized kitchens in the back or basement, thus separating cooking and eating spaces. Matthew Johnson, *An Archeology of Capitalism* (Oxford: Blackwell, 1996), 143, 176.

24. Upton, "Vernacular Domestic Architecture," 320. Also see Kathleen M. Brown, *Good Wives, Nasty Wenches, and Anxious Patriarchs: Gender, Race, and Power in Colonial Virginia* (Chapel Hill: University of North Carolina Press, 1996), 250, 262–263.

25. Cary Carson, "Doing History with Material Culture," in *Material Culture and the Study of American Life*, ed. Ian M. G. Quimby (New York: W. W. Norton, 1978), 54. Larry McKee suggests that well into the eighteenth century "the typical domestic arrangement for slaves was a haphazard array of reused buildings, large, dormitory-style dwellings, and various kinds of unsettled quarters." Larry McKee, "The Ideals and Realities behind the Design and Use of 19th Century Virginia Slave Cabins," in *The Art and Mystery of Historical Archeology: Essays in Honor of James Deetz*, ed. Anne Elizabeth Yentsch and Mary C. Beaudry (Boca Raton, FL: CRC, 1992), 196–197.

26. Johnson, *Archeology of Capitalism*, 143. Also see Rhys Isaac, *The Transformation of Virginia, 1740–1790* (Chapel Hill: University of North Carolina Press, 1982), 72–74, 302–305.

27. Kenneth E. Lewis, "Plantation Layout and Function in the South Carolina Lowcountry," in *The Archeology of Slavery and Plantation Life*, ed. Theresa A. Singleton (San Diego, CA: Academic Press, 1985), 35–65, 38. Also see Stephen Hague, "Building Status in the British Atlantic World: The Gentleman's House in the English West Country and Pennsylvania," in *Building the British Atlantic World: Spaces, Places, and Material Culture, 1600–1850*, ed. Daniel Maudlin and Bernard L. Herman (Chapel Hill: University of North Carolina Press, 2016).

28. Bankoff and Winter, "Archeology of Slavery," 291; Dell Upton, "White and Black Landscapes in Eighteenth-Century Virginia," *Places* 2, no. 2 (1984): 64; Deborah Rothman, "Introduction," in *Shared Spaces and Divided Place: Material Dimensions of Gender Relations and the American Historical Landscape*, ed. Deborah Rothman and Ellen-Rose Savulis (Knoxville: University of Tennessee Press, 2003), 7. Others who have discussed this include Mark P. Leone, "Interpreting Ideology in Historical Archeology: Using

the Rules of Perspective in William Paca Garden in Annapolis, Maryland," in *Ideology, Power, and Prehistory*, ed. Daniel Miller and Christopher Tilley (Cambridge: Cambridge University Press, 1984); Johnson, *Archeology of Capitalism*, 149; Brown, *Good Wives*, 261; Epperson, "Race," 31.

29. *Heads of Families at the First Census of the United States taken in the Year 1790: New York*, 12.

30. References to the people enslaved by the Schuyler family can be found throughout his correspondence, the Philip Schuyler Papers at the New York Public Library. A runaway slave advertisement reveals that Claas, or Nicholas, fled Schuyler's Saratoga Estate in 1782. *New York Gazetteer* (Saratoga, NY), November 4, 1782.

31. John Jay to Schuyler, February 19, 1780, box 1, folder 6, 8, Schuyler Family Collection, SC19811, New York State Library.

32. John Jay to Schuyler, February 19, 1780, box 1, folder 6, 8, Schuyler Family Collection, SC19811, New York State Library.

33. "Schuyler Mansion," 18.

34. "Schuyler Mansion," 22, 27, 29. When the British tried to kidnap Schuyler in the evening of August 7, 1781, they entered the home through the outdoor kitchen, which according to at least one account had a passageway to the main house. George Clinton, *Public Papers of George Clinton: First Governor of New York, 1777–1795–1801–1804* (Albany: Oliver A. Quayle State Legislature Printer, 1904), 7: 184–185.

35. "Schuyler Mansion," 22, 29; Clinton, *Public Papers*, 7: 185.

36. "The Ten Broeck Mansion Existing Conditions Report" (Compiled for the Albany County Historical Association, 2015), 4.

37. "Ten Broeck Mansion," 83.

38. James Deetz, *Flowerdew Hundred: The Archeology of a Virginia Plantation* (Charlottesville: University Press of Virginia, 1993), 145. Vlach shows how nineteenth-century southern planters tended to hide their enslaved laborers' work and living areas unless their labor and living quarters appeared clean and organized. John Michael Vlach, "'Snug Li'l House with Flue and Oven': Nineteenth-Century Reforms in Plantation Slave Housing," in *Gender, Class, and Shelter: Perspectives in Vernacular Architecture, V* (Knoxville: University of Tennessee Press, 1995), 118–120. Also see Theresa A. Singleton, "Slavery and Spatial Dialectics on Cuban Coffee Plantations," *World Archeology* 33, no. 1 (2001): 102–103.

39. Architects' Emergency Committee, *Great Georgian Houses of America*, vol. 1 (New York: Dover, 1970), 25, 95–97.

40. Brown, *Good Wives*, 250, 262–263; Epperson, "Race," 32.

41. Foucault, *Discipline and Punish*, 195–230.

42. Delle, *Archeology of Social Space*, 159. In his study of Jamaica plantations, Louis Nelson found "the overseer's house at Good Hope had almost no capacity for surveillance over the slave village." Instead, surveillance focused on the plantation's work areas. Louis P. Nelson, *Architecture and Empire in Jamaica* (New Haven, CT: Yale University Press, 2016), 124.

43. Epperson, "Panopticon Plantations," 58–77.

44. Singleton, "Slavery," 106.

45. Lincoln, Johnson, and Northrup, *Colonial Laws of New York*, 1:631; Jessica Kross, *The Evolution of an American Town: Newtown, New York, 1642–1775* (Philadelphia: Temple University Press, 1983), 156, 176; Hodges, *Root & Branch*, 64.

46. For more on the 1741 Slave Conspiracy, see Daniel Horsmanden, *The New York Conspiracy* (Boston: Beacon, 1971); Rucker, *River Flows On*, 59–90; Lepore, *New York Burning*; Linebaugh and Rediker, *Many-Headed Hydra*, 174–210.

47. Minutes, February 2, 1715, GLC3107.01103, Gilder Lehrman Collection; A. J. Williams-Meyers, "Re-examining Slavery in New York," *New York Archives* 1, no. 3 (Winter 2002): 15–18. Nicole Maskiell discusses this case in greater detail in her dissertation and in her forthcoming manuscript. She points out that Dijkemans survived the attack. Maskiell, "Bound by Bondage," 56; Accusation, April 1730, Justices Court, H box no. 4, Ulster County Clerk, Archives Division; Kenneth Scott, "Ulster County, New York, Court Records, 1693–1775," *National Genealogical Society Quarterly* 61, no. 1 (1973): 62.

48. N.d., Isaac Cortelyou family notebook, 1974.137, Brooklyn Historical Society (BHS).

49. Bankoff, Ricciardi, and Loorya, "Remembering Africa," 40.

50. Roderic H. Blackburn, *Dutch Colonial Homes in America* (New York: Rizzoli International Publications, 2002), 162.

51. Strickland, *Journal of a Tour in the United States of America*, 119.

52. Truth, *Narrative of Sojourner Truth*, 3.

53. Hardesty, *Unfreedom*, 74.

54. The examination of Bet a Negro Female Slave of Philip S. Van Rensselaer Esquire taken the 28th day of November 1793, 2–3, NYSL.

55. Delle, *Archeology of Social Space*, 161–163.

56. Epperson, "Race," 34.

57. Epperson, 34; Singleton, "Slavery," 108. Also see Patricia Samford, "The Archeology of African-American Slavery and Material Culture," *William and Mary Quarterly* 53, no. 1 (January 1996): 100, https://doi.org/10.2307/2946825; Warren R. DeBoer, "Subterranean Storage and the Organization of Surplus: The View from Eastern North America," *Southeastern Archeology* 7 (1988): 1–20.

58. Bankoff, Ricciardi, and Loorya, "Remembering Africa," 36–40; Ricciardi, *Changing through the Century*, 188–189.

59. Mark P. Leone and Gladys-Marie Fry, "Conjuring in the Big House Kitchen: An Interpretation of African American Belief Systems Based on the Uses of Archaeology and Folklore Sources," *Journal of American Folklore* 112, no. 445 (1999): 377; Diana diZerega Wall, "Twenty Years After: Re-examining Archeological Collection for Evidence of New York City's Colonial African Past," *African Diaspora Archeology Newsletter* 7, no. 2 (April 2000): 2.

60. Walter Richard Wheeler, "Magical Dwelling: Apotropaic Building Practices in the New World Dutch Cultural Hearth," in *Religion, Cults & Rituals in the Medieval Rural Environment, Ruralia XI*, ed. C. Bis-Worch and C. Theune (Leiden: Sidestone Press, 2017), 389–390.

61. Laurie Wilkie, "Secret and Sacred: Contextualizing the Artifacts of African-American Magic in Religion," *Historical Archeology* 31, no. 4 (1997): 89–90; Robert Farris Thompson, *Flash of the Spirit* (New York: Vintage Books, 1984), 129–131; James Sweet, *Recreating Africa: Culture, Kinship, and Religion in the African-Portuguese World, 1441–1770* (Chapel Hill: University of North Carolina Press, 2003), 179–185; Laurie Wilkie, "Magic and Empowerment on the Plantation: An Archeological Consideration of African-American Worldview," *Southeastern Archeology* 14, no. 2 (1995): 145;

Samford, "Archeology," 107–109. For more about the *minkisi*, see Wyatt MacGaffey, *Religion and Society in Central Africa: The BaKongo of Lower Zaire* (Chicago: University of Chicago Press, 1986); Jason R. Young, *Rituals of Resistance: African Atlantic Religion in Kongo and the Lowcountry South in the Era of Slavery* (Baton Rouge: Louisiana State University, 2007), 105–145; Michael Gomez, *Exchanging Our Country Marks: The Transformation of African Identities in the Colonial and Antebellum South* (Chapel Hill: University of North Carolina Press, 1998), 43–45; Rucker, *River Flows On*, 35–37 and 164–167; Carolyn E. Fick, *The Making of Haiti: Saint Domingue Revolution from Below* (Knoxville: University of Tennessee Press, 1990), 57–58. In his description of the seventeenth-century Senegambia, Jean Barbot claimed that "one grigri will save them from drowning at sea, and another from being killed in war; another again will give a woman a safe childbirth, another will prevent fires, another heal fevers, and so on." Barbot, *Barbot on Guinea*, 1:85–86.

62. Patricia Samford has argued that these items would be most effective when buried in the dirt. She explains that among the Igbo, for example, "earth is one of the most important sacred places." Other scholars have pointed out that even though that may have been more common practice variety exists. For example, similar bags have been hidden below floorboards. It is possible that enslaved people adjusted these practices to their circumstances: if their living quarters only had floorboards, as would be the case in garret spaces, they would likely have used these. Patricia Samford, *Subfloor Pits and the Archeology of Slavery in Colonial Virginia* (Tuscaloosa: University of Alabama Press, 2007), 181; Young, *Rituals of Resistance*, 125–127; Wheeler, "Magical Dwelling," 389; Matthew Kirk, "Out of the Ashes of Craft, the Fires of Consumerism: A 1797 Deposit in Downtown Albany," in *People, Places, and Material Things: Historical Archeology of Albany, New York*, ed. Charles L. Fisher (Albany: New York State Museum, 2003), 53.

63. Wheeler, "Magical Dwelling," 381.

64. Wheeler, 391.

65. Joseph points out that "both the X and cross-in-circle marks have European as well as African contexts and meanings." J. W. Joseph, "'. . . All of Cross'—African Potters, Marks, and Meanings in the Folk Pottery of Edgefield District, South Carolina," *Historical Archeology* 45, no. 2 (2011): 134, 149.

66. Archeologists also found what appears to be a *dikenga* carved on the northeast side of a hearth, located in the basement where enslaved laborers lived in present-day Germantown, NY. Christopher Lindner, "West African Cosmogram Recognized adjacent to Probably Hearth Concealment at 19th-century Slave Quarter in mid-Hudson Valley Settlement of early German Americans," *SHA Newsletter: Quarterly News on Historical Archeology from around the Globe* 49, no. 1 (Spring 2016): 28–30.

67. Thompson, *Flash of the Spirit*, 109; Leland Ferguson, *Uncommon Ground: Archeology and Early African America, 1650–1800* (Washington, DC: Smithsonian Institution Press, 1992), 110; Fromont, *Art of Conversion*, 76, 150; Leone and Fry, "Conjuring in the Big House Kitchen," 377; Wall, "Twenty Years After," 1. See chap. 6 for a more detailed discussion on the religious meaning of these items.

68. Marla Miller similarly shows that domestic workers in New England gained some autonomy when their workspaces were segregated from the main living areas of the rural New England gentry homes. Miller, "Labor and Liberty," 15–31.

69. Sibley notes that the home is not often seen as a space of exclusion. David Sibley, *Geographies of Exclusion: Society and Difference in the West* (London: Routledge,

1995), 91–92. Elizabeth Maddock Dillon's analysis of Olaudah Equiano's narrative shows how the meaning of spaces changes. Dillon, "Sea of Texts," 38–39.

70. Stoler, *Carnal Knowledge and Imperial Power*, 183.

71. Peter Lowe to unidentified friend, 1788, Reverend Peter Lowe Correspondence, 1782–1818, ArMs 1974.008, BHS. Also see Andrea Mosterman, "'I Thought They Were Worthy': A Dutch Reformed Church Minister and His Congregation Debate African American Membership in the Church," *Early American Studies* 14, no. 3 (Summer 2016): 610–616.

72. Maria Louw to Peter Louw, July 6, 1786, Misc. Mss. Peter Lowe, New-York Historical Society (N-YHS); *U.S. Census, 1790: Heads of Families*, 172. See chap. 6 for more about Peter Lowe.

73. Grant, *Memoirs of an American Lady*, 58.

74. Lisa Anderson, "Update on the Schuyler Flatts Burial Ground," *Legacy: The Magazine of the New York State Museum* 5, no. 1 (Summer 2009): 9; Esther J. Lee et al., "MtDNA Origins of an Enslaved Labor Force from the 18th Century Schuyler Flatts Burial Ground in Colonial Albany, NY: Africans, Native Americans, and Malagasy?," *Journal of Archeological Science* 36 (2009): 2805–2810, https://doi.org/10.1016/j.jas.2009.09.008.

75. Prince to Mrs. Schuyler, 1776, Schuyler Family Slavery Records (copies), Schuyler Mansion.

76. Marisa Fuentes has shown how such scars can be used to learn about the people. Fuentes, *Dispossessed Lives*, 14.

77. Stessin-Cohn and Hurlburt-Biagini, *In Defiance*, 74.

78. Stessin-Cohn and Hurlburt-Biagini, 197.

79. Stessin-Cohn and Hurlburt-Biagini, 48.

80. Clinton, "'Southern Dishonor,'" 54.

81. Van Laer, *Minutes of the Court of Albany, Rensselaerswijck, and Schenectady*, 1:254; Sullivan, *Punishment*, f. 319.

82. Grant, *Memoirs of an American Lady*, 36.

83. Several scholars have discussed these silences in the archives. See, for instance, Hartman, "Venus in Two Acts," 1–14; Fuentes, *Dispossessed Lives*.

84. Block, "Lines of Color," 142.

85. Harriet Jacobs, *Incidents in the Life of a Slave Girl* (Garden City, NY: Dover Publications, 2001). Amanda Flather describes similar circumstances for female servants in England. Amanda Flather, "Gender, Space and Place: The Experience of Servants in Rural Households 1550–1750," *Mundo Agragrio* 18, no. 39 (December 2017): 171–188. Also see Terri Snyder, *Brabbling Women: Disorderly Speech and the Law in Early Virginia* (Ithaca, NY: Cornell University Press, 2003), 45–66.

86. For more about enslaved women and sexuality, see Washington, "'From Motives of Delicacy,'" 57–73.

87. Block, "Lines of Color," 142.

88. Marisa Fuentes provides an important discussion of enslaved women and the violence enacted upon them. She also explains the challenges of discussing enslaved women's agency when researching their sexual relations with free, white men. Fuentes, *Dispossessed Lives*, 9–11.

89. Grant, *Memoirs of an American Lady*, 58.

90. Truth, *Narrative of Sojourner Truth*, 7–8.

91. Gerardus Duyckinck to Henry Van Rensselaer, April 29, 1738, Van Rensselaer Miscellaneous Papers, I/3/9, HL80-30, AIHA.

92. Slave Bill of Sale, September 2, 1752, Van Schaick Family Papers, SC10837, NYSL.

93. Slave Bill of Sale (formerly folder 1815), Seaman Family Papers, 19.74.005, BHS. For more on the trade of enslaved people in the nineteenth century, see, among others, Walter Johnson, *Soul by Soul: Life Inside the Antebellum Slave Market* (Cambridge, MA: Harvard University Press, 1999); Daina Ramey Berry, *The Price for Their Pound of Flesh: The Value of the Enslaved, from Womb to Grave, in the Building of a Nation* (Boston: Beacon, 2017); Edward E. Baptist, *The Half Has Never Been Told: Slavery and the Making of American Capitalism* (New York: Basic Books, 2014).

94. Grant, *Memoirs of an American Lady*, 18.

95. Gustave Anjou, ed., *Ulster County, N.Y. Probate Records in the Office of the Surrogate, and in the County Clerk's Office At Kingston, N.Y.: A Careful Abstract and Translation of the Dutch and English Wills* (Rhinebeck, NY: Palatine Transcripts, 1980): 1:106–110.

96. Anjou, 2:89.

97. Anjou, 2:15.

98. Will of Nikus Jans, December 19, 1712, GLC 3107.00947, GLC.

99. For more on motherhood, mothering, and slavery, see Wilkie, *Archeology of Mothering*, 49–78; Sasha Turner, "The Nameless and the Forgotten: Maternal Grief, Sacred Protection, and the Archive of Slavery," *Slavery & Abolition* 38, no. 2 (2017): 232–250, https://doi.org/10.1080/0144039X.2017.1316962; Sasha Turner, *Contested Bodies: Pregnancy, Childrearing, and Slavery in Jamaica* (Philadelphia: University of Pennsylvania Press, 2017).

100. O'Callaghan, *Census of Slaves, 1755.*

101. R. Bleecker to John Elmendorp, November 27, 1773, box 6, folder 4, Kingston Collection, CV10181, NYSL.

102. Truth, *Narrative of Sojourner Truth*, 15.

103. Stessin-Cohn and Hurlburt-Biagini, *In Defiance*, 48.

104. Stessin-Cohn and Hurlburt-Biagini, 286, 290.

105. Stessin-Cohn and Hurlburt-Biagini, 120.

106. Stessin-Cohn and Hurlburt-Biagini, 190.

107. Stessin-Cohn and Hurlburt-Biagini, 130.

108. Bett and the children lived in Albany while Bill resided in Troy. Their enslavers suspected that they had fled to Massachusetts together. Stessin-Cohn and Hurlburt-Biagini, 127.

109. Stessin-Cohn and Hurlburt-Biagini, 178.

110. Runaway Slave Advertisement, *New York Evening Post*, October 8, 1808.

111. Frederick Douglass, *Narrative of the Life of Frederick Douglass, an American Slave* (Boston: Published at the Anti-Slavery Office, 1845), 28. Larry McKee has used archeological evidence to show that enslaved Africans on southern plantations had little to no emotional attachment to the places in which they lived. McKee, "Ideals and Realities," 207.

5. Slavery and Social Power in Dutch Reformed Churches

1. Will of David Johnston, 1809, 2, Historic Huguenot Street [copy; original is located at the Dutchess County Surrogate's Office]; Russell Gasero, *Historical Directory of the Reformed Church in America* (Grand Rapids, MI: Wm. B. Eerdmans, 2001), 280; letter to the Rev. Particular, Synod of Albany, concerning "The Memorial of Ann Bevier and Rachel Westbrook, members of the Reformed Protestant Dutch Church of Rochester," 1823, Philip Dubois Bevier Family Papers (1685–1910), Historic Huguenot Street.

2. Dirk Mouw discusses that a Dutch Reformed Church minister had significant power not just in the church but in the community at large. Dirk Edward Mouw, *"Moederkerk* and *Vaderland*: Religion and Ethnic Identity in the Middle Colonies, 1690–1772" (PhD diss., University of Iowa, 2009), 155–156. Gerald De Jong describes the ritual of the minister climbing the steps of the elevated pulpit. De Jong, *Dutch Reformed Church*, 131.

3. Letter to the Rev. Particular, Synod of Albany, concerning "The Memorial of Ann Bevier and Rachel Westbrook, members of the Reformed Protestant Dutch Church of Rochester," 1823, Philip Dubois Bevier Family Papers (1685–1910), Historic Huguenot Street.

4. Minutes, April 7, 1823, Classis Ulster, 1:419, ARCA.

5. For more on religious pluralism in early New York, see Patricia Bonomi, *Under the Cope of Heaven: Religion, Society, and Politics in Colonial America* (Oxford: Oxford University Press, 1986); Kyle T. Bulthuis, *Four Steeples over the City Streets: Religion and Society in New York's Early Republic Congregations* (New York: New York University Press, 2014); Bonomi, "'Swarms of Negroes'"; Goodfriend, *Before the Melting Pot*.

6. In fact, Kingston church members requested that the church hire a Dutch-speaking minister for Dutch sermons as late as 1811. Consistory Minutes 1795–1841, October 14, 1811; November 27, 1811; December 9, 1811; January 1812; June 20, 1812; July 3, 1812; Kingston Church Records, Ulster County Clerk, Archives Division. Also see Randall H. Balmar, *A Perfect Babel of Confusion: Dutch Religion and English Culture in the Middle Colonies* (New York: Oxford University Press, 1989); Goodfriend, *Before the Melting Pot*; De Jong, *Dutch Reformed Church*; Hackett, *Rude Hand of Innovation*.

7. For a more detailed discussion of the church's institutional organization, see Mouw, *"Moederkerk* and *Vaderland*," 163–172.

8. Bonomi notes the important social and political function of colonial churches: "Churches in both country and town were vital centers of community life, as government proclamations were broadcast from the pulpit and news of prices and politics was exchanged in the churchyard." Bonomi, *Under the Cope of Heaven*, 88. Also see Joyce D. Goodfriend, "The Social Dimensions of Congregational Life in Colonial New York City," *William and Mary Quarterly* 46, no. 2 (April 1989): 252–278, https://doi.org/10.2307/1920254; David D. Hall, *Worlds of Wonder, Days of Judgment: Popular Religious Belief in Early New England* (Cambridge, MA: Harvard University Press, 1990), 165; Beasley, *Christian Ritual*, 10; Isaac, *Transformation of Virginia*, 120.

9. As David Hall explains, "the everyday meaning of religion thus involved the social experience of withdrawing from one kind of community and uniting with another." Hall, *Worlds of Wonder, Days of Judgment*, 117–118. Also see Olwell, *Masters, Slaves, and Subjects*, 107–108.

10. For discussions of social power and church life, see, Olwell, *Masters, Slaves, and Subjects*; Frances E. Dolan, "Gender and the 'Lost' Spaces of Catholicism," *Journal of Interdisciplinary History* 32, no. 4 (Spring 2002): 641–665; Isaac, *Transformation of Virginia*; Beasley, *Christian Ritual*; Andrew Spicer and Sarah Hamilton, eds., *Defining the Holy: Sacred Space in Medieval and Early Modern Europe* (Burlington, VT: Ashgate, 2005); Gretchen Townsend Buggeln, *Temples of Grace: The Material Transformation of Connecticut's Churches, 1790–1840* (Hanover, NH: University Press of New England, 2003); Andrew Spicer, *Calvinist Churches in Early Modern Europe* (Manchester: Manchester University Press, 2007); Will Coster and Andrew Spicer, eds., *Sacred Space in Early Modern Europe* (Cambridge: Cambridge University Press, 2005); Jeanne Halgren Kilde, *Sacred Power, Sacred Space: An Introduction to Christian Architecture and Worship* (Oxford: Oxford University Press, 2008); Peter Benes, "The New England Meetinghouse: An Atlantic Perspective," in *Building the British Atlantic World: Spaces, Places, and Material Culture*, ed. Daniel Maudlin and Bernard L. Herman (Chapel Hill: University of North Carolina Press, 2016), 119–120; Peter Benes and Philip D. Zimmerman, *New England Meeting House and Church: 1630–1850; A Loan Exhibition Held at the Currier Gallery of Art, Manchester, New Hampshire* (Boston: Boston University Scholarly Publications, 1979).

11. See, among others, Katharine Gerbner, *Christian Slavery: Conversion and Race in the Protestant Atlantic World* (Philadelphia: University of Pennsylvania Press, 2019), 25–28; Bonomi, "'Swarms of Negroes'"; D. L. Noorlander, *Heaven's Wrath: The Protestant Reformation and the Dutch West India Company in the Atlantic World* (Ithaca, NY: Cornell University Press, 2019), 166–191; Joosse, *Geloof in de Nieuwe Wereld*; Frijhoff, *Wegen van Evert Willemsz*, 765–794; Frans Leonard Schalkwijk, *The Reformed Church in Dutch Brazil, 1630–1654* (Zoetermeer: Boekencentrum, 1998). Gerald De Jong discusses some of the more practical aspects of having enslaved people in the church. De Jong, *Dutch Reformed Church*, chap. ix; De Jong, "Dutch Reformed Church," 423–436.

12. Mircea Eliade, *The Sacred and the Profane: The Nature of Religion*, trans. Willard R. Trask (Boston: Mariner Books, 1968); Coster and Spicer, *Sacred Space*; Spicer and Hamilton, *Defining the Holy*; James P. Walsh, "Holy Time and Sacred Space in Puritan New England," *American Quarterly* 32, no. 1 (Spring 1980): 79–95, https://doi.org/10.2307/2712497; Anthony Garvan, "The Protestant Plain Style before 1630," *Journal of the Society of Architectural Historians* 9, no. 2 (October 1950): 4–13, https://doi.org/10.2307/987455; Kevin M. Sweeney, "Meetinghouses, Town Houses, and Churches: Changing Perceptions of Sacred and Secular Space in Southern New England, 1720–1850," *Winterthur Portfolio* 28, no.1 (Spring 1993): 59–93; Buggeln, *Temples of Grace*; Spicer, *Calvinist Churches*; Isaac, *Transformation of Virginia*.

13. Hall, *Worlds of Wonder, Days of Judgment*.

14. Dell Upton, *Holy Things and Profane: Anglican Parish Churches in Colonial Virginia* (New Haven, CT: Yale University Press, 1997); Isaac, *Transformation of Virginia*; Beasley, *Christian Ritual*; Spicer and Hamilton, *Defining the Holy*; Buggeln, *Temples of Grace*; Spicer, *Calvinist Churches*; Coster and Spicer, *Sacred Space*; Kilde, *Sacred Power, Sacred Space*; Benes, "New England Meetinghouse," 119–120; Louis P. Nelson, *The Beauty of Holiness: Anglicanism and Architecture in Colonial South Carolina* (Chapel Hill: University of North Carolina Press, 2008).

15. For more about slavery, race, and Protestant Christianity in the Americas, see, among others, Heather Miyano Koppelson, *Faithful Bodies: Performing Religion and Race in the Puritan Atlantic* (New York: New York University Press, 2014); Rebecca Anne Goetz,

The Baptism of Early Virginia: How Christianity Created Race (Baltimore: Johns Hopkins University Press, 2012); Gerbner, *Christian Slavery*; Jon F. Sensbach, *Rebecca's Revival: Creating Black Christianity in the Atlantic World* (Cambridge, MA: Harvard University Press, 2005); Jon J. Sensbach, *A Separate Canaan: The Making of an Afro-Moravian World in North Carolina, 1763–1840* (Chapel Hill: University of North Carolina Press, 1998); Bonomi, "'Swarms of Negroes'"; Richard J. Boles, "Dividing the Faith: The Rise of Racially Segregated Northern Churches, 1730–1850" (PhD diss., George Washington University, 2013); Olwell, *Masters, Slaves, and Subjects*, chap. 3.

16. See De Jong, *Dutch Reformed Church*, 164; Hodges, *Root & Branch*, 22–24; Foote, *Black and White Manhattan*, 49; Goodfriend, *Before the Melting Pot*, 125–126; Frijhoff and J. Jacobs, "Dutch, New Netherland, and Thereafter," 46; Graham Russell Hodges, "The Pastor and the Prostitute: Sexual Power among Africans and Germans in Colonial New York," in *Sex, Love, Race: Crossing Boundaries in North American History*, ed. Martha Hodes (New York: New York University Press, 1999), 63; Washington, *Sojourner Truth's America*, 19.

17. Kilde, *Sacred Power, Sacred Space*, 117.

18. William Durell, ed., *The Constitution of the Reformed Dutch Church in the United States of America* (New York: William Durell, 1793), 78.

19. Robert S. Alexander, *Albany's First Church and Its Role in the Growth of the City* (Delmar, NY: Newgraphics Printers, 1988), 56.

20. Consistory Minutes, 1704, Kingston Reformed Churchbook, vol. 2, Ulster County Clerk, Archives Division.

21. Alexander, *Albany's First Church*, 56.

22. Nicholas Beasley observed that marriage and baptism in colonial Anglican churches could advance the social positions of free and enslaved Africans and African descendants. Beasley, *Christian Ritual*, 79–80. Also see Hardesty, *Unfreedom*, 160–161; Gerbner, *Christian Slavery*, 22–28.

23. Selijns to the Classis Amsterdam, June 9, 1664, Amsterdam Correspondence, nr. 46, ARCA.

24. See chap. 2.

25. Baptismal Records, September 5, 1703, Churchbook/Volume 2 of the Kingston Dutch Reformed Church, 67, Ulster County Clerk, Archives Division; Roswell Randall Hoes, ed. and trans., *Baptismal and Marriage Registers of the Dutch Church of Kingston, Ulster County, New York, 1660–1809* (Baltimore: Genealogical Publishing Co., 1980), 70.

26. Lincoln, Johnson, and Northrup, *Colonial Laws of New York from the year 1664 to the Revolution*, 1:598. Beasley discusses how similar concerns caused English colonists to be hesitant about baptizing their enslaved laborers. Beasley, *Christian Ritual*, 80, 84–108.

27. Hoes, *Baptismal and Marriage Registers*, 351.

28. Together with his colleague Martinus Schoonmaker, Lowe rotated between the Collegiate Churches of Kings County, and eventually he became responsible for the English services at these churches. In 1808, he accepted a call from the Flatbush and Flatlands churches, where he stayed until his death in June of 1818 at the age of fifty-four. From 1805 to 1818, Lowe also served as the principal of the Erasmus Hall Academy in Brooklyn. De Jong, *Reformed Church*, 224; Thomas M. Strong, *The History of the Town Flatbush in Kings County, Long Island* (New York: T. R. Mercein, Jr., printer, 1842), 94; Gasero, *Historical Directory of the Reformed Church in America*, 241.

29. It appears the letter remained unsent. The letter does not detail whether these men were free or enslaved, but considering the congregants' objections and Kings County's demographics at the time of their request, these men were most likely enslaved. Peter Lowe to unidentified friend, 1788, Reverend Peter Lowe Correspondence, 1782–1818, ArMs 1974.008, BHS.

30. Peter Lowe to unidentified friend, 1788, Reverend Peter Lowe Correspondence, 1782–1818, ArMs 1974.008, BHS.

31. Peter Lowe to unidentified friend, 1788, Reverend Peter Lowe Correspondence, 1782–1818, ArMs 1974.008, BHS.

32. David D. Demarest, *The Reformed Church in America: Its origin, development and characteristics* (New York: Board of Publication of the Reformed Church in America, 1889), 181.

33. Peter Lowe to unidentified friend, 1788, Reverend Peter Lowe Correspondence, 1782–1818, ArMs 1974.008, BHS.

34. Peter Lowe to unidentified friend, 1788, Reverend Peter Lowe Correspondence, 1782–1818, ArMs 1974.008, BHS.

35. Both Lowe and his colleague Martinus Schoonmaker held people in bondage, as had been common among Dutch Reformed Church ministers. At the time of the 1790 census, Lowe included two enslaved people as part of his household and Schoonmaker held one person in bondage. *Heads of Families at the First Census of the United States taken in the Year 1790: New York*, 97; Advertisement, *Republican Watch-Tower*, August 20, 1800.

36. Peter Lowe to unidentified friend, 1788, Reverend Peter Lowe Correspondence, 1782–1818, ArMs 1974.008, BHS.

37. Ryan Hanley, "Calvinism, Proslavery and James Albert Ukawsaw Gronniosaw," *Slavery & Abolition* 36, no. 2 (2015): 362, https://doi.org/10.1080/0144039X.2014.920973.

38. Jacobus Elisa Johannes Capitein, *The Agony of Asar: A Thesis on Slavery by the Former Slave, Jacobus Elisa Johannes Capitein, 1717–1747*, ed. and trans. Grant Parker (Princeton, NJ: Markus Wiener, 1999).

39. Edward T. Corwin, trans. and ed., *Ecclesiastical Records: State of New York* (Albany: J. B. Lyon, state printer, 1901), 4:3109.

40. Peter Lowe to unidentified friend, 1788, Reverend Peter Lowe Correspondence, 1782–1818, ArMs 1974.008, BHS. Other denominations also professed that Christianity would make enslaved people better servants. See, for instance, Olwell, *Masters, Slaves, and Subjects*, 103–139.

41. Consideratie des E. Classis van Amsteldam, Archief van de Classis Amsterdam van de Nederlandse Hervormde Kerk (access no. 379), inventory no. 160, 6–8, SAA; Extra Ord. Classis, November 5, 1743, Classis Amsterdam van de Nederlandse Hervormde Kerk (access number 379), inventory no. 159, 589–592, SAA.

42. Classis ordinaria, April 12, 1779, Archief Classis Asd (379), inventory no. 161, 231–235, SAA.

43. Extra Ord. Classis, November 5, 1743, Classis Amsterdam van de Nederlandse Hervormde Kerk (accessnumber 379), inventory no. 159, 589–592, SAA; Extract from letter Henr. Muller to Classis, June 15, 1775, Archief Classis Asd (379), inventory no. 166, 502–505, SAA; Henricus Muller to the Classis Amsterdam, March 10, 1779, Archief Classis Asd (379), inventory no. 166, 604, SAA.

44. Peter Lowe to unidentified friend, 1788, Reverend Peter Lowe Correspondence, 1782–1818, ArMs 1974.008, BHS.

45. E. T. Corwin, ed., *A Digest of Constitutional and Synodical Legislation of the Reformed Church in America: Formerly the Ref. Prot. Dutch Church* (New York: Board of Publication of the Reformed Church in America, 1906), 679–680, ARCA.

46. Corwin, *Digest*, 680, ARCA.

47. Sypher, *Liber A of the Collegiate Churches of New York*, part 2. These black families include the Bastiaenszen, Luykasse, Dee, Salomons, and Pouwelse families. Also see Goodfriend, *Before the Melting Pot*, 116.

48. Thomas Grier Evans, ed., *Records of the Reformed Dutch Church in New Amsterdam and New York: Baptisms from 25 December, 1639, To 27 December, 1730* (New York: Printed for the Society, 1901), 329, 351.

49. Louis Duermeyer, ed., *Records of the Reformed Dutch Church of Albany, New York, 1683–1809* (Baltimore: Genealogical Publishing Co., 1978), 1:52, 55, 56, 58, 67, 68, 71, 80, 110; 2:17, 22, 29, 32, 61, 70; 3: 14, 45, 55. Also see Mouw, "*Moederkerk* and *Vaderland*, 99; Maskiell, "Bound by Bondage," 207–210.

50. List of Members, December 21, 1750, Kingston Church Records, 3:319, Ulster County Clerk, Archives Division; Hoes, *Baptismal and Marriage Registers*, 70, 17, 307.

51. First Book of Records of the Dutch Reformed Church at Caughnawaga, Fonda, NY, 158, ARCA.

52. See, for example, the Kingston consistory minutes: Consistory Minutes, April 3, 1739, Kingston Church book, vol. 2, Ulster County Clerk, Archives Division; Consistory Minutes, October 7, 1789, Kingston Church book, 3:438, Ulster County Clerk, Archives Division.

53. Mouw, "*Moederkerk* and *Vaderland*," 97.

54. Not only Dutch Reformed Church congregants proved reluctant to admit enslaved men and women to their church. Nelson discusses similar hesitancies in the eighteenth-century Anglican Church. Nelson, *Beauty of Holiness*, 178–179.

55. *The Acts and Proceedings of the General Synod, of the Reformed Dutch Church, in North America at New York, June 1816* (Albany: Websters and Skinners, 1816), 18–19, ARCA.

56. Firth Haring Fabend, *Zion on the Hudson: Dutch New York and New Jersey in the Age of Revivals* (New Brunswick, NJ: Rutgers University Press, 2000), 39; Minutes of the Particular Synod of New-York, October 1826, 12, Flatbush Reformed Church Collection, located at the Flatbush Church.

57. Olwell provides an interesting discussion on the meaning of accepting enslaved people in communion. Olwell, *Masters, Slaves, and Subjects*, 115–139.

58. Gerald De Jong discusses communion in North America's Dutch Reformed Church. De Jong, *Dutch Reformed Church*, 134–135. As is evident from Nelson's study of South Carolina's Anglican churches, slavery and social hierarchy did not necessarily prohibit sharing communion with enslaved men and women. He found that in these churches black and white communicants usually had the Lord's Supper together, even when these black congregants were enslaved by the white men or women with whom they shared this meal. Nelson, *Beauty of Holiness*, 179, 200.

59. Peter Lowe to unidentified friend, 1788, Reverend Peter Lowe Correspondence, 1782–1818, ArMs 1974.008, BHS.

60. Kilde, *Sacred Power, Sacred Space*, 112.

61. Joyce Goodfriend, "The Social and Cultural Life of Dutch Settlers, 1664–1776," in *Four Centuries of Dutch-American Relations, 1609–2009*, ed. Hans Krabbendam, Cornelis A. van Minnen, and Giles Scott-Smith (Albany: State University of New York Press, 2009), 124.

62. Extra Ord. Classis, November 5, 1743, Classis Amsterdam van de Nederlandse Hervormde Kerk (access no. 379), inventory no. 159, 589–592, SAA; Extract from letter, Henr. Muller to Classis, June 15, 1775, Archief Classis Asd (379), inventory no. 166, 502–505, SAA; Henricus Muller to the Classis Amsterdam, March 10, 1779, Archief Classis Asd (379), inventory no. 166, 604, SAA.

63. Classis of Ulster meeting, October 19, 1814, Classis Ulster, 1:309, 313, 317, 419–425, ARCA.

64. Minutes, April 7, 1823, Classis Ulster, 1:419–425, ARCA.

65. *The Acts and Proceedings of the General Synod of the Reformed Dutch Church, in North America at Albany, June 1823* (New York: Abraham Paul, 1823), 47–48, ARCA.

66. *The Acts and Proceedings of the particular Synod of Albany, Convened in the city of Albany, May 19, 1824* (Albany: Printed at the office of the Daily Advertiser, 1824), 7, ARCA.

67. Gasero, *Historical Directory*, 688. Susan Stessin-Cohn and Rose Rudnitski are currently working on a biography and documentary about James Murphy. In an interview, Stessin-Cohn suggests that his background would eventually catch up with him. Lynn Woods, "A Pastor's Double Life Unearthed," Hudson Valley online, accessed June 6, 2019, https://hudsonvalleyone.com/2013/05/05/the-mystery-of-james-murphy/.

68. Examination of Students, 1822, Minutes of the Classis of New York, 5:95–96, ARCA.

69. Minutes, April 1823, Minutes of the Classis of New York, 5:111–112, ARCA.

70. Examination of Students, May 26, 1823, Minutes of the Classis of New York, 5:119, ARCA; Grievances, October 1823, Minutes of the Classis of New York, 5:134, ARCA.

71. Samuel Cornish still did not give up on his objections. Minutes of the Classis of New York, 5:122, 134, 205–207, ARCA.

72. *Inventory of the Church Archives in New York City: Reformed Church in America* (New York: Historical Records Survey, 1939), 43.

73. Hodges, *Root & Branch*, 214.

74. Kilde, *Sacred Power, Sacred Space*, 3, 9.

75. Coster and Spicer explain that in European churches, seating "was sometimes used to separate men from women, the young from the old, but most frequently it reflected the hierarchical social structure of early modern society." Will Coster and Andrew Spicer, "Introduction: Dimensions of Sacred Space," in *Sacred Space in Early Modern Europe*, ed. Will Coster and Andrew Spicer, *Sacred Spaces in Early Modern Europe* (Cambridge: Cambridge University Press, 2005), 9. Louis Nelson points out in his work that Anglican churches in the eighteenth-century British colonies often had "differentiated entrances, honorific seating, internal burials, elite wall memorials." Nelson, *Beauty of Holiness*, 277. Beasley discusses seating in Anglican churches in British slave societies: "Applicants for seats in newly pewed spaces desired to be able to see and hear the officiating minister above all but also desired seats that reflected their understanding of their proper place in the parish hierarchy, especially as revealed by one's ability to pay." Beasley, *Christian Ritual*, 27. Also see Isaac, *Transformation of Virginia*, 64–65.

76. Derek A. Rivard, *Blessing the World: Ritual and Lay Piety in Medieval Religion* (Washington, DC: Catholic University of America Press, 2011), 45–46; Christian Grosse, "Places

of Sanctification: The Liturgical Sacrality of Genevan Reformed Churches," in *Sacred Space in Early Modern Europe*, ed. Andrew Spicer and Will Coster (Cambridge: Cambridge University Press, 2005), 73; Henk van Nierop, "Sacred Space Contested: Amsterdam in the Age of the Reformation," in *The Power of Space in Late Medieval and Early Modern Europe: The Cities of Italy, Northern France, and the Low Countries*, ed. Marc Boone and Martha Howell (Turnhout, Belium: Brepols, 2013), 154–155, 157; Walsh, "Holy Time," 79.

77. Coster and Spicer, "Introduction," 4; Buggeln, *Temples of Grace*, 44.

78. Sarah Hamilton and Andrew Spicer, "Defining the Holy: The Delineation of Sacred Space," in *Defining the Holy: Sacred Space in Medieval and Early Modern Europe*, ed. Sarah Hamilton and Andrew Spicer (New York: Ashgate, 2005), 19; Van Nierop, "Sacred Space Contested," 154–155; Coster and Spicer, "Introduction," 5; Walsh, "Holy Time," 90.

79. Frijhoff, *Wegen van Evert Willemsz*, 589.

80. Spicer, *Calvinist Churches*; T. S. Doolittle, "The Architecture of the Reformed Church," in *A manual of the Reformed Church in America: formerly Ref. Prot. Dutch Church, 1628–1902*, ed. Edward Tanjore Corwin (New York: Reformed Church in America, 1879), 153–154. See also Pehr or Peter Kalm's description of the Dutch Reformed Church in Albany: "It is built of stone; and in the middle it has a small steeple, with a bell." Pehr Kalm, *Travels into North America; containing its natural history, and a circumstantial account of its plantations and agriculture in general, with the civil, ecclesiastical and commercial state of the country, the manners of the inhabitants, and several curious and important remarks on various subjects*, trans. Johann Reinhold Forster (London: The editor, 1770–1771), 2:256.

81. Kilde, *Sacred Power, Sacred Space*, 113–114; Buggeln, *Temples of Grace*, 76.

82. In 1681, Cornelis Dircksen's estate included "a Church seate." Inventory and Appraisal of Cornelis Dirckse Estate, August 10, 1681, JLP no. 2158, NNA Wills 18: 24–26, Jacob Leisler Institute. Many thanks to David Willem Voorhees for sharing this reference. Also see Garvan, "Protestant Plain Style before 1630," 4–13.

83. Kilde, *Sacred Power, Sacred Space*, 120.

84. Benes, "New England Meetinghouse," 128.

85. Barry L. Stiefel, *Jews and the Renaissance of Synagogue Architecture, 1450–1730* (New York: Routledge, 2016), 109–110. For more about gender segregation, see Van Swighen, *Protestants Kerk Interieur* (1984), 223, Willem Frederick (Eric) Nooter Papers, box 2, folder Q, Jacob Leisler Institute; Wells, *Quarter Millennial Anniversary of the Reformed Dutch Church of Flatbush*, 15–16, Jacob Leisler Institute.

86. Some of the Kingston Church records suggest that women still had separate seats in the early nineteenth century. Consistory Minutes 1795–1841, February 1816, Kingston Church records, vol. 5B, p. 63, Ulster County Clerk, Archives Division; Consistory Minutes 1795–1841, 20 April 1819, Kingston Church records, vol. 5B, 80, Ulster County Clerk, Archives Division. The church of Caughnawaga also continued its gender divisions into the early nineteenth century. Royden Woodward Vosburgh, ed., *Records of the Reformed Protestant Dutch Church of Caughnawaga, now the Reformed Church of Fonda, in the village of Fonda, Montgomery County, N.Y. / transcribed by the New York Genealogical and Biographical Society* (New York City: [s.n.], 1917) 2:160–166.

87. Dr. John Coulbourn, *A History of the Reformed Church of Claverack* (1966), Claverack Church, Mary Hallenbeck Collection, Jacob Leisler Institute.

88. Kalm, *Travels into North America*, 1:251.

89. Alexander, *Albany's First Church*, 38.

90. Alexander, 106; Munsell, *Collections*, 2:384; Arthur James Weisse, *History of the City of Albany, New York: From the Discovery of the Great River in 1524, by Verrazzano, to the Present Time* (Albany: E. H. Bender, 1884), 282.

91. Kilde, *Sacred Power, Sacred Space*, 125.

92. Consistory Minutes, April 18, 1754, Kingston Church book, vol. 3, 448, Ulster County Clerk, Archives Division.

93. Wells, *Quarter Millennial Anniversary of the Reformed Dutch Church of Flatbush, New York*, 15, Jacob Leisler Institute.

94. Alexander, *Albany's First Church*, 107. Also see Demarest, *Reformed Church in America*, 181–182.

95. Kilde, *Sacred Power, Sacred Space*, 120.

96. Beasley introduces the concept of "permanent guests" when he discusses how free and enslaved black people in the Anglican churches he studies never had designated seats or owned pews. Beasley, *Christian Ritual*, 33–34.

97. Alexander, *Albany's First Church*, 105. Also see Munsell, *Collections*, 2:384–385.

98. Alexander, *Albany's First Church*, 106.

99. Beasley notices the same thing in American Anglican churches. He also found evidence of enslaved people who waited outside the churches. Beasley, *Christian Ritual*, 31–32, 34.

100. Francis J. Sypher, ed. and trans., *Liber A of the Collegiate Churches of New York, part 1* (Grand Rapids: William B. Eerdmans, 2015), 140–145.

101. William B. Rhoads, *An Architectural History of the Reformed Church New Paltz, New York* (Tricentennial Committee of the Church, 1983), 12; Buggeln, *Temples of Grace*, 88; Benes, "New England Meetinghouse," 119–120.

102. Benes, "New England Meetinghouse," 133–136; Benes and Zimmerman, *New England Meeting House and Church*, 1.

103. Benes and Zimmerman, *New England Meeting House and Church*, 28.

104. Rhoads, *Architectural History*, 6.

105. Benes and Zimmerman, *New England Meeting House and Church*, 31; Buggeln, *Temples of Grace*, 77–79.

106. Nelson, *Beauty of Holiness*, 50; Buggeln, *Temples of Grace*, 75.

107. Buggeln, *Temples of Grace*, 146; Rhoads, *Architectural History*, 8; D. D. Cornelius L. Wells, *Quarter Millennial Anniversary of the Reformed Dutch Church of Flatbush, New York* (1904), 39, Willem Frederick (Eric) Nooter Papers, box 2, folder F.

108. Available pews would often be sold at a public auction that would take place in the church. Consistory Minutes, March 1810, Kingston Church records, vol. 5B, Ulster County Clerk, Archives Division; Consistory Minutes, June 15, 1811, Kingston Church records, vol. 5B, Ulster County Clerk, Archives Division; Ame Vennema, *History of the Reformed Church of New Paltz, Ulster County, NY from 1683 to 1883* (Rondout, NY: Kingston Freeman Steam Printing House, 1884), 29.

109. Alexander, *Albany's First Church*, 187.

110. In Consistory, January 22, 1799, Consistory Minutes, 1795–1801, First Reformed Church of Albany, NYSL; In Consistory, February 25, 1811, Consistory Minutes, 1809–1815, First Reformed Church of Albany, NYSL; In Consistory, May 2, 1815, Consistory Minutes, 1809–1815, First Reformed Church of Albany, NYSL; Alexander, *Albany's First Church*, 106.

111. Consistorial Record, 1839, Reformed Dutch Church of New Paltz, Ulster County, NY, bk. 4, 424, located at the New Paltz Reformed Church, New Paltz. Many thanks to the New Paltz Church historian Kevin Cook for showing me these records. According to Richard Hasbrouck, the New Paltz church became part of the Dutch Reformed Church in 1773. Richard Hasbrouck, *A Brief History of the New Paltz Reformed Church* (published by the Tricentennial Committee on the occasion of the 300th Anniversary, 1982), 3.

112. Rhoads, *Architectural History*, 7. When a congregation planned to build a new church, congregants would usually raise money, supplies, and labor. Several church records show that some congregants would offer the labor of the men they enslaved to build these churches. For instance, when the New Paltz congregation built a new church, Petrus van Wagenen contributed the labor of Tam. Alexander notes in his book on the Albany church that when they gathered contributions for a new church in 1714, several prominent Dutch Americans, including Jonas Douw, Hendrick Douw, Cornelis Schemmerhorn, and Peter Schuyler, had some of their enslaved laborers work on the building. Receipts, Abraham Deyo (1771–1775), New Paltz Reformed Church Records, Huguenot Historical Society Library and Archives; Dingman Versteeg trans., Peter R. Christoph, Kenneth Scott, and Kenn Stryker-Rodda, eds., *Records of the Reformed Dutch Church of New Paltz, New York: Containing an Account of the Organization of the Church and the Registers of the Consistories, Members, Marriages, and* Baptisms (Baltimore: Genealogical Publishing Co., 1977), 33; Alexander, *Albany's First Church*, 103–104. Buggeln points out that among church builders were often the enslaved men who were excluded from worshipping in these buildings. Buggeln, *Temples of Grace*, 32.

113. Nelson, *Beauty of Holiness*, 317–318; Olwell, *Masters, Slaves, and Subjects*, 110–111; Upton, "White and Black Landscapes," 69.

114. Nelson, *Beauty of Holiness*, 317.

115. Nelson, 362–363.

116. Upton, "White and Black Landscapes," 69. Beasley comes to a similar conclusion. Beasley, *Christian Ritual*, 35. Also see Paula Wheeler Carlo, *Huguenot Refugees in Colonial New York: Becoming American in the Hudson Valley* (Brighton: Sussex Academic Press, 2005), 164.

117. Sensbach, *Separate Canaan*, 211–215.

118. In Consistory, January 22, 1799, Consistory Minutes, 1795–1801, First Reformed Church of Albany, NYSL.

119. In Consistory, February 5, 1811, Consistory Minutes, 1809–1815, First Reformed Church of Albany, NYSL.

120. In Consistory, February 25, 1811, Consistory Minutes, 1809–1815, First Reformed Church of Albany, NYSL.

121. In Consistory, May 2, 1815, Consistory Minutes, 1809–1815, First Reformed Church of Albany, NYSL.

122. In Consistory, May 2, 1815, Consistory Minutes, 1809–1815, First Reformed Church of Albany, NYSL.

123. Diary of James Kent [or Kant], pt. 9, New York March 6, 1822, BV Diary vol. 1, N-YHS.

124. Frederick Douglass, *My Bondage and My Freedom* (New York: Miller, Orton & Co., 1857), 352–353.

125. Cato Pearce, *Jailed for Preaching: The Autobiography of Cato Pearce, a Freed Slave from Washington County, Rhode Island* (Kingstown, RI: Pettaquamscutt Historical Society, 2006), 15, 27. Many thanks to Richard Boles for bringing the Cato Pearce and William Brown narratives to my attention.

126. William J. Brown, *The Life of William J. Brown, of Providence, R.I.; with Personal Recollections of Incidents in Rhode Island* (Freeport, NY: Books for Libraries Press, 1971), 46.

127. Andrew D. Mellick, *The Story of an Old farm; or, life in New Jersey* (Somerville, NJ: Unionist-Gazette, 1889), 5–7.

128. Mellick, 437. Also see De Jong, *Reformed Church*, 133.

129. Dell Upton discusses such practices in Virginia and notes that announcements included runaway slave notices. There is no reason to believe such announcements would not be posted in Dutch Reformed churchyards. Upton, *Holy Things and Profane*, 204; Kilde, *Sacred Power, Sacred Space*, 112; Benes and Zimmerman, *New England Meeting House and Church*, 64.

130. Upton, *Holy Things and Profane*, 203; Nelson, *Beauty of Holiness*, 246–247; Isaac, *Transformation of Virginia*, 61; Gerbner, *Christian Slavery*, 32.

131. Lillian Dockstader van Dusen, *A History of the Reformed Church of Fonda, N.Y. beginning with the old Caughnawaga Church* (Ladies Aid Society, 1925).

132. Sypher, *Liber A of the Collegiate Churches of New York, 1628–1700, part 1*, 42.

133. Sypher, *Liber A of the Collegiate Churches of New York, 1628–1700, part 1*, 12–13. These were common practices in various denominations in the colonies and in Europe. For instance, Louis Nelson shows that South Carolina planters had family mausoleums built in the most prominent parts of the cemetery, usually close to the church's main entrance. Nelson, *Beauty of Holiness*, 272. Will Coster details how money determined the place of a burial in medieval England. Will Coster, "A Microcosm of Community: Burial, Space and Society in Chester, 1598 to 1633," in *Sacred Space in Early Modern Europe*, ed. Andrew Spicer and Will Coster (Cambridge: Cambridge University Press, 2005): 124–143, 135.

134. A plaque at the Shawangunk church marks the place where these ministers were interred.

135. Will Coster highlights the ways in which the medieval English church cemetery served as a place of exclusion. Coster, "Microcosm of Community," 135–136.

136. Beasley discusses how "limited space and deepening racism led to increasingly racialized control of burial ground by the middle of the eighteenth century." Beasley, *Christian Ritual*, 125.

137. Maika, "Slavery, Race, and Culture," 30.

138. *The New York African Burial Ground: Unearthing the African Presence in Colonial New York* (Washington, DC: Howard University Press, 2009), 43.

139. Venema, *Beverwijck*, 117, 353.

140. Stiles, *History of the City of Brooklyn*, 1:389; Vanderbilt, *Social History of Flatbush*, 165–168.

141. Cohen, *Ramapo Mountain People*, 63.

142. Maika, "Slavery, Race, and Culture," 30; Fitts, "Landscapes of Northern Bondage," 54–73.

143. Joseph E. Diamond, "Owned in Life, Owned in Death: The Pine Street African and African American Burial Ground in Kingston, New York," *Northeast Historical Archeology* 25, no. 1, art. 6 (2006), https://doi.org/10.22191/neha/vol35/iss1/22.

144. Peter Lowe to anonymous friend, 1788, ArMs 1974.008 Peter Lowe Correspondence, BHS.

145. *Brooklyn Minerva*, December 9, 1807.

146. Boles, "Dividing the Faith," 224.

147. Boles, 249; Graham Russell Hodges, ed., *Black Itinerants of the Gospel: The Narratives of John Jea and George White* (Madison: Madison House Publishers, 1993), 70.

148. Bonomi, "'Swarms of Negroes,'" 52–53; Foote, *Black and White Manhattan*, 129–131; Hodges, *Root & Branch*, 54.

149. Dubois and Larison, *Sylvia Dubois*, 96.

150. Bankoff, Ricciardi, and Loorya, "Remembering Africa," 36–40; Ricciardi, "Changing through the Century," 188–189.

151. Leone and Fry, "Conjuring in the Big House Kitchen," 377; Wall, "Twenty Years After," 2; Laurie Wilkie, "Secret and Sacred: Contextualizing the Artifacts of African-American Magic and Religion," *Historical Archeology* 31, no. 4 (1997): 89–90; Thompson, *Flash of the Spirit*, 129–131; Sweet, *Recreating Africa*, 179–185; Wilkie, "Magic and Empowerment," 145; Young, *Rituals of Resistance*, 118–120; Robert Farris Thompson, "Kongo Influences on African-American Artistic Culture," in *Africanisms in American Culture*, ed. Joseph E. Holloway (Bloomington: Indiana University Press, 1990), 148–184; Finch, *Rethinking Slave Rebellion*, chap. 7.

152. Joseph, "'. . . All of Cross,'" 134, 149–150; Wheeler, "Magical Dwelling," 382; Young, *Rituals of Resistance*, 88. Leland Ferguson acknowledges that even though the X-marked South Carolina bowls were very likely rooted in BaKongo cosmology, "we know that the cross was an important symbol, and the cross and circle were important symbols to Native Americans. We also know that both Native Americans and African Americans made varieties of colonoware. So, circle-and-cross symbols on colonoware could be syncretic, incorporating Christian and Native American as well as African and newly created African-American meanings." Leland Ferguson, "'The Cross Is a Magic Sign': Marks on Eighteenth-Century Bowls from South Carolina," in *"I, Too, Am America": Archeological Studies of African-American Life*, ed. Theresa Singleton (Charlottesville: University Press of Virginia, 1999), 124.

153. Ricciardi, "Changing through the Century," 136–137.

154. Ferguson, *Uncommon Ground*, 18–22; Deetz, *Flowerdew Hundred*, 26–29, 80–81.

155. Ferguson, *Uncommon Ground*, 113–115.

156. Paul Huey, "A New Look at an Old Object," *New York State Preservationist* 8, no. 2 (2004): 22; Covart, "Collision on the Hudson," 127; Inquisition on the body of Bat a Negro Wench of Folkert Veeder, August 16, 1799, The Abbott Collection, box 4, item 602, NYSL.

157. Fromont, *Art of Conversion*, 150–151. Many thanks to John K. Thornton for bringing these findings to my attention. James Davidson points out that in medieval Europe perforated coins were used as charms, though there is only scant evidence that European descendants in North America used such coins. James M. Davidson, "Rituals Captured in Context and Time: Charm Use in North Dallas Freedman's Town (1869–1907)," *Historical Archeology* 38, no. 2 (2004): 49, https://doi.org/10.1007/BF03376641.

158. Davidson, "Rituals Captured," 23; Wilkie, "Secret and Sacred," 89, 101; Wilkie, "Magic and Empowerment on the Plantation," 144; Theresa A. Singleton, "The Ar-

cheology of Slavery in North America," *Annual Review of Anthropology* 24 (1995): 131; Samford, "Archeology," 102; Nelson, *Beauty of Holiness*, 159.

159. Anne-Marie Cantwell and Diana diZerega Wall, *Unearthing Gotham: The Archeology of New York City* (New Haven, CT: Yale University Press, 2001), 290; Dapper, *Naukeurige Beschrijvinge der Afrikaensche Gewesten*, 349, 607; Bosman, *Nauwkeurige Beschryving Van De Guinese Goud-Tand-En Slavekust*, 2:12.

160. Dapper, *Naukeurige Beschrijvinge der Afrikaensche Gewesten*, 607.

161. *New York African Burial Ground*, 153–154.

162. *New York African Burial Ground*, 167.

163. Bosman, *Nauwkeurige Beschryving Van De Guinese Goud-Tand-En Slavekust*, 2:147–149. According to religious scholar Albert Raboteau, "improper or incomplete funeral rites can interfere with or delay the entrance of the deceased into the spiritual world and may cause his soul to linger about, as a restless and malevolent ghost." Albert J. Raboteau, *Slave Religion: The "Invisible Institution" in the Antebellum South* (New York: Oxford University Press, 2004), 13. Similarly, Laurie Wilkie points to the significance of a proper burial among Africans and their descendants. Wilkie, "Secret and Sacred," 90. Also see Sweet, *Recreating Africa*, 179; Young, *Rituals of Resistance*, chap. 4.

164. Murphy, *Working the Spirit*, 143.

165. Olwell, *Masters, Slaves, and Subjects*, 116.

Conclusion

1. Cooper, *Satanstoe*, 77–78.

2. For more about the ways in which historical narratives and silences are often created, see Trouillot, *Silencing the Past*.

Bibliography

Archives

Albany County Hall of Records, Albany
Albany Institute of History and Art (AIHA), Albany
Brooklyn Historical Society (BHS), New York
Collegiate Church Records, New York
Flatbush Church Records, New York
Gilder Lehrman Collection (GLC), New York
Historic Huguenot Street, New Paltz, NY
International Institute of Social History (IISG), Amsterdam
Jacob Leisler Institute, Hudson, New York
Nationaal Archief (Nat. Arch.), The Hague, The Netherlands
New York City Municipal Archives (NYCMA)
New-York Historical Society (N-YHS), New York
New York Public Library (NYPL), New York
New York State Archives (NYSA), Albany
New York State Library (NYSL), Albany
Reformed Church of America Archives (RCA), New Brunswick, NJ
Reformed Church of New Paltz Records, New Paltz, NY
Stadsarchief Amsterdam (SAA), Amsterdam, The Netherlands
Ulster County Clerk, Archives Division, Kingston, NY

Published Primary Sources

Abstract of the Returns of the Fifth Census, showing the number of free people, the number of slaves, the Federal or Representative Number; and the Aggregate of Each County of Each State of the United States. Prepared from the corrected returns of the Secretary of Congress, By the Clerk of the House of Representatives. Washington, DC: Duff Green, 1832.

The Acts and Proceedings of the General Synod of the Reformed Dutch Church, in North America at Albany, June 1823. New York: Abraham Paul, 1823.

The Acts and Proceedings of the General Synod, of the Reformed Dutch Church, in North America at New York, June 1816. Albany: Websters and Skinners, 1816.

The Acts and Proceedings of the particular Synod of Albany, Convened in the city of Albany, May 19, 1824. Albany: Printed at the office of the Daily Advertiser, 1824.

"Albany Fifty Years Ago." *Harper's Magazine.* March 1857.

Anjou, Gustave, ed. *Ulster County, New York, Probate Records in the Office of the Surrogate, and in the County Clerk's Office At Kingston, N.Y.: A Careful Abstract and Translation of the Dutch and English Wills.* Vol. 1. Rhinebeck, NY: Palatine Transcripts, 1980.

Architects' Emergency Committee. *Great Georgian Houses of America.* New York: Dover, 1970.

Barbot, Jean. *Barbot on Guinea: The Writings of Jean Barbot on West Africa 1678–1712.* Edited by P. E. H. Hair, Adam Jones, and Robin Law. 2 vols. London: Hakluyt Society, 1992.

Bosman, Willem. *Nauwkeurige Beschryving Van De Guinese Goud-Tand-En Slavekust.* Utrecht: Anthony Schouten, 1704.

Brown, William J. *The life of William J. Brown, of Providence, R.I.: with personal recollections of incidents in Rhode Island.* Freeport, N Y: Books for Libraries, 1971.

Capitein, Jacobus Elisa Johannes. *The Agony of Asar: A Thesis on Slavery by the Former Slave, Jacobus Elisa Johannes Capitein, 1717–1747.* Edited and translated by Grant Parker. Princeton, NJ: Markus Wiener, 1999.

Carli, Dionigi de, and R.R.F.F. Michele Angelo Guattini. "A Curious and Exact Account of a Voyage to Congo, in the years 1666 and 1667, By the R.R.F. Michael Angelo of Cattina, and Denis De Carli of Piacenza, Capuchins, and Apostolic Missioners into the said Kingdom of Congo." In *A General Collection of the Best and Most Interesting Voyages and Travels in All Parts of the World; Many of which are now first Translated into English.* Edited by John Pinkerton. London: Longman, 1814.

Cavazzi, Giovanni Antonio. "Missione evagelica nel Regno de Congo." Central African History (blog). Translated by John K. Thornton, http://centralafricanhistory .blogspot.com/2008/08/book-i-chapter-3.html.

Clinton, George. *Public Papers of George Clinton: First Governor of New York, 1777–1795 1801–1804.* Albany: Oliver A. Quayle State Legislature Printer, 1904.

Compendium of the Enumeration of the Inhabitants and Statistics of the United States, as obtained at the Department of State, from the returns of the sixth census, by counties and principal towns exhibiting the population, wealth, and resources of the country. Washington, DC: Printed by Thomas Allen, 1841.

Cooper, James Fenimore. *Satanstoe; Or, the Family of Littlepage: A Tale of the Colony.* New York: Burgess, Stringer, 1845.

Corwin, E. T. *A Digest of Constitutional and Synodical Legislation of the Reformed Church in America: Formerly the Ref. Prot. Dutch Church.* New York: Board of Publication of the Reformed Church in America, 1906.

Corwin, Edward T., trans. and ed. *Ecclesiastical Records: State of New York.* 7 vols. Albany: J. B. Lyon, state printer, 1901–1916.

Coventry, Alexander. *Memoirs of an Emigrant: The Journal of Alexander Coventry, M.D.; in Scotland, the United States and Canada during the Period 1783–1831.* Albany: Albany Institute of History and Art and the New York State Library, 1978.

Damhouder, Joost. *Practycke in Civile Saecken, seer nut/profijtelijck ende nodigh allen Schouten, Borghemeesteren Magistraten ende andere Rechteren.* 's Gravenhage: Ordinaris Druckers vande Ho.Mo. Heeren Staten Generael, 1626.

Danckaerts, Jasper. *Journal of Jasper Danckaerts, 1679–1680.* New York: C. Scribner's Sons, 1913.

Dapper, Olfert. *Naukeurige Beschrijvinge der Afrikaensche Gewesten*. Amsterdam: Jacob van Meurs, 1668.

Douglass, Frederick. *My Bondage and My Freedom*. New York: Miller, Orton & Co., 1857.

Douglass, Frederick. *Narrative of the Life of Frederick Douglass, an American Slave*. Boston: Published at the Anti-Slavery Office, 1845.

Dubois, Sylvia, and C. W. Larison. *Sylvia Dubois, a Biography of the Slav Who Whipt Her Mistres and Gand Her Freedom*. Edited by Jared C. Lobdell. Oxford: Oxford University Press, 1988.

Duermeyer, Louis, ed. *Records of the Reformed Dutch Church of Albany, New York, 1683–1809*. Baltimore: Genealogical Publishing Co., 1978.

Dunlap, William. *Diary of William Dunlap, 1766–1839; the Memoirs of a Dramatist, Theatrical Manager, Painter, Critic, Novelist, and Historian*. Edited by Dorothy C. Barck. New York: C. Scribner's Sons, 1913.

Durell, William, ed. *The Constitution of the Reformed Dutch Church in the United States of America*. New York: William Durell, 1793.

Evans, Thomas Grier ed. *Records of the Reformed Dutch Church in New Amsterdam and New York: Baptisms from 25 December, 1639, To 27 December, 1730*. New York: Printed for the Society, 1901.

Gasero, Russell L., ed. *Historical Directory of the Reformed Church in America 1628–2000*. Grand Rapids, MI: Wm. B. Eerdmans, 2001.

Gehring, Charles T., trans. and ed. *Correspondence, 1647–1653*. Syracuse, NY: Syracuse University Press, 2000.

Gehring, Charles T., trans. and ed. *Correspondence 1654–1658*. Syracuse, NY: Syracuse University Press, 2003.

Gehring, Charles T., ed. *Council Minutes, 1652–1654*. Baltimore: Genealogical Pub. Co., 1983.

Gehring, Charles T., ed. *Council Minutes, 1655–1656*. Syracuse, NY: Syracuse University Press, 1995.

Gehring, Charles T., trans. and ed. *Curaçao Papers 1640–1665*. Albany: New Netherland Research Center and the New Netherland Institute, 2011.

Gehring, Charles T. "The Dutch Language in Colonial New York: An Investigation of a Language in Decline and Its Relationship to Social Change." PhD diss., Indiana University Press, 1973.

Gehring, Charles T., trans. and ed. *Minutes of the Court of Fort Orange and Beverwijck, 1652–1660*. Syracuse, NY: Syracuse University Press, 1990.

Grant, Anne MacVicar. *Memoirs of an American Lady, With Sketches of Manners and Scenery in America*. New York: D. Appleton, 1846.

Hastings, Hugh, et al., eds. *Ecclesiastical Records, State of New York*. Vol. 1. Albany: James B. Lyon, State Printer, 1901.

Heads of Families at the First Census of the United States taken in the Year 1790: New York. Washington, DC: Government Printing Office, 1908.

Hodges, Graham Russell. *Black Itinerants of the Gospel: The Narratives of John Jea and George White*. Madison, WI: Madison House Publishers, 1993.

Hodges, Graham Russell. *"Pretends to Be Free": Runaway Slave Advertisements from Colonial and Revolutionary New York and New Jersey*. New York: Garland, 1994.

Hoes, Roswell Randall, ed. and trans. *Baptismal and Marriage Registers of the Dutch Church of Kingston, Ulster County, New York, 1660–1809*. Baltimore: Genealogical Publishing Co., 1980.

Horsmanden, Daniel. *The New York Conspiracy*. Boston: Beacon, 1971.

Inventory of the Church Archives in New York City: Reformed Church in America. New York: Historical Records Survey, 1939.

Jacobs, Harriet. *Incidents in the Life of a Slave Girl*. Garden City, NY: Dover, 2001.

Jameson, J. Franklin, ed. *Narratives of New Netherland, 1609–1664*. New York: Charles Scribner's Sons, 1909.

Jogues, Isaac. "Novum Belgium." In *Narratives of New Netherland*. Edited by Franklin J. Jameson. New York: Charles Scribner's Sons, 1909.

Kalm, Pehr. *Travels into North America; containing its natural history, and a circumstantial account of its plantations and agriculture in general, with the civil, ecclesiastical and commercial state of the country, the manners of the inhabitants, and several curious and important remarks on various subjects*. Translated by Johann Reinhold Forster. London: The editor, 1770–1771.

Laan, K. ter. *Folkloristisch Woordenboek Van Nederland En Vlaams België*. 's Gravenhage: GB van Goor Zonen, 1949.

Laer, A. J. van, trans. and ed. *Correspondence of Jeremias Van Rensselaer*. Albany: University of the State of New York Press, 1932.

Laer, A. J. van, trans. and ed. *Council Minutes 1638–1649* (New York Historical Manucripts: Dutch, vol. 4). Baltimore: Genealogical Publishing Co., 1974.

Laer, A. J. van, trans. and ed. *Minutes of the Court of Rensselaerswyck, 1648–1652*. Albany: University of the State of New York, 1922.

Laer, A. J. van., trans. and ed. *Register of the Provincial Secretary, 1638–1642* (New York Historical Manucripts: Dutch, vol. 1). Baltimore: Genealogical Publishing Co., 1974.

Laer, A. J. van, trans. and ed. *Register of the Provincial Secretary, 1642–1647* (New York Historical Manucripts: Dutch, vol. 2). Baltimore: Genealogical Publishing Co., 1974.

Laer, A. J. van, trans. and ed. *Register of the Provincial Secretary, 1648–1660* (New York Historical Manucripts: Dutch, vol. 3). Baltimore: Genealogical Publishing Co., 1974.

Laet, Johannes de. *Historie ofte Iaerlijck Verhael van de Verrichtinghen der Geoctroyeerde West-Indische Compagnie, Zedert haer Begin/ tot het eynde van 't jaer sesthienhondert ses-en-dertich*. Leiden: Bonaventuer ende Abraham Elsevier, 1644.

Lincoln, Charles Zebina, William H. Johnson, and Ansel Judd Northrup, eds. *The Colonial Laws of New York from the year 1664 to the Revolution, Including the Charters to the Duke of York, the Commission and Instructions to Colonial Governors, the Dukes Laws, the Laws of the Donagan and Leisler Assemblies, the Charters of Albany and New York and the Acts of the Colonial Legislature from 1691 to 1775*. Vols. 1–3. Minneapolis: J. B. Lyon, State Printer, 1894.

Mellick, Andrew D. *The story of an old farm; or, life in New Jersey*. Somerville, NJ: Unionist Gazette, 1889.

Munsell, J. *Collections on the history of Albany: from its discovery to the present time; with notices of its public institutions, and biographical sketches of citizens deceased*. Albany: J. Munsell, 1865–81.

O'Callaghan, Edmund Bailey. *Census of Slaves, 1755*. New York, 1850.

O'Callaghan, Edmund Bailey, ed. *Documentary History of the State of New York (1849–1851)*. Albany: Weed, Parsons & Co., Public Printers, 1849.

O'Callaghan, Edmund Bailey. *History of New Netherland; or, New York Under the Dutch*. Vol. 1. New York: D. Appleton, 1846.

O'Callaghan, Edmund Bailey, trans. and ed. *Laws and Ordinances of New Netherland, 1638–1674*. Albany: Weed, Parsons and Company, printers and stereotypers, 1868.

O'Callaghan, Edmund Bailey, trans. and ed. *Voyages of the slavers St. John and Arms of Amsterdam, 1659, 1663: together with additional papers illustrative of the slave trade under the Dutch*. Albany: J. Munsell, 1867.

O'Callaghan, Edmund Bailey, and Berthold Fernow, trans. and ed. *Documents Relative to the Colonial History of the State of New-York: new ser., v. 2. Documents relating to the history and settlements of the towns along the Hudson and Mohawk Rivers (with the exception of Albany), from 1630 to 1684*. Albany: Weed & Parsons, 1881.

O'Callaghan, Edmund Bailey, trans., Berthold Fernow, ed. *The Records of New Amsterdam from 1653 to 1674 Anno Domini*. New York: Knickerbocker, 1897.

O'Callaghan, Edmund Bailey, trans., Kenneth Scott, and Kenn Stryker-Rodda, eds. *The Register of Salomon Lachaire, Notary Public of New Amsterdam, 1661–1662. Translated from the original Dutch Manuscript in the Office of the Clerk of the Common Council of New York* (New York Historical Manuscripts: Dutch). Baltimore, 1978.

Oldendorp, C. G. A., and Gudrun Meier, eds. *Historie Der Caribischen Inseln Sanct Thomas, Sanct Crux Und Sanct Jan: Insbesondere Der Dasigen Neger Und Der Mission De Evangelischen Brüder Unter Denselben*. Berlin: VWB, Verlag für Wissenschaft und Bildung, 2000.

Osgood, Herbert L., et al., eds. *Minutes of the Common Council of the City of New York, 1675–1776*. New York: Dodd, Mead, 1905.

Pearce, Cato. *Jailed for Preaching: The Autobiography of Cato Pearce, a freed slave from Washington County, Rhode Island*. Kingstown, RI: Pettaquamscutt Historical Society, 2006.

Pearson, Jonathan, A.J.F. van Laer, trans. and ed., *Early Records of the City and County of Albany and Colony of Rensselaerswyck*, vol. 4. Albany: University of the State of New York, 1919.

Pleat, Geraldine R., and Agnes N. Underwood. "Pinkster Ode, Albany, 1803." *New York Folklore Quarterly* 8, no. 1 (Spring 1952): 31–45.

Proceedings of the General Court of Assizes held in the City of New York, October 6, 1680, to October 6, 1682. New York: New-York Historical Society, 1913.

Records of the Reformed Dutch Church of Albany, New York, 1683–1809. Baltimore: Genealogical Publishing Co., 1978.

Scott, Kenneth, ed. *New York City Court Records, 1684–1760: Genealogical Data from the Court of Quarter Sessions*. Washington, DC: National Genealogical Society, 1982.

Scott, Kenneth. "Ulster County, New York, Court Records, 1693–1775." *National Genealogical Society Quarterly* 60, no. 4 (December 1972): 276–285.

Scott, Kenneth. "Ulster County, New York, Court Records, 1693–1775." *National Genealogical Society Quarterly* 61, no. 1 (1973): 60-68.

Stessin-Cohn, Susan, and Ashley Hurlburt-Biagini, eds. *In Defiance: Runaways from Slavery in New York's Hudson River Valley, 1735–1831.* Delmar: Black Dome Press, 2016.

Strickland, William. *Journal of a Tour in the United States of America, 1794–1795.* New York: New-York Historical Society, 1971.

Struys, Jan Janszoon. *Drie aanmerkelijke en seer rampspoedige Reysen door Italien, Griekenlandt, Lijslandt, Mascovien, Tartarijen, Meden, Persien, Oost-Indien, Japan, en verscheyden andere Gewesten.* Amsterdam: Jacob van Meurs, 1676.

Sypher, Francis J., Jr., ed. and trans. *Liber A of the Collegiate Churches of New York, part 1.* Grand Rapids, MI: William B. Eerdmans, 2009.

Sypher, Francis J., Jr., ed. and trans. *Liber A of the Collegiate Churches of New York, part 2.* Grand Rapids, MI: William B. Eerdmans, 2015.

"The Ten Broeck Mansion Existing Conditions Report." Compiled for the Albany County Historical Association, 2015.

Truth, Sojourner. *Narrative of Sojourner Truth.* Mineola: Dover, 1999.

Versteeg, Dingman, trans., Peter R. Christoph, Kenneth Scott, and Kenn Stryker-Rodda, eds. *Records of the Reformed Dutch Church of New Paltz, New York: Containing an account of the organization of the church and the registers of the Consistories, members, marriages, and baptisms.* Baltimore: Genealogical Publishing Co., 1977.

Vosburgh, Royden Woodward, ed. *Records of the Reformed Protestant Dutch Church of Caughnawaga, now the Reformed Church of Fonda, in the village of Fonda, Montgomery County, N.Y. / transcribed by the New York Genealogical and Biographical Society.* New York: [s.n.], 1917.

Voyages database, 2013. *Voyages: The Trans-Atlantic Slave Trade Database.* http://www.slavevoyages.org.

Wassenaer, Nicolaes van. "Historisch Verhael." In *Narratives of New Netherland, 1609–1664,* edited by J. Franklin Jameson. New York: Charles Scribner's Sons, 1909.

Wassenaer, Nicolaes van. *Historisch verhael aldaer ghedenck-weerdichste geschienidenisse, die vanden beginner des jaers 1621 (tot 1932) voorgevallens yn (Amsterdam, 1622–1635).*

Secondary Sources

Adams, Julia. *The Familial State: Ruling Families and Merchant Capitalism in Early Modern Europe.* Ithaca, NY: Cornell University Press, 2005.

Alexander, Robert S. *Albany's First Church and Its Role in the Growth of the City.* Delmar, NY: Newgraphics Printers, 1988.

Allen, Richard B. "Satisfying the 'Want for Labouring People': European Slave Trading in the Indian Ocean, 1500–1850." *Journal of World History* 21, no. 1 (2010): 45–73. https://doi.org/10.1353/jwh.0.0100.

Anderson, Elijah. "Cosmopolitan Canopy." *Annals of the American Academy of Political and Social Science* 595 (September 2004): 14–31. https://doi.org/10.1177/0002716204266833.

Anderson, Elijah. "The White Space." *Sociology of Race and Ethnicity* 1, no. 1 (2015): 10–21. https://doi.org/10.1177/2332649214561306.

Anderson, Lisa. "Update on the Schuyler Flatts Burial Ground." *Legacy: The Magazine of the New York State Museum 5*, no. 1 (Summer 2009): 9.

Andrade, Tonio. *How Taiwan Became Chinese: Dutch, Spanish, and Han Colonization in the Seventeenth Century.* New York: Columbia University Press, 2008 [Gutenberg-e].

Andrade, Tonio. "The Rise and Fall of Dutch Taiwan, 1624–1662: Cooperative Colonization and the Statist Model of European Expansion." *Journal of World History* 17, no. 4 (December 2006): 429–450. https://doi.org/10.1353/jwh.2006.0052.

Antunes, Cátia. "From Binary Narratives to Diversified Tales: Changing the Paradigm in the Study of Dutch Colonial Participation." *TVGESCH* 131, no. 3 (2018): 393–407. https://doi.org/110.5117/TVGESCH2018.3.001.ANTU.

Apeldoorn, L. J. van. *Geschiedenis van het Nederlandsche Huwelijksrecht voor de invoering van de Fransche wetgeving.* Amsterdam: Uitgeversmaatschappij Holland, 1925.

Armstead, Myra B. Young, ed. *Mighty Change, Tall Within: Black Identity in the Hudson Valley.* Albany: State University of New York Press, 2003.

Bakker, G. Murray. "Iets over de stichters van Nieuw-Nederland en hunne afstammelingen." *Eigen Haard*, no. 32 (1888).

Balandier, Georges. *Daily Life in the Kingdom of the Kongo: From the Sixteenth to the Eighteenth Century.* New York: Pantheon Books, 1968.

Balmar, Randall H. *A Perfect Babel of Confusion: Dutch Religion and English Culture in the Middle Colonies.* New York: Oxford University Press, 1989.

Bankoff, H. Arthur, Christopher Ricciardi, and Alyssa Loorya. "Remembering Africa under the Eaves." *Archeology* 54, no. 3 (May–June 2001): 36–40. https://jstor.org/stable/i40083354.

Bankoff, H. Arthur, and Frederick A. Winter. "The Archeology of Slavery at the Van Cortlandt Plantation in the Bronx, New York." *International Journal of Historical Archeology* 9, no. 4 (December 2005): 291–318. https://doi.org/10.1007/s10761-005-9302-5.

Baptist, Edward E. *The Half Has Never Been Told: Slavery and the Making of American Capitalism.* New York: Basic Books, 2014.

Beasley, Nicholas. *Christian Ritual and the Creation of British Slave Societies.* Athens: University of Georgia Press, 2009.

Belmessous, Saliha, ed. *Native Claims: Indigenous Law against Empire, 1500–1920.* Oxford: Oxford University Press, 2012.

Benes, Peter. "The New England Meetinghouse: An Atlantic Perspective." In *Building the British Atlantic World: Spaces, Places, and Material Culture*, edited by Daniel Maudlin and Bernard L. Herman, 119–141. Chapel Hill: University of North Carolina Press, 2016.

Benes, Peter, and Philip D. Zimmerman. *New England Meeting House and Church: 1630–1850. A Loan Exhibition Held at the Currier Gallery of Art, Manchester, New Hampshire.* Boston: Boston University Scholarly Publications, 1979.

Benton, Lauren. *Law and Colonial Cultures: Legal Regimes in World History, 1400–1900.* Cambridge: Cambridge University Press, 2001.

Benton, Lauren, and Richard Ross, eds. *Legal Pluralism and Empires, 1500–1850.* New York: New York University Press, 2013.

Berlin, Ira. "From Creole to African: Atlantic Creoles and the Origins of African-American Society in Mainland North America." *William and Mary Quarterly* 53, no. 2 (1996): 251–288. https://doi.org/102307/2947401.

Berlin, Ira. *Generations of Captivity: A History of African-American Slaves.* Cambridge, MA: Belknap Press, 2003.

Berlin, Ira. *Many Thousands Gone: The First Two Centuries of Slavery in North America.* Cambridge, MA: Belknap Press, 1998.

Berlin, Ira, and Leslie Harris, eds. *Slavery in New York.* New York: New Press, 2005.

Berry, Daina Ramey. *The Price for Their Pound of Flesh: The Value of the Enslaved, from Womb to Grave, in the Building of a Nation.* Boston: Beacon, 2017.

Birmingham, David. *Trade and Conflict in Angola: The Mbundu and Their Neighbours under the Influence of the Portuguese, 1483–1790.* Oxford: Clarendon, 1966.

Blackburn, Roderic H. *Dutch Colonial Homes in America.* New York: Rizzoli International Publications, 2002.

Blackburn, Roderic H., and Ruth Piwonka. *Remembrance of Patria: Dutch Arts and Culture in Colonial America, 1609–1776.* Albany: Albany Institute of History and Art, 1988.

Block, Sharon. "Lines of Color, Sex, and Service: Comparative Sexual Coercion in Early America." In *Sex, Love, Race: Crossing Boundaries in North American History,* edited by Martha Hodes, 141–163. New York: New York University Press, 1999.

Block, Sharon, and Kathleen M. Brown. "Clio in Search of Eros: Redefining Sexualities in Early America." *William and Mary Quarterly* 60, no. 1 (January 2003): 5–12. https://doi.org/10.2307/3491493.

Blussé, Leonard. "Batavia: 1619–1740: The Rise and Fall of a Chinese Colonial Town." *Journal of Southeast Asian Studies* 12, no. 1 (March 1981): 159–178.

Boles, Richard J. "Dividing the Faith: The Rise of Racially Segregated Northern Churches, 1730–1850." PhD diss., George Washington University, 2013.

Bonomi, Patricia U. "'Swarms of Negroes Comeing about My Door': Black Christianity in Early Dutch and English North America." *Journal of American History* 103, no. 1 (June 2016): 34–58. https://doi.org/10.1093/jahist/jaw007.

Bonomi, Patricia U. *Under the Cope of Heaven: Religion, Society, and Politics in Colonial America.* Oxford: Oxford University Press, 2003 [Updated Edition].

Boogaart, Ernst van den. "The Servant Migration to New Netherland, 1624–1664." In *Colonialism and Migration; Indentured Labour before and after Slavery,* edited by P. C. Emmer, 67–97. Dordrecht: Martinus Nijhoff, 1986.

Boogaart, Ernst van den. "The Trade between Western Africa and the Atlantic World, 1600–90: Estimates of Trends in Composition and Value." *Journal of African History* 33, no. 2 (November 1992): 369–385.

Boogaart, Ernst van den, and Pieter Emmer. *The Dutch Participation in the Atlantic Slave Trade.* Leiden: Centre for the History of European Expansion, 1979.

Brandon, Pepijn, and Karwan Fatah-Black. "'For the Reputation and Respectability of the State': Trade, the Imperial State, Unfree Labor, and Empire in the Dutch Atlantic." In *Building the Atlantic Empires: Unfree Labor and Imperial States in the Political Economy of Capitalism, ca. 1500–1914,* edited by John Donoghue and Evelyn Jennings, 84–108. Leiden: Brill, 2016.

Brooks, Lisa. *The Common Pot: The Recovery of Native Space in the Northeast.* Minneapolis: University of Minnesota Press, 2008.

Brown, Kathleen M. *Good Wives, Nasty Wenches, and Anxious Patriarchs: Gender, Race, and Power in Colonial Virginia.* Chapel Hill: University of North Carolina Press, 1996.

Brown, Vincent. "Slave Revolt in Jamaica, 1760–1761: A Cartographic Narrative." http://revolt.axismaps.com/project.html.

Brown, Vincent. *Tacky's Revolt: The Story of an Atlantic Slave War.* Cambridge, MA: Belknap Press, 2020.

Buggeln, Gretchen Townsend. *Temples of Grace: The Material Transformation of Connecticut's Churches, 1790–1840.* Hanover, NH: University Press of New England, 2003.

Bulthuis, Kyle T. *Four Steeples over the City Streets: Religion and Society in New York's Early Republic Congregations.* New York: New York University Press, 2014.

Burke, Peter. *Popular Culture in Early Modern Europe.* New York: New York University Press, 1978.

Camp, Stephanie. *Closer to Freedom: Enslaved Women & Everyday Resistance in the Plantation South.* Chapel Hill: University of North Carolina Press, 2004.

Cantwell, Anne-Marie, and Diana diZerega Wall. *Unearthing Gotham: The Archeology of New York City.* New Haven, CT: Yale University Press, 2001.

Carlo, Paula Wheeler. *Huguenot Refugees in Colonial New York: Becoming American in the Hudson Valley.* Brighton: Sussex Academic Press, 2005.

Carson, Cary. "Doing History with Material Culture." In *Material Culture and the Study of American Life,* edited by Ian M. G. Quimby, 41–64. New York: W. W. Norton, 1978.

Certeau, Michel de. *The Practice of Everyday Life.* Translated by Steven Rendall. Berkeley: University of California Press, 1984.

Chan, Alexandra. *Slavery in the Age of Reason: Archeology at a New England Farm.* Knoxville: University of Tennessee Press, 2007.

Christoph, Peter. "The Freedmen of New Amsterdam." In *A Beautiful and Fruitful Place: Selected Rensselaerswijck Seminar Papers,* edited by N. A. McClure Zeller, 157–170. N.p.: 1991.

Clark-Pujara, Christy. *Dark Work: The Business of Slavery in Rhode Island.* New York: New York University Press, 2016.

Clinton, Catherine. "'Southern Dishonor': Flesh, Blood, Race, and Bondage." In *In Joy and In Sorrow: Women, Family, and Marriage in the Victorian South, 1830–1900,* edited by Carol Bleser, 52–68. Oxford: Oxford University Press, 1991.

Clulow, Adam. *Amboina, 1623: Fear and Conspiracy on the Edge of Empire.* New York: Columbia University Press, 2019.

Clulow, Adam. "The Art of Claiming: Possession and Resistance in Early Modern Asia." *American Historical Review* 121, no. 1 (February 2016): 17–38. https://doi.org/10.1093/ahr/121.1.17.

Cohen, David S. *The Ramapo Mountain People.* New Brunswick, NJ: Rutgers University Press, 1986.

Cohen, David Steven. *The Dutch-American Farm.* New York: New York University Press, 1993.

Cohen, David Steven. "In Search of Carolus Africanus Rex: Afro-Dutch Folklore in New York and New Jersey." *Journal of Afro-American Historical and Genealogical Society* 5 (Fall & Winter 1984): 147–162.

Coster, Will. "A Microcosm of Community: Burial, Space and Society in Chester, 1598 to 1633." In *Sacred Space in Early Modern Europe*, edited by Will Coster and Andrew Spicer, 124–143. Cambridge: Cambridge University Press, 2005.

Coster, Will, and Andrew Spicer. "Introduction: Dimensions of Sacred Space in Reformation Europe." In *Sacred Space in Early Modern Europe*, edited by Will Coster and Andrew Spicer, 1–16. Cambridge: Cambridge University Press, 2005.

Coster, Will, and Andrew Spicer, eds. *Sacred Space in Early Modern Europe*. Cambridge: Cambridge University Press, 2005.

Covart, Elizabeth. "Collision on the Hudson: Identity, Migration, and the Improvement of Albany, New York, 1730–1830." PhD diss., University of California, Davis, 2011.

Cowling, Camillia. *Conceiving Freedom: Women of Color, Gender, and the Abolition of Slavery in Havana and Rio de Janeiro*. Chapel Hill: University of North Carolina Press, 2013.

Cowling, Camillia. "Gendered Geographies: Motherhood, Slavery, Law, and Space in Mid-Nineteenth-Century Cuba." *Women's History Review* 27, no. 6 (2018): 939–953. https://doi.org/10.1080/09612025.2017.1336845.

Cronon, William. *Changes in the Land: Colonists and the Ecology of New England*. New York: Hill & Yang, 1983.

Crum, F. S. "A Century of Population Growth, 1790–1900 (1909)." In *Publications of the American Statistical Association* 12, no. 92 (1910): 376–379.

Cummings, Abbott Lowell. *The Framed Houses of Massachusetts Bay, 1625–1725*. Cambridge, MA: Belknap Press of Harvard University Press, 1979.

Dantzig, Albert van. *Het Nederlandse aandeel in de slavenhandel*. Bussum: Fibula-van Dishoeck, 1968.

Davidson, James M. "Rituals Captured in Context and Time: Charm Use in North Dallas Freedman's Town (1869–1907)." *Historical Archeology* 38, no. 2 (2004): 22–54. https://doi.org/10.1007/BF03376641.

Davis, Natalie Zemon. *Society and Culture in Early Modern France*. Stanford, CA: Stanford University Press, 1975.

Davis, Thomas J. "These Enemies within Their Own Household: A Note on the Troublesome Slave Population in Eighteenth-Century New York City." *Journal of the Afro American Historical and Genealogical Society* 5, nos. 3 & 4 (Fall and Winter 1984): 133–157.

DeBoer, Warren R. "Subterranean Storage and the Organization of Surplus: The View from Eastern North America." *Southeastern Archeology* 7 (1988): 1–20. https://jstor.org/stable/40712860.

Deetz, James. *Flowerdew Hundred: The Archeology of a Virginia Plantation*. Charlottesville: University Press of Virginia, 1993.

Deetz, James. *In Small Things Forgotten: An Archeology of Early American Life*. New York: Doubleday Dell, 1996.

De Jong, Gerald F. "The Dutch Reformed Church and Negro Slavery in Colonial America." *Church History* 4, no. 4 (1971): 423–436.

De Jong, Gerald F. *The Dutch Reformed Church in the American Colonies*. Grand Rapids. MI: Eerdmans, 1978.

Delle, James A. *An Archeology of Social Space: Analyzing Coffee Plantations in Jamaica's Blue Mountains*. New York: Plenum, 1998.

Demarest, David D. *The Reformed Church in America: Its Origin, Development and Characteristics*. New York: Board of Publication of the Reformed Church in America, 1889.

Deursen, A. Th. van. *Mensen van Klein Vermogen: Het Kopergeld van de Gouden Eeuw*. Amsterdam: Prometheus, 1999.

Dewulf, Jeroen. "Emulating a Portuguese Model: The Slave Policy of the West India Company and the Dutch Reformed Church in Dutch Brazil (1630–1654) and New Netherland (1614–1664) in Comparative Perspective." *Journal of Early American History* 4 (2014): 3–36. https://doi.org/10.1163/18770703 -00401006.

Dewulf, Jeroen. *The Pinkster King and the King of Kongo: The Forgotten History of America's Dutch-Owned Slaves*. Jackson: University Press of Mississippi, 2016.

Dewulf, Jeroen. "'A Strong Barbaric Accent': America's Dutch-Speaking Black Community from Seventeenth-Century New Netherland to Nineteenth-Century New York and New Jersey." *American Speech* 90, no. 2 (May 2015): 131–153. https://doi .org/10.1215/00031283-3130302.

Diamond, Joseph E. "Owned in Life, Owned in Death: The Pine Street African and African American Burial Ground in Kingston, New York." *Northeast Historical Archeology* 25, no. 1, art. 6 (2006): 47–62. https://doi.org/10.22191/neha/vol35 /iss1/22.

Dillon, Elizabeth Maddock. "A Sea of Texts: The Atlantic World, Spatial Mapping, and Equiano's *Narrative*." In *Religion, Space, and the Atlantic World*, edited by John Corrigan, 25–54. Columbia: University of South Carolina Press, 2017.

Dolan, Frances E. "Gender and the 'Lost' Spaces of Catholicism." *Journal of Interdisciplinary History* 32, no. 4 (Spring 2002): 641–665. https://www.jstor.org/stable /3656149.

Doolittle, T. S. "The Architecture of the Reformed Church." In *A Manual of the Reformed Church in America: Formerly Ref. Prot. Dutch Church, 1628–1902*, edited by Edward Tanjore Corwin, 152–160. New York: Reformed Church in America, 1879.

Egmond, Florike. "Fragmentatie rechtverscheidenheid en rechtsongelijkheid in de Noordelijke Nederlanden tijdens de zeventiende en acttiende eeuw." In *Nieuw Licht op Oude Justitie: Misdaad en straf ten tijde van de republiek*, edited by Sjoerd Faber, 9–23. Muiderberg: Dick Coutinho, 1989.

Egmond, Florike. *Underworlds: Organized Crime in the Netherlands, 1650–1800*. Cambridge: Polity, 1993.

Eliade, Mircea. *The Sacred and the Profane: The Nature of Religion*. Translated by Willard R. Trask. Boston: Mariner Books, 1968.

Ellis, Clifton, and Rebecca Ginsberg, eds. *Slavery in the City: Architecture and Landscapes of Urban Slavery in North America*. Charlottesville: University of Virginia Press, 2017.

Emmer, P. C. *De Nederlandse Slavenhandel, 1500–1850*. Amsterdam: Uitgeverij De Arbeidspers, 2000.

Emmer, P. C. "De Slavenhandel van en naar Nieuw-Nederland." *Economisch- en social- historisch jaarboek 35*, no. 1 (1972): 94–147.

Emmer, Pieter, and Ernst van den Boogaart. *The Dutch in the Atlantic Economy, 1580–1880: Trade, Slavery and Emancipation*. Aldershot: Ashgate, 1998.

Epperson, Terrence W. "Panopticon Plantations: The Garden Sights of Thomas Jefferson and George Mason." In *Lines that Divide: Historical Archaeologies of Race, Class, and Gender*, edited by James A. Delle, Stephen Mrozowski, and Robert Paynter, 58–77. Knoxville: University of Tennessee Press, 2000.

Epperson, Terrence W. "Race and the Disciplines of the Plantation." *Historical Archeology* 24, no. 4 (1990): 29–36.

Fabend, Firth Haring. *Zion on the Hudson: Dutch New York and New Jersey in the Age of Revivals*. New Brunswick, NJ: Rutgers University Press, 2000.

Ferguson, Leland. "'The Cross Is a Magic Sign': Marks on Eighteenth-Century Bowls from South Carolina." In *"I, Too, Am America": Archeological Studies of African-American Life*, edited by Theresa Singleton, 116–131. Charlottesville: University Press of Virginia, 1999.

Ferguson, Leland. *Uncommon Ground: Archeology and Early African America, 1650–1800*. Washington, DC: Smithsonian Institution Press, 1992.

Fick, Carolyn E. *The Making of Haiti: Saint Domingue Revolution from Below*. Knoxville: University of Tennessee Press, 1990.

Finch, Aisha. *Rethinking Slave Rebellion in Cuba: La Escalera and the Insurgency of 1841–1844*. Chapel Hill: University of North Carolina Press, 2015.

Fischer, Kirsten, and Jennifer Morgan. "Sex, Race, and the Colonial Project." *William and Mary Quarterly* 60, no. 1 (January 2003): 197–198. https://doi.org/10.2307/3491504.

Fiske, John. "Surveilling the City: Whiteness, the Black Man and Democratic Totalitarianism." *Theory, Culture & Society* 15, no. 2: 67–88. https://doi.org/10.1177/026327698015002003.

Fitts, Robert K. "The Landscapes of Northern Bondage." *Historical Archeology* 30, no. 2 (1996): 54–73. https://doi.org/10.1007/BF03373588.

Flather, Amanda. "Gender, Space and Place: The Experience of Servants in Rural Households 1550–1750." *Mundo Agragrio* 18, no. 39 (December 2017): 171–188. https://www.jstor.org/stable/24542990.

Foote, Thelma Wills. *Black and White Manhattan: The History of Racial Formation in Colonial New York City*. Oxford: Oxford University Press, 2004.

Foucault, Michel. *Discipline and Punish: The Birth of the Prison*. Translated by Alan Sheridan. New York: Pantheon Books, 1977.

Foucault, Michel. "Of Other Spaces." *Diacritics* 16 (Spring 1986): 22–27. https://doi.org/10.2307/464648.

Fox, J. "'For Good and Sufficient Reasons': An Examination of Early Dutch East India Company Ordinances on Slaves and Slavery." In *Slavery, Bondage, & Dependency in Southeast Asia*, edited by Anthony Reid, 246–262. New York: St. Martin's, 1983.

Frijhoff, Willem. *Wegen van Evert Willemsz.: Een Hollands weeskind op zoek naar zichzelf, 1607–1647*. Nijmegen: SUN, 1995.

Frijhoff, Willem, and Jaap Jacobs. "The Dutch, New Netherland, and Thereafter (1609–1780s)." In *Four Centuries of Dutch-American Relations, 1609–2009*, edited by Hans Krabbendam, Cornelis A. van Minnen, and Giles Scott-Smith, 31–48. Albany: State University of New York Press, 2009.

Fromont, Cécile. *The Art of Conversion: Christian Visual Culture in the Kingdom of Kongo*. Chapel Hill: University of North Carolina Press, 2014.

Fuente, Alejandro de la. "Slaves and the Creation of Legal Rights in Cuba: Coartacion and Papel." *Hispanic American Historical Review* 87, no. 4 (2007): 659–692. https://doi.org/10.1215/00182168.

Fuentes, Marisa. *Dispossessed Lives: Enslaved Women, Violence, and the Archive*. Philadelphia: University of Pennsylvania Press, 2018.

Furman, Gabriel. *Antiquities of Long Island*. New York: J. W. Bouton, 1875.

Games, Alison. "Cohabitation, Suriname-Style: English Inhabitants in Dutch Suriname after 1667." *William and Mary Quarterly*, 3d ser., 72, no. 2 (April 2015): 195–242. https://doi.org/10.5309/Willmaryquar.72.2.0195.

Garofalo, Leo. "Afro-Iberian Subjects: Petitioning the Crown at Home, Serving the Crown Abroad, 1590s–1630s." In *Afro-Latino Voices: Narratives from the Early Modern Ibero-Atlantic World, 1550–1812*, edited by Kathryn McKnight and Leo Garofalo, 52–63. Indianapolis: Hackett, 2009.

Garvan, Anthony. "The Protestant Plain Style before 1630." *Journal of the Society of Architectural Historians* 9, no. 3 (October 1950): 4–13. https://doi.org/10.2307/987455.

Gehring, Charles T. "The Dutch Language in Colonial New York: An Investigation of a Language in Decline and Its Relationship to Social Change." PhD diss., Indiana University Press, 1973.

Gehring, Charles T. "New Netherland: The Formative Years, 1609–1632." In *Four Centuries of Dutch-American Relations, 1609–2009*, edited by Hans Krabbendam, Cornelis A. van Minnen, and Giles Scott-Smith, 74–84. Albany: State University of New York Press, 2009.

Gellman, David N. *Emancipating New York: The Politics of Slavery and Freedom, 1777–1827*. Baton Rouge: Louisiana State University Press, 2006.

Gerbner, Katharine. *Christian Slavery: Conversion and Race in the Protestant Atlantic World*. Philadelphia: University of Pennsylvania Press, 2019.

Gerlach, Don R. "Black Arson in Albany, New York: November 1793." *Journal of Black Studies* 7, no. 3 (1977): 301–312. https://www.jstor.org/stable/2783709.

Gigantino II, James J. *The Ragged Road to Abolition: Slavery and Freedom in New Jersey, 1775–1865*. Philadelphia: University of Pennsylvania Press, 2014.

Goetz, Rebecca Anne. *The Baptism of Early Virginia: How Christianity Created Race*. Baltimore: Johns Hopkins University Press, 2012.

Gomez, Michael A. *Exchanging Our Country Marks: The Transformation of African Identities in the Colonial and Antebellum South*. Chapel Hill: University of North Carolina Press, 1998.

Goodfriend, Joyce. *Before the Melting Pot: Society and Culture in Colonial New York City, 1644–1730*. Princeton, NJ: Princeton University Press, 1992.

Goodfriend, Joyce. "Black Families in New Netherland." In *A Beautiful and Fruitful Place*, edited by Nancy McClure Zeller, 147–156. N.p., 1991.

Goodfriend, Joyce. "Burghers and Blacks: The Evolution of a Slave Society at New Amsterdam." *New York History* 59, no. 2 (1978): 125–144. https://www.jstor.org/stable/23169655.

Goodfriend, Joyce. "Slavery in Colonial New York." *Journal of Urban History* 35, no. 3 (December 2008): 485–496. https://jstor.org/stable/44613788.

Goodfriend, Joyce. "The Social and Cultural Life of Dutch Settlers, 1664–1776." In *Four Centuries of Dutch-American Relations, 1609–2009*, edited by Hans Krabbendam, Cornelis A. van Minnen, and Giles Scott-Smith, 120–131. Albany: State University of New York Press, 2009.

Goodfriend, Joyce. "The Social Dimensions of Congregational Life in Colonial New York City." *William and Mary Quarterly* 46, no. 2 (April 1989): 252–278. https://doi.org/10.2307/1920254.

Goodfriend, Joyce. "The Souls of African American Children: New Amsterdam." *Common-Place* 3, no. 4 (July 2003). http://www.common-place-archives.org/vol-03/no-04/new-york/.

Goodfriend, Joyce. *Who Should Rule at Home?: Confronting the Elite in British New York City.* Ithaca, NY: Cornell University Press, 2017.

Goodfriend, Joyce. "Why New Netherland Matters." In *Explorers, Fortunes, & Love Letters: A Window on New Netherland*, edited by Martha Dickinson Shattuck, 148–161. New York: New Netherland Institute and Mount Ida Press, 2009.

Goslinga, Cornelis Ch. *The Dutch in the Caribbean and on the Wild Coast 1580–1680.* Assen: Van Gorcum, 1971.

Gouw, Jan ter. *De Volksvermaken.* Haarlem: Erven F. Bohn, 1871.

Greenberg, Douglas. "Patterns of Criminal Prosecution in Eighteenth Century New York." In *Courts and Law in Early New York: Selected Essays*, edited by Leo Hershkowitz and Milton M. Klein, 133–153. Port Washington, NY: Kennikat, 1978.

Greene, Lorenzo J. "The New England Negro as Seen in Advertisements for Runaway Slaves." *Journal of Negro History* 29, no. 2 (April 1944): 125–146. https://doi.org/10.2307/2715307.

Grey, Cam. "Slavery in the Late Roman World." In *The Cambridge World History of Slavery.* Vol. 1, *The Ancient Mediterranean World*, edited by Keith Bradley and Paul Cartledge, 482–509. Cambridge: Cambridge University Press, 2011.

Grivno, Max. *Gleanings of Freedom: Free and Slave Labor along the Mason-Dixon Line, 1790–1860.* Urbana: University of Illinois Press, 2011.

Grosse, Christian. "Places of Sanctification: The Liturgical Sacrality of Genevan Reformed Churches." In *Sacred Space in Early Modern Europe*, edited by Andrew Spicer and Will Coster, 60–80. Cambridge: Cambridge University Press, 2005.

Groth, Michael E. *Slavery and Freedom in the Mid-Hudson Valley.* Albany: State University of New York Press, 2017.

Haan, F. de. *Oud Batavia.* Vol. 1. Batavia: G. Kolff, 1922.

Hacker, Barton C. "Firearms, Horses, and Slave Soldiers: The Military History of African Slavery." *Icon* 14 (2008): 62–83. https://www.jstor.org/stable/23787162.

Hackett, David G. *The Rude Hand of Innovation: Religion and Social Order in Albany, New York, 1652–1836.* Oxford: Oxford University Press, 1991.

Hadden, Sally E. *Slave Patrols: Law and Violence in Virginia and the Carolinas.* Cambridge, MA: Harvard University Press, 2001.

Haefeli, Evan. *New Netherland and the Dutch Origins of American Religious Liberty.* Philadelphia: University of Pennsylvania Press, 2012.

Hague, Stephen. "Building Status in the British Atlantic World: The Gentleman's House in the English West Country and Pennsylvania." In *Building the British Atlantic World: Spaces, Places, and Material Culture, 1600–1850,* edited by Daniel Maudlin and Bernard L. Herman, 231–252. Chapel Hill: University of North Carolina Press, 2016.

Hall, David D. *Worlds of Wonder, Days of Judgement: Popular Religious Belief in Early England.* Cambridge, MA: Harvard University Press, 1990.

Hall, Gwendolyn Midlo. *Africans in Colonial Louisiana: The Development of Afro-Creole Culture in the Eighteenth Century.* Baton Rouge: Louisiana State University Press, 1995.

Hamer, Deborah. "Creating an Orderly Society: The Regulation of Marriage and Sex in the Dutch Atlantic World, 1621–1674." PhD diss., Columbia University, 2014.

Hamer, Deborah. "Marriage and the Construction of Colonial Order: Jurisdiction, Gender, and Class in Seventeenth Century Dutch Batavia." *Gender & History* 29, no. 3 (November 2017): 622–640. https://doi.org/10.1111/1468-0424.12316.

Hamilton, Sarah, and Andrew Spicer. "Defining the Holy: The Delineation of Sacred Space." In *Defining the Holy: Sacred Space in Medieval and Early Modern Europe,* edited by Sarah Hamilton and Andrew Spicer, 1–26. New York: Ashgate, 2005.

Hanley, Ryan. "Calvinism, Proslavery and James Albert Ukawsaw Gronniosaw." *Slavery & Abolition* 36, no. 2 (2015): 360–381. https://doi.org/10.1080/0144039X.2014.920973.

Hardesty, Jared. *Unfreedom: Slavery and Dependence in Eighteenth-Century Boston.* New York: New York University Press, 2016.

Harris, Leslie M. *In the Shadow of Slavery: African Americans in New York City, 1626–1863.* Chicago: University of Chicago Press, 2003.

Hart, Simon. "The City-Colony of New Amstel on the Delaware: II." *de Halve Maen: Journal of The Holland Society of New York* 40, no. 1 (April 1965): 5–6, 13–14.

Hartman, Saidiya V. *Lose Your Mother: A Journey along the Atlantic Slave Route.* New York: Farrar, Straus and Giroux, 2007.

Hartman, Saidiya V. *Scenes of Subjection: Terror, Slavery, and Self-Making in Nineteenth-Century America.* Oxford: Oxford University Press, 1997.

Hartman, Saidiya V. "Venus in Two Acts." *Small Axe* 26, v. 12, no. 2 (June 2008): 1–14. https://www.muse.jhu/article/241115.

Hasbrouck, Richard. *A Brief History of the New Paltz Reformed Church.* Published by the Tricentennial Committee on the occasion of the 300th Anniversary, 1982.

Hatfield, April Lee. "Dutch and New Netherland Merchants in the Seventeenth-Century English Chesapeake." In *The Atlantic Economy during the Seventeenth and Eighteenth Centuries: Organization, Operation, Practice, and Personnel,* edited by Peter A. Coclanis, 205–228. Columbia: University of South Carolina Press, 2005.

Hayes, Katherine Howlett. *Slavery before Race: Europeans, Africans, and Indians at Long Island's Sylvester Manor Plantation, 1651–1884.* New York: New York University Press, 2013.

Heijer, Henk den. *De geschiedenis van de WIC*. Zutphen: Walburg Pers, 2002.

Heijer, Henk den. "The Dutch West India Company, 1621–1791." In *Riches from the Atlantic Commerce: Dutch Transatlantic Trade and Shipping, 1585–1817*, edited by Johannes Postma and Victor Enthoven, 77–114. Leiden: Brill, 2003.

Heijer, Henk den. "Goud, ivoor en slaven. Scheepvaart en handel van de Tweede Westindische Compagnie of Afrika, 1674–1740." PhD diss., Universiteit van Leiden, 1997.

Herman, Bernard L. "Slave and Servant Housing in Charleston, 1770–1820." *Historical Archeology* 33, no. 3 (1999): 88–101. https://jstor.org/stable/25616727.

Herskowitz, L. "The Troublesome Turk: An Illustration of the Judicial Process in New Amsterdam." *New York History* 46, no. 4 (1965): 299–310. https://jstor.org/stable/23162613.

Heywood, Linda M. "Queen Njinga Mbandi Ana De Sousa of Ndongo/Matamba: African Leadership, Diplomacy, and Ideology, 1620s–1650s." In *Afro-Latino Voices: Narratives from the Early Modern Ibero-Atlantic World, 1550–1812*, edited by Kathryn McKnight and Leo Garofalo, 38–51. Indianapolis: Hackett, 2009.

Heywood, Linda M., and John K. Thornton. *Central Africans, Atlantic Creoles, and the Foundation of the Americas, 1585–1660*. Cambridge: Cambridge University Press, 2007.

Heywood, Linda M., and John K. Thornton. "Intercultural Relations between Europeans and Blacks in New Netherland." In *Four Centuries of Dutch-American Relations: 1609–2009*, edited by Hans Krabbendam, Cornelis A. van Minnen, and Giles Scott-Smith, 192–203. Albany: State University of New York Press, 2009.

Heywood, Linda M., and John K. Thornton. "The Treason of Dom Pedro Nkanga a Mvemba against Dom Diogo, King of Kongo, 1550." In *Afro-Latino Voices: Narratives from the Early Modern Ibero-Atlantic World, 1550–1812*, edited by Kathryn McKnight and Leo Garofalo, 2–29. Indianapolis: Hackett, 2009.

Higginbotham, A. Leon. *In the Matter of Color: Race and the American Legal Process: The Colonial Period*. Oxford: Oxford University Press, 1978.

Higman, Barry. *Slave Populations of the British Caribbean*. Mona, Jamaica: University of West Indies Press, 1995.

Hilton, Anne. *The Kingdom of Kongo*. Oxford: Clarendon, 1985.

Hodges, Graham Russell. "The Pastor and the Prostitute: Sexual Power among African Americans and Germans in Colonial New York." In *Sex, Love, Race: Crossing Boundaries in North American History*, edited by Martha Hodes, 60–71. New York: New York University Press, 1999.

Hodges, Graham Russell. *Root & Branch: African Americans in New York & East Jersey*. Chapel Hill: University of North Carolina Press, 1999.

Hodges, Graham Russell. *Slavery and Freedom in the Rural North: African Americans in Monmouth County, New Jersey, 1665–1865*. Madison: Madison House, 1997.

Hoff, Henry, B. "A Colonial Black Family in New York and New Jersey: Pieter Santomee and His Descendants." *Journal of the Afro-American Historical and Genealogical Society* 9 (1998): 101–134.

Hoff, Henry B. "Swan Janse Van Luane: A Free Black in Seventeenth Century Kings County." *New York Genealogical and Biographical Record* 125 (April 1994): 74–77.

Horton, James Oliver, and Lois E. Horton. *In Hope of Liberty: Culture, Community, and Protest among Northern Free Blacks, 1700–1860*. New York: Oxford University Press, 1997.

Howell, George R., ed. *History of the County of Albany, N.Y., from 1609–1886. With Portraits, Biographies and Illustrations*. New York: W. W. Munsell, 1886.

Huey, Paul. "A New Look at an Old Object." *New York State Preservationist* 8, no. 2 (2004): 22–23.

Humphrey, Thomas J. "Agrarian Rioting in Albany County, New York: Tenants, Markets and Revolution in the Hudson Valley, 1751–1801." PhD diss., Northern Illinois University, 1997.

Isaac, Rhys. *The Transformation of Virginia, 1740–1790*. Chapel Hill: University of North Carolina Press, 1982.

Ittersum, Martine Julia van. "The Long Goodbye: Hugo Grotius' Justification of Dutch Expansion Overseas, 1615–1645." *History of European Idea* 36 (2010): 386–411. https://doi.org/10.1016/j.histeuroideas.2010.05.003.

Jacobs, Bart. "The Upper Guinea Origins of Papiamentu: Linguistic and Historical Evidence." *Diachronica* 26, no. 3 (2009): 319–379. https://doi.org/10.1075/dia.26.3.02jac.

Jacobs, Jaap. *The Colony of New Netherland: A Dutch Settlement in Seventeenth-Century America*. Ithaca, NY: Cornell University Press, 2009.

Jacobs, Jaap. "Dutch Proprietary Manors in America: The Patroonships in New Netherland." In *Constructing Early Modern Empires: Proprietary Ventures in the Atlantic World*, edited by Lou Roper, 301–326. Leiden: Brill, 2007.

Jacobs, Jaap. "Migration, Population, and Government in New Netherland." In *Four Centuries of Dutch-American Relations, 1609–2009*, edited by Hans Krabbendam, Cornelis A. van Minnen, and Giles Scott-Smith, 85–96. Albany: State University of New York Press, 2009.

Jacobs, Jaap. *New Netherland: A Dutch Colony in Seventeenth-Century America*. Leiden: Brill Academic, 2015.

Jacobs, Jaap. "'To Favor This New and Growing City of New Amsterdam with a Court of Justice': The Relations between Rulers and Ruled in New Amsterdam." In *Amsterdam-New York: Transatlantic Relations and Urban Identities since 1653*, edited by George Harinck and Hans Krabbendam, 17–29. Amsterdam: VU Uitgeverij, 2005.

Jacobs, Jaap. "Van Angola naar Manhattan. Slavernij in Nieuw-Nederland in de seventiende Eeuw." In *Slaven en schepen. Enkele reis, bestemming onbekend*, edited by Remmelt Daalder, Andrea Kieskamp, and Dirk J. Tang, 69–75. Leiden: Primavera, 2001.

Johnson, Matthew. *An Archeology of Capitalism*. Oxford: Blackwell, 1996.

Johnson, Rashauna. *Slavery's Metropolis: Unfree Labor in New Orleans during the Age of Revolutions*. Cambridge: Cambridge University Press, 2016.

Johnson, Walter. *Soul by Soul: Life inside the Antebellum Slave Market*. Cambridge, MA: Harvard University Press, 1999.

Jones, Martha. *Birthright Citizens: A History of Race and Rights in Antebellum America*. Cambridge: Cambridge University Press, 2018.

Joosse, Leendert. *Geloof in de Nieuwe Wereld: Ontmoeting met Afrikanen en Indianen (1600–1700)*. Kampen: Uitgeverij Kok, 2008.

Joseph, J. W. "'. . . All of Cross'—African Potters, Marks, and Meanings in the Folk Pottery of Edgefield District, South Carolina." *Historical Archeology* 45, no. 2 (2011): 134–155. https://www.jstor.org/stable/23070092.

Judd, Jacob. "Frederick Philipse and the Madagascar Trade." *New York Historical Society Quarterly* 55, no. 4 (September 1971): 354–374.

Kehoe, Marsely L. "Dutch Batavia: Exposing the Hierarchy of the Dutch Colonial City." *Journal of Historians of Netherlandish Art* 7, no. 1 (Winter 2015): 1–28. https://doi.org/10.5092/jhna.2015.7.1.3.

Kennington, Kelly. *In the Shadow of Dred Scott: St. Louis Freedom Suits and the Legal Culture of Slavery in Antebellum America*. Athens: University of Georgia Press, 2017.

Kilde, Jeanne Halgren. *Sacred Power, Sacred Space: An Introduction to Christian Architecture and Worship*. Oxford: Oxford University Press, 2008.

Kirk, Matthew. "Out of the Ashes of Craft, the Fires of Consumerism: A 1797 Deposit in Downtown Albany." In *People, Places, and Material Things: Historical Archeology of Albany, New York*, edited by Charles L. Fisher, 47–56. Albany: New York State Museum, 2003.

Klooster, Wim. "The Dutch in the Atlantic." In *Four Centuries of Dutch-American Relations, 1609–2009*, edited by Hans Krabbendam, Cornelis A. van Minnen, Giles Scott-Smith, 63–73. Albany: State University of New York Press, 2009.

Klooster, Wim. *The Dutch Moment: War, Trade, and Settlement in the Seventeenth-Century Atlantic World*. Ithaca, NY: Cornell University Press, 2016.

Knaap, Gerrit. "Kasteel, stad en land: Het begin van het Nederlandse Imperium in de Oost." *Leidschrift* 21, no. 2 (September 2006): 17–30.

Koot, Christian. "Anglo-Dutch Trade in the Chesapeake and the British Caribbean, 1621–1733." In *Dutch Atlantic Connections, 1680–1800: Linking Empires, Bridging Borders*, edited by Gert Oostindie and Jessica V. Roitman, 72–99. Leiden: Brill, 2014.

Kooten, Rogier van. "'Like a Child in Their Debt, and Consequently Their Slave?' Power Structures in the Commercial Circuits of a Colonial Agro-System near New York around 1675." Master's thesis, University of Antwerp, 2016.

Koppelson, Heather Miyano. *Faithful Bodies: Performing Religion and Race in the Puritan Atlantic*. New York: New York University Press, 2014.

Kothari, Uma. "Geographies and Histories of Unfreedom: Indentured Labourers and Contract Workers in Mauritius." *Journal of Development Studies* 49, no. 8 (2013): 1042–1057. https://doi.org/10.1080/00220388.2013.780039.

Krabbendam, Hans, Cornelius A. van Minnen, and Giles Scott-Smith, eds. *Four Centuries of Dutch American Relations, 1609–2009*. Albany: State University of New York Press, 2009.

Kramer, Erin. "New York's Unrighteous Beginnings." Gotham Center Blog. August 5, 2020. https://www.gothamcenter.org/blog/new-yorks-unrighteous-beginnings.

Kross, Jessica. *The Evolution of an American Town: Newtown, New York, 1642–1775*. Philadelphia: Temple University Press, 1983.

Kruger, Vivienne. "Born to Run: The Slave Family in Early New York, 1626 to 1827." PhD diss., Columbia University, 1985.

Kruijtzer, Gijs. "European Migration in the Dutch Sphere." In *Dutch Colonialism, Migration and Cultural Heritage*, edited by Gert Oostindie, 97–154. Leiden: KITLV, 2008.

Landers, Jane. *Black Society in Spanish Florida*. Urbana: University of Illinois Press, 1999.

Landers, Jane. "Traditions of African American Freedom and Community in Spanish Colonial Florida." In *The African American Heritage of Florida*, edited by David R. Colburn and Jane L. Landers, 17–41. Gainesville: University Press of Florida, 1995.

Lanier, Gabrielle M. *Everyday Architecture of the Mid-Atlantic: Looking at Buildings and Landscapes*. Baltimore: Johns Hopkins University Press, 1997.

Law, Robin. "Horses, Firearms, and Political Power in Pre-Colonial West Africa." *Past and Present Society*, no. 72 (August 1979): 119–120. https://www.jstor.org/stable/650330.

Lee, Esther J., et al. "MtDNA Origins of an Enslaved Labor Force from the 18th Century Schuyler Flatts Burial Ground in Colonial Albany, NY: Africans, Native Americans, and Malagasy?" *Journal of Archeological Science* 36 (2009): 2805–2810. https://doi.org/10.1016/j.jas.2009.09.008.

Lefebvre, Henri. *The Production of Space*. Translated by Donald Nicholson-Smith. Oxford, UK: Blackwell, 1991. First published in French in 1974.

Leone, M. P., and G.-M. Fry. "Conjuring in the Big House Kitchen: An Interpretation of African American Belief Systems Based on the Use of Archaeology and Folklore Sources." *Journal of American Folklore* 112, no. 445 (1999): 372–403. https://www.jstor.org/stable/541368.

Leone, Mark P. "Interpreting Ideology in Historical Archeology: Using the Rules of Perspective in William Paca Garden in Annapolis, Maryland." In *Ideology, Power, and Prehistory*, edited by Daniel Miller and Christopher Tilley, 25–36. Cambridge: Cambridge University Press, 1984.

Lepore, Jill. *New York Burning: Liberty, Slavery and Conspiracy in Eighteenth-Century Manhattan*. New York: Alfred A. Knopf, 2005.

Lepore, Jill. "The Tightening Vise: Slavery and Freedom in British New York." In *Slavery in New York*, edited by Ira Berlin and Leslie Harris, 57–89. New York: New Press, 2005.

Lewis, Kenneth E. "Plantation Layout and Function in the South Carolina Lowcountry." In *The Archeology of Slavery and Plantation Life*, edited by Theresa A. Singleton, 35–65. San Diego: Academic Press, 1985.

Lieburg, Fred van. "The Dutch and Their Religion." In *Four Centuries of Dutch-American Relations, 1609–2009*, edited by Hans Krabbendam, Cornelis A. van Minnen, and Giles Scott-Smith, 154–165. Albany: State University of New York Press, 2009.

Lindner, Christopher. "West African Cosmogram Recognized Adjacent to Probably Hearth Concealment at 19th-Century Slave Quarter in Mid-Hudson Valley Settlement of Early German Americans." *SHA Newsletter: Quarterly News on Historical Archeology from around the Globe* 49, no. 1 (Spring 2016): 28–29.

Linebaugh, Peter, and Marcus Rediker. *The Many-Headed Hydra: Sailors, Slaves, Commoners, and the Hidden History of the Revolutionary Atlantic*. Boston: Beacon, 2000.

Lipman, Andrew. *The Saltwater Frontier: Indians and the Contest for the American Coast.* New Haven, CT: Yale University Press, 2015.

Mabee, Carleton. *Sojourner Truth: Slave, Prophet, Legend.* New York: New York University Press, 1995.

MacGaffey, Wyatt. *Religion and Society in Central Africa: The BaKongo of Lower Zaire.* Chicago: Chicago University Press, 1986.

Maika, Dennis. "Encounters: Slavery and Philipse Family: 1680–1751." In *Dutch New York: The Roots of Hudson Valley Culture*, edited by Roger Panetta, 35–72. Yonkers, NY: Hudson River Museum/Fordham University Press, 2009.

Maika, Dennis. "Slavery, Race, and Culture in Early New York." *de Halve Maen: Magazine of the Dutch Colonial Period in America* (Summer 2000): 27–33.

Maika, Dennis. "To 'Experiment with a Parcel of Negros': Incentive, Collaboration, and Competition in New Amsterdam's Slave Trade." *Journal of Early American History* 10, no. 1 (2020): 33–69.

Manca, Joseph. "Erasing the Dutch: The Critical Reception of Hudson Valley Dutch Architecture, 1670–1840." In *Going Dutch: The Dutch Presence in America, 1609–2009*, edited by Joyce D. Goodfriend, Benjamin Schmidt, and Annette Stott, 59–84. Leiden: Brill, 2008.

Maskiell, Nicole. "Bound by Bondage: Slavery among Elites in Colonial Massachusetts and New York." PhD diss., Cornell University, 2013.

Mbeki, Linda, and Matthias van Rossum. "Private Slave Trade in the Dutch Indian Ocean World: A Study into the Networks and Backgrounds of the Slavers and the Enslaved in South Asia and South Africa." *Slavery & Abolition* 38, no. 1 (2017): 95–116.

McGill, Joseph. "There Is Something Special about Sleepovers." The Slave Dwelling Project Blog, November 8, 2019. https://slavedwellingproject.org/there-is-something-special-about-sleepovers/.

McKee, Larry. "The Ideals and Realities behind the Design and Use of 19th Century Virginia Slave Cabins." In *The Art and Mystery of Historical Archeology: Essays in Honor of James Deetz*, edited by Anne Elizabeth Yentsch and Mary C. Beaudry, 195–214. Boca Raton, FL: CRC, 1992.

McKinley, Michelle A. *Fractional Freedoms: Slavery, Intimacy, and Legal Mobilization in Colonial Lima.* Cambridge: Cambridge University Press, 2016.

McKittrick, Katherine. *Demonic Grounds: Black Women and the Cartographies of Struggle.* Minneapolis: University of Minnesota Press, 2006.

McKnight, Kathryn, and Leo Garofalo, eds. *Afro-Latino Voices: Narratives from the Early Modern Ibero-Atlantic World, 1550–1812.* Indianapolis: Hackett, 2009.

McLaughlin, William. "Dutch Rural New York: Community, Economy and Family in Colonial Flatbush." PhD diss., Columbia University, 1981.

McManus, Edgar J. *A History of Negro Slavery in New York.* Syracuse, NY: Syracuse University Press, 1996.

Meischke, Ir. R. *Het Nederlandse Woonhuis van 1300–1800: Vijftig jaar Vereniging 'Hendrick de Keyser.* Haarlem: H. D. Tjeenk Willink & Soon N.V., 1969.

Meischke, Ir. R., H. J. Zantkuijl, W. Raue, and P.T.E.E. Rosenberg. *Huizen in Nederland: Amsterdam. Architectuurhistorische verkenningen aan de hand van het bezit van de Vereniging Hendrick de Keyser*, deel 1. Zwolle: Waanders Uitgevers, 1995.

Mello, José Antônio Gonsales de. *Nederlanders in Brazilië (1624–1654): De invloed van de Hollandse besetting op het leven en de cultuur in Noord-Brazilië*. Translated by G. N. Visser. Zutphen: Walburg, 2001 [repr. ed.].

Merlin-Faucquez, Anne-Claire. "De la Nouvelle-Néerlande à New York: La naissance d'une société esclavagiste (1624–1712)." Ph.D. diss., Université Paris VIII–Vincennes Saint Denis, 2011.

Merwick, Donna. *The Shame and the Sorrow: Dutch-Amerindian Encounter in New Netherland*. Philadelphia: University of Pennsylvania Press, 2006.

Meuwese, Mark. *Brothers in Arms, Partners in Trade: Dutch-Indigenous Alliances in the Atlantic World, 1595–1674*. Leiden: Brill, 2012.

Miller, Daniel. *Unwrapping Christmas*. Oxford: Oxford University Press, 1993.

Miller, Joseph. *Kings and Kinsmen: Early Mbundu States in Angola*. Oxford: Clarendon, 1976.

Miller, Marla. "Labor and Liberty in the Age of Refinement: Gender, Class, and the Built Environment." *Perspectives in Vernacular Architecture* 10 (2005): 15–31.

Mol, Hans de. "Het Huwelyck is goddelyck van aart, wanneer men tsaam uyt reine liefde paart." In *Kent, en Versint eer datje Mint: Vrijen en trouwen 1500–1800*, edited by Petra van Boheemen et al. Zwolle: Waanders Uitgeverij, 1989.

Molen, S. J. van der. *Levend Volksleven: Een Eigentijdse Volkskunde Van Nederland*. Van Gorcum: HJ Prakke & HMG Prakke, 1961.

Moore, Christopher. "A World of Possibilities: Slavery and Freedom in Dutch New Amsterdam." In *Slavery in New York*, edited by Ira Berlin and Leslie M. Harris, 29–56. New York: New Press, 2005.

Morgan, Jennifer. *Laboring Women: Reproduction and Gender in New World Slavery*. Philadelphia: University of Pennsylvania Press, 2004.

Mosterman, Andrea C. "Een slavenschip voor Nieuwer-Amstel, stadskolonie aan de Delaware." In *Amsterdam en de Slavernij in Oost en West*, edited by Pepijn Brandon, Guno Jones, Nancy Jouwe, and Matthias van Rossum, 164–171. Amsterdam: Uitgeverij Het Spectrum, 2020.

Mosterman, Andrea C. "'I Thought They Were Worthy': A Dutch Reformed Church Minister and His Congregation Debate African American Membership in the Church." *Early American Studies* 14, no. 3 (Summer 2016): 610–616.

Mosterman, Andrea C. "Sharing Spaces in a New World Environment: African-Dutch Contributions to North American Culture, 1626–1826." PhD diss., Boston University, 2012.

Mouritsen, Henrik. *The Freedman in the Roman World*. Cambridge: Cambridge University Press, 2015.

Mouw, Dirk Edward. "*Moederkerk* and *Vaderland*: Religion and Ethnic Identity in the Middle Colonies, 1690–1772." PhD diss., University of Iowa, 2009.

Murphy, Joseph M. *Working the Spirit: Ceremonies of the African Diaspora*. Boston: Beacon, 1994.

Murphy, Larry G. *Sojourner Truth: A Biography*. Santa Barbara, CA: Greenwood, 2011.

Nelson, Louis P. *Architecture and Empire in Jamaica*. New Haven, CT: Yale University Press, 2016.

Nelson, Louis P. *The Beauty of Holiness: Anglicanism & Architecture in Colonial South Carolina*. Chapel Hill: University of North Carolina Press, 2008.

Newell, Margaret Ellen. *Brethren by Nature: New England Indians, Colonists, and the Origins of American Slavery*. Ithaca, NY: Cornell University Press, 2015.

Newman, Oscar. *Defensible Space: Crime Prevention through Urban Design*. New York: Macmillan, 1972.

Newman, Simon. *A New World of Labor: The Development of Plantation Slavery in the British Atlantic*. Philadelphia: University of Pennsylvania Press, 2013.

The New York African Burial Ground: Unearthing the African Presence in Colonial New York. Washington, DC: Howard University Press, 2009.

Niaah, Sonjah Stanley. "Mapping Black Atlantic Performance Geographies: From Slave Ship to Ghetto." In *Black Geographies and the Politics of Place*, edited by Katherine McKittrick and Clyde Woods, 193–217. Boston: South End, 2007.

Niemeijer, Hendrik E. *Batavia: Een koloniale samenleving in de zeventiende eeuw*. Amsterdam: Uitgeverij Balans, 2005.

Nierop, Henk van. "Sacred Space Contested: Amsterdam in the Age of the Reformation." In *The Power of Space in Late Medieval and Early Modern Europe: The Cities of Italy, Northern France, and the Low Countries*, edited by Marc Boone and Martha Howell, 153–161. Turnhout, Belgium: Brepols, 2013.

Noorlander, D. L. *Heaven's Wrath: The Protestant Reformation and the Dutch West India Company in the Atlantic World*. Ithaca, NY: Cornell University Press, 2019.

Northrup, Ansel Judd. *Slavery in New York: A Historical Sketch*. Albany: University of the State of New York, 1900.

Olson, Edwin. "The Slave Code in Colonial New York." *Journal of Negro History* 29, no. 2 (1944): 147–165. https://doi.org/10.2307/2715308.

Olwell, Robert. *Masters, Slaves, and Subjects: The Culture of Power in the South Carolina Low Country, 1740–1790*. Ithaca, NY: Cornell University Press, 1998.

O'Malley, Gregory E. *Final Passages: The Intercolonial Slave Trade of British America, 1619–1807*. Chapel Hill: University of North Carolina Press, 2014.

Otto, Paul. *The Dutch-Munsee Encounter in America*. New York: Berghahn Books, 2006.

Painter, Nell Irvin. *Sojourner Truth: A Life, a Symbol*. New York: W. W. Norton, 1997.

Panetta, Roger, ed. *Dutch New York: The Roots of Hudson Valley Culture*. New York: Fordham University Press, 2009.

Phillips, William D., Jr. "Manumission in Metropolitan Spain and the Canaries." In *Paths to Freedom: Manumission in the Atlantic World*, edited by Rosemary Brana-Shute and Randy J. Sparks, 31–50. Columbia: University of South Carolina Press, 2009.

Piersen, William D. *Black Yankees: The Development of an Afro-American Subculture in Eighteenth-Century New England*. Amherst: University of Massachusetts Press, 1988.

Postma, Johannes. "The Dimensions of the Dutch Slave Trade from Western Africa." *Journal of African History* 13 (1972): 237–248.

Postma, Johannes. *The Dutch in the Atlantic Slave Trade, 1600–1815*. Cambridge: Cambridge University Press, 1990.

Postma, Johannes. "A Reassessment of the Dutch Atlantic Slave Trade." In *Riches from Atlantic Commerce: Dutch Transatlantic Trade and Shipping, 1585–1817*, edited by Johannes Postma and Victor Enthoven, 115–138. Leiden: Brill, 2003.

Prude, Jonathan. "To Look upon the 'Lower Sort': Runaway Ads and the Appearance of Unfree Laborers in America, 1750–1800." *Journal of American History* 78, no. 1 (June 1991): 124–159. https://doi.org/10.2307/2078091.

Purvis, Thomas L. *Colonial America to 1763*. Edited by Richard Balkin. New York: Infobase, 2014.

Raben, Remco. "Cities and the Slave Trade in Early-Modern Southeast Asia." In *Linking Destinies: Trade, Towns and Kin in Asian Histories*, edited by Peter Boomgaard, Dick Kooiman, and Henk Schulte Nordholt, 129–151. Leiden: KITLV, 2008.

Raben, Remco. "Facing the Crowd: The Urban Ethnic Policy of the Dutch East India Company, 1600–1800." In *Mariners, Merchants, and Oceans: Studies in Maritime History*, edited by Skaria Mathew Kuzhippallil, 209–245. New Delhi: Manohar, 1995.

Raboteau, Albert J. *Slave Religion: The "Invisible Institution" in the Antebellum South*. Oxford: Oxford University Press, 2004.

Ratelband, Klaas. *Nederlanders in West-Afrika 1600–1650*. Zutphen: Uitgeverijmaatshappij Walburg Pers, 2000.

Reid, A. "'Closed' and 'Open' Slave Systems in Pre-Colonial Asia." In *Slavery, Bondage, & Dependency in Southeast Asia*, edited by Anthony Reid, 156–181. New York: St. Martin's, 1983.

Reidy, Joseph P. "'Negro Election Day' & Black Community Life in New England, 1750–1860." *Marxist Perspectives* 1, no. 3 (Fall 1978): 102–117.

Rhoads, William B. *An Architectural History of the Reformed Church New Paltz, New York*. Tricentennial Committee of the Church (1983).

Ricciardi, Christopher Gerard. "Changing through the Century: Life at the Lott Family Farm in the Nineteenth-Century Town of Flatlands, Kings County, New York." PhD diss., Syracuse University, 2004.

Rivard, Derek A. *Blessing the World: Ritual and Lay Piety in Medieval Religion*. Washington, DC: Catholic University of America Press, 2011.

Rockman, Seth. *Scraping By: Wage Labor, Slavery, and Survival in Early Baltimore*. Baltimore: Johns Hopkins University Press, 2009.

Romney, Susanah Shaw. *New Netherland Connections: Intimate Networks and Atlantic Ties in Seventeenth-Century America*. Chapel Hill: University of North Carolina Press, 2014.

Romney, Susannah Shaw. "'With & alongside his housewife': Claiming Ground in New Netherland and the Early Modern Dutch Empire." *William and Mary Quarterly* 73, no. 2 (April 2016): 187–224. https://doi.org/10.5309/willmaryquar.73.2.0187.

Ross, Robert. *Status and Respectability in the Cape Colony, 1750–1870: A Tragedy of Manners*. Cambridge: Cambridge University Press, 1999.

Rossum, Matthias van. "Labouring Transformations of Amphibious Monsters: Exploring Early Modern Globalization, Diversity, and Shifting Clusters of Labour Relations in the Context of the Dutch East India Company (1600–1800)." *IRSH* 64 (2019): 19–42. https://doi.org/10.1017/S0020859019000014.

Rothman, Deborah. "Introduction." In *Shared Spaces and Divided Place: Material Dimensions of Gender Relations and the American Historical Landscape*, edited by

Deborah Rothman and Ellen-Rose Savulis, 1–23. Knoxville: University of Tennessee Press, 2003.

Rucker, Walter. *The River Flows On: Black Resistance, Culture, and Identity Formation in Early America*. Baton Rouge: Louisiana State University, 2006.

Rupert, Linda. "Marronage, Manumission and Maritime Trade in the Early Modern Caribbean." *Slavery and Abolition* 30, no. 3 (September 2009): 361–382. https://doi.org/10.1080/01440390903098003.

Samford, Patricia. "The Archeology of African-American Slavery and Material Culture." *William and Mary Quarterly* 53, no. 1 (January 1996): 87–114. https://doi.org/10.2307/2946825.

Samford, Patricia. *Subfloor Pits and the Archeology of Slavery in Colonial Virginia*. Tuscaloosa: University of Alabama Press, 2007.

Sawyer, Sean E. "Constructing the Tradition of Dutch American Architecture, 1609–2009." In *Dutch New York: The Roots of Hudson Valley Culture*, edited by Roger Panetta, 93–136. New York: Fordham University Press, 2009.

Schalkwijk, Frans Leonard. *The Reformed Church in Dutch Brazil, 1630–1654*. Zoetermeer: Boekencentrum, 1998.

Schmidt, Benjamin. "The Dutch Atlantic: From Provincialism to Globalism." In *Atlantic History: A Critical Appraisal*, edited by Jack P. Greene and Philip D. Morgan. Oxford: Oxford University Press, 2009.

Schmidt, Benjamin. "Exotic Allies: The Dutch-Chilean Encounter and the Failed Conquest of America." *Renaissance Quarterly* 52, no. 2 (Summer 1999): 440–473. https://doi.org/10.2307/2902060.

Schmidt, Benjamin. *Innocence Abroad: The Dutch Imagination and the New World, 1570–1670*. New York: Cambridge University Press, 2001.

Schuyler Mansion: A Historic Structure Report. N.p.: The Division for Historic Preservation Bureau of Historic Sites, 1977.

Sensbach, Jon F. *Rebecca's Revival: Creating Black Christianity in the Atlantic World*. Cambridge, MA: Harvard University Press, 2005.

Sensbach, Jon F. *A Separate Canaan: The Making of an Afro-Moravian World in North Carolina, 1673–1840*. Chapel Hill: University of North Carolina Press, 1998.

Shattuck, Martha Dickinson. "A Civil Society: Court and Community in Beverwijck, New Netherland, 1652–1664." PhD diss., Boston University, 1993.

Shattuck, Martha Dickinson. "Dutch Jurisprudence in New Netherland and New York." In *Four Centuries of Dutch-American Relations: 1609–2009*, edited by Hans Krabbendam, Cornelis A. van Minnen, and Giles Scott-Smith, 143–153. Albany: State University of New York Press, 2009.

Sibley, David. *Geographies of Exclusion: Society and Difference in the West*. London: Routledge, 1995.

Silva, Filipa Ribeiro da. *Dutch and Portuguese in Western Africa: Empires, Merchants and the Atlantic System, 1580–1674*. Leiden: Brill, 2011.

Singleton, Theresa A. ed. *The Archeology of Slavery and Plantation Life*. San Diego: Academic Press, 1985.

Singleton, Theresa A. "The Archeology of Slavery in North America." *Annual Review of Anthopology* 24 (1995): 119–140.

Singleton, Theresa A. "Slavery and Spatial Dialectics on Cuban Coffee Plantations." *World Archeology* 33, no. 1 (2001): 98–114. https://www.jstor.org/stable/827891.

Smallwood, Stephanie. "The Politics of the Archive and History's Accountability to the Enslaved." *History of the Present: A Journal of Critical History* 6, no. 2 (Fall 2016): 117–132. https://doi.org/10.5406/historypresent.6.2.0117.

Snyder, Terri. *Brabbling Women: Disorderly Speech and the Law in Early Virginia*. Ithaca, NY: Cornell University Press, 2003.

Soja, Edward. *Postmodern Geographies: The Reassertion of Space in Critical Theory*. London: Verso, 1989.

Spicer, Andrew. *Calvinist Churches in Early Modern Europe*. Manchester: Manchester University Press, 2007.

Spicer, Andrew, and Sarah Hamilton eds. *Defining the Holy: Sacred Space in Medieval and Early Modern Europe*. Burlington, VT: Ashgate, 2005.

Spierenburg, Pieter. "Judicial Violence in the Dutch Republic: Corporal Punishment, Executions and Torture in Amsterdam, 1650–1750." PhD diss., University of Amsterdam, 1978.

Spierenburg, Pieter. *The Spectacle of Suffering: Executions and the Evolution of Repression: From a Preindustrial Metropolis to the European Experience*. Cambridge: Cambridge University Press, 2008.

Stevenson, Brenda. "What's Love Got to Do with It? Concubinage and Enslaved Women and Girls in the Antebellum South." In *Sexuality & Slavery: Reclaiming Intimate Histories in the America*, ed. Daina Ramey Berry and Leslie M. Harris, 159–188. Athens: University of Georgia Press, 2018.

St. George, Robert Blair. "'Set Thine House in Order': The Domestication of the Yeomanry in Seventeenth-Century New England." In *Common Places: Readings in American Vernacular Architecture*, edited by Dell Upton and John Michael Vlach, 336–364. Athens: University of Georgia Press, 1986.

Stiefel, Barry L. *Jews and the Renaissance of Synagogue Architecture, 1450–1730*. New York: Routledge, 2016.

Stiles, Henry Reed. *A History of the City of Brooklyn*. Brooklyn, NY: Subscription, 1869.

Stokes, I. N. Phelps. *The Iconography of Manhattan Island, 1498–1909*. Vol. 2. New York: Robert H. Dodd, 1916.

Stoler, Ann Laura. *Carnal Knowledge and Imperial Power: Race and the Intimate in Colonial Rule*. Berkeley: University of California Press, 2010 [repr. ed.].

Strong, Thomas M. *The History of the Town Flatbush in Kings County, Long Island*. New York: T. R. Mercein, Jr., printer, 1842.

Stuckey, Sterling. *Slave Culture: Nationalist Theory and the Foundations of Black America*. New York: Oxford University Press, 1987.

Sullivan, Dennis. *The Punishment of Crime in Colonial New York: The Dutch Experience in Albany during the Seventeenth Century*. New York: Peter Lang, 1997.

Swan, Robert. "The Black Presence in Seventeenth-Century Brooklyn." *de Halve Maen* 63, no. 4 (December 1990): 3–5

Swan, Robert. "Slaves and Slaveholding in Dutch New York, 1628–1664." *Journal of Afro American Historical and Genealogical Society* 17, no. 1 (1998): 46–81.

Sweeney, Kevin M. "Meetinghouses, Town Houses, and Churches: Changing Perceptions of Sacred and Secular Space in Southern New England, 1720–1850." *Winterthur Portfolio* 28, no.1 (Spring 1993): 59–93.

Sweet, James. *Recreating Africa: Culture, Kinship, and Religion in the African-Portuguese World, 1441–1770*. Chapel Hill: University of North Carolina Press, 2003.

Tally, Robert T. *Spatiality*. New York: Routledge, 2012.

Taylor, Jean Gelman. *The Social World of Batavia: Europeans and Eurasians in Colonial Indonesia*. Madison: University of Wisconsin Press, 2009.

Thompson, Mark L. *The Contest for the Delaware Valley: Allegiance, Identity, and Empire in the Seventeenth Century*. Baton Rouge: Louisiana State University Press, 2013.

Thompson, Robert Farris. *Flash of the Spirit*. New York: Vintage Books, 1984.

Thompson, Robert Farris. "Kongo Influences on African-American Artistic Culture." In *Africanisms in American Culture*, edited by Joseph E. Holloway, 148–184. Bloomington: Indiana University Press, 1990.

Thornton, John K. *Africa and Africans in the Making of the Atlantic World, 1400–1680*. Cambridge: Cambridge University Press, 1992.

Thornton, John K. "Afro-Christian Syncretism in the Kingdom of Kongo." *Journal of African History* 54, no. 1 (2013): 53–77.

Thornton, John K. *The Kingdom of Kongo: Civil War and Transition, 1641–1718*. Madison: University of Wisconsin Press, 1983.

Thornton, John K. *The Kongolese Saint Anthony: Dona Beatriz Kimpa Vita and the Antonian Movement, 1684–1706*. Cambridge: Cambridge University Press, 1998.

Thornton, John K. "Religious and Ceremonial Life in the Kongo and Mbundu Areas, 1500–1700." In *Central Africans and Cultural Transformations in the American Diaspora*, edited by Linda Heywood, 71–90. Cambridge: Cambridge University Press, 2002.

Thornton, John K. *Warfare in Atlantic Africa, 1500–1800*. London: Routledge, 2000.

Thornton, John K., and Andrea C. Mosterman. "A Re-Interpretation of the Kongo-Portuguese War of 1622 According to New Documentary Evidence." *Journal of African History* 51 (2010): 235–248.

Tomlins, Christopher. *Freedom Bound: Law, Labor, and Civic Identity in Colonizing English America, 1580–1865*. Cambridge: Cambridge University Press, 2010.

Trouillot, Michel-Rolph. *Silencing the Past: Power and the Production of History*. Boston: Beacon, 1995.

Turner, Sasha. *Contested Bodies: Pregnancy, Childrearing, and Slavery in Jamaica*. Philadelphia: University of Pennsylvania Press, 2017.

Turner, Sasha. "The Nameless and the Forgotten: Maternal Grief, Sacred Protection, and the Archive of Slavery." *Slavery & Abolition* 38, no. 2 (2017): 232–250. https://doi.org/10.1080/0144039X.2017.1316962.

Twitty, Anne. *Before Dred Scott: Slavery and Legal Culture in the American Confluence, 1787–1857*. Cambridge: Cambridge University Press, 2018.

Upton, Dell. *Holy Things and Profane: Anglican Parish Churches in Colonial Virginia*. New Haven, CT: Yale University Press, 1997.

Upton, Dell. "Vernacular Domestic Architecture in Eighteenth-Century Virginia." In *Common Places: Readings in American Vernacular Architecture*, edited by Dell Upton and John Michael Vlach, 315–335. Athens: University of Georgia Press, 1986.

Upton, Dell. "White and Black Landscapes in Eighteenth-Century Virginia." *Common Places* 2, no. 2 (1984): 357–369.

Upton, Dell, and John Michael Vlach, eds. *Common Places: Readings in American Vernacular Architecture*. Athens: University of Georgia Press, 1986.

Van Dusen, Lillian Dockstader. *A History of the Reformed Church of Fonda, N.Y. beginning with the old Caughnawaga Church*. Ladies Aid Society, 1925.

Van Zandt, Cynthia Jean. *Brothers among Nations: The Pursuit of Intercultural Alliances in Early America, 1580–1660.* Oxford: Oxford University Press, 2008.

Van Zandt, Cynthia Jean. "Negotiating Settlement: Colonialism, Cultural Exchange, and Conflict in Early Colonial Atlantic North America, 1580–1660." PhD diss., University of Connecticut, 1998.

Vanderbilt, Gertrude Lefferts. *The Social History of Flatbush: And Manners and Customs of the Dutch Settlers in Kings County.* New York: D. Appleton, 1881.

Vandervelde, Lea. *Redemption Songs: Suing for Freedom before Dred Scott.* Oxford: Oxford University Press, 2014.

Venema, Janny. *Beverwijck: A Dutch Village on the American Frontier, 1652–1664.* Albany: State University of New York Press, 2003.

Vennema, Ame. *History of the Reformed Church of New Paltz, Ulster County, NY from 1683 to 1883.* Rondout, NY: Kingston Freeman Steam Printing House, 1884.

Verter, Bradford. "Interracial Festivity and Power in Antebellum New York: The Case of Pinkster." *Journal of Urban History* 28, no. 4 (2002): 398–428. https://doi.org/10.1177/0096144202028004002.

Vink, Markus. "'The World's Oldest Trade': Dutch Slavery and Slave Trade in the Indian Ocean in the Seventeenth Century." *Journal of World History* 14, no. 2 (June 2003): 131–177. https://doi.org/10.1353/jwh.2003.0026.

Vlach, John Michael. "'Snug Li'l House with Flue and Oven': Nineteenth-Century Reforms in Plantation Slave Housing." In *Gender, Class, and Shelter: Perspectives in Vernacular Architecture*, V, edited by Elizabeth Collins Cromley and Carter L. Hudgins, 118–129. Knoxville: University of Tennessee Press, 1995.

Vos, Jelmer, David Eltis, and David Richardson. "The Dutch in the Atlantic World: New Perspectives from the Slave Trade with Particular Reference to African Origins of the Traffic." In *Extending the Frontiers: Essay on the New Transatlantic Slave Trade Database*, edited by David Eltis and David Richardson, 228–249. New Haven, CT: Yale University Press, 2008.

Vries, Jan de. "The Dutch Atlantic Economies." In *The Atlantic Economy during the Seventeenth and Eighteenth Centuries: Organization, Operation, Practice, and Personnel*, edited by Peter A. Coclanis, 1–29. Columbia: University of South Carolina Press, 2005.

Wade, Melvin. "'Shining in Borrowed Plumage': Affirmation of Community in the Black Coronation Festivals of New England (c. 1750–c. 1850)." *Western Folklore* 40, no. 3 (July 1981): 211–231. https://doi.org/10.2307/1499693.

Wagman, Morton. "Corporate Slavery in New Netherland." *Journal of Negro History* 65, no. 1 (Winter 1980): 34–42. https://doi.org/10.2307/3031546.

Waldstreicher, David. "Reading the Runaways: Self-Fashioning, Print Culture, and Confidence in Slavery in the Eighteenth-Century Mid-Atlantic." *William and Mary Quarterly* 56, no. 2 (April 1999): 243–272. https://doi.org/10.2307/2674119.

Wall, Diana diZerega. "Twenty Years After: Re-examining Archeological Collection for Evidence of New York City's Colonial African Past." *Southeastern Archeology* 18, no. 1 (Summer 1999): 57–68.

Walsh, James P. "Holy Time and Sacred Space in Puritan New England," *American Quarterly* 32, no. 1 (Spring 1980): 79–95. https://doi.org/10.2307/2712497.

Warren, Wendy. *New England Bound: Slavery and Colonization in Early America.* New York: Liveright, 2016.

Washington, Margaret. "'From Motives of Delicacy': Sexuality and Morality in the Narratives of Sojourner Truth and Harriet Jacobs." *Journal of African American History* 92, no. 1 (Winter 2007): 57–73. https://jstor.org/stable/20064154.

Washington, Margaret. *Sojourner Truth's America*. Champaign: University of Illinois Press, 2009.

Weisse, Arthur James. *The History of the City of Albany, New York: From the Discovery of the Great River in 1524, by Verrazzano, to the Present Time*. Albany: E. H. Bender, 1884.

Welch, Kimberly M. *Black Litigants in the Antebellum South*. Chapel Hill: University of North Carolina Press, 2018.

Welie, Rik van. "Patterns of Slave Trading and Slavery in the Dutch Colonial World, 1596–1863." In *Dutch Colonialism, Migration and Cultural Heritage*, edited by Gert Oostindie, 155–259. Leiden: KITLV, 2008.

Welie, Rik van. "Slave Trading and Slavery in the Dutch Colonial Empire: A Global Comparison." *New West Indian Guide/Nieuwe West-Indische Gids* 82, nos. 1 & 2 (2008): 47–96. https://doi.org/10.1163/13822373-90002465.

Wells, D. D. Cornelius L. *Quarter Millennial Anniversary of the Reformed Dutch Church of Flatbush, New York* (1904).

Weslager, C. A. "The City of Amsterdam's Colony on the Delaware, 1656–1664." *Delaware History* 20 (1982): 1–25, 73–97.

Weststeijn, Arthur. "Republican Empire: Colonialism, Commerce and Corruption in the Dutch Golden Age." *Renaissance Studies* 26, no. 2 (September 2012): 491–509. https://jstor.com/stable/24420170.

Wheeler, Walter Richard. "Magical Dwelling: Apotropaic Building Practices in the New World Dutch Cultural Hearth." In *Religion, Cults & Rituals in the Medieval Rural Environment, Ruralia XI*, edited by C. Bis-Worch and C. Theune, 373–396. Leiden: Sidestone, 2017.

Where Slavery Died Hard: The Forgotten History of Ulster County and the Shawangunk Mountain Region. DVD. Directed by Wendy Harris and Arnold Pickman. Cragsmoor Consultants, 2018.

White, Shane. "'It was a Proud Day': African Americans, Festivals, and Parades in the North." *Journal of American History* 81, no. 1 (June 1994): 13–50. https://doi.org/10.2307/2080992.

White, Shane. "Pinkster: Afro-Dutch Syncretization in New York City and the Hudson Valley." *Journal of American Folklore* 102, no. 403 (January–March 1989): 68–75. https://doi.org/10.2307/540082.

White, Shane. *Somewhat More Independent: The End of Slavery in New York City, 1770–1810*. Athens: University of Georgia Press, 1991.

Whitfield, Harvey Amani. *North to Bondage: Loyalist Slavery in the Maritimes*. Vancouver: UBC Press, 2016.

Wilcoxen, Charlotte. *Seventeenth Century Albany: A Dutch Profile*. Albany: Education Dept., Albany Institute History and Art, 1984.

Wilder, Craig Steven. *A Covenant with Color: Race and Social Power in Brooklyn*. New York: Columbia University Press, 2000.

Wilder, Craig Steven. *In the Company of Black Men: The African Influence on African American Culture in New York City*. New York: New York University Press, 2001.

Wilkie, Laurie. "Magic and Empowerment on the Plantation: An Archeological Consideration of African-American Worldview." *Southeastern Archeology* 14, no. 2 (1995): 136–148.

Wilkie, Laurie. "Secret and Sacred: Contextualizing the Artifacts of African-American Magic in Religion." *Historical Archeology* 31, no. 4 (1997): 81–106.

Wilkie, Laurie A. *The Archeology of Mothering: An African-American Midwife's Tale.* New York: Routledge, 2003.

Williams, James Homer. "Dutch Attitudes towards Indians, Africans, and Other Europeans in New Netherland, 1624–1664." In *Connecting Cultures: The Netherlands in Five Centuries of Transatlantic Exchange*, edited by Rosemarijn Hoefte and Johanna Kardux, 23–43. Amsterdam: VU University Press, 1994.

Williams, Oscar. *African Americans and Colonial Legislation in the Middle Colonies.* Milton Parks, UK: Routledge, 2014.

Williams, Oscar. "Slavery in Albany, New York, 1624–1827." *Afro-Americans in New York Life and History* 34, no. 2 (July 2010): 154–168.

Williams-Myers, A. J. *Long Hammering: Essays on the Forging of an African American Presence in the Hudson River Valley to the Early Twentieth.* Trenton, NJ: Africa World Press, 1994.

Williams-Myers, A. J. "Pinkster Carnival: Africanisms in the Hudson River Valley." *Afro-Americans in New York Life and History* 9, no. 1 (1985): 7–17.

Williams-Meyers, A. J. "Re-examining Slavery in New York." *New York Archives* 1, no. 3 (Winter 2002): 15–18.

Wingens, Marc. "De Pinksterkroon is Weer in 'T Land, Hoezee! Het Pinksterkroon Feest in Deventer." *Volkscultuur* 6, no. 2 (1989): 7–30.

Woods, Lynn. "A Pastor's Double Life Unearthed." Hudson Valley online. Accessed June 6, 2019. https://hudsonvalleyone.com/2013/05/05/the-mystery-of-james-murphy/.

Worden, Nigel. "Space and Identity in VOC Cape Town." *Kronos* 25 (1998–99): 72–87.

Young, Jason R. *Rituals of Resistance: African Atlantic Religion in Kongo and the Lowcountry South in the Era of Slavery.* Baton Rouge: Louisiana State University, 2007.

Zabin, Serena R. *Dangerous Economies: Status and Commerce in Imperial New York.* Philadelphia: University of Pennsylvania Press, 2009.

Zelnick-Abramovitz, Rachel. *Not Wholly Free: The Concept of Manumission and the Status of Manumitted Slaves in the Ancient Greek World.* Boston: Brill, 2005.

Zuesse, Evan M. "Perseverance and Transmutation in African Traditional Religions." In *African Traditional Religions In Contemporary Society*, edited by Jacob K. Olupona, 167–184. New York: Paragon House, 1991.

Zuidhoek, Arne. *Zeerovers van de Gouden Eeuw.* Bussum: De Boer, 1977.

Zwieten, Adriana E. van. "The Orphan Chamber of New Amsterdam." *William and Mary Quarterly* 53, no. 2 (April 1996): 319–340. https://doi.org/10.2307/2947403.

INDEX

abolition, 4–5, 54, 57, 67, 135; gradual, 4, 57
abuse, 45, 74, 80, 94, 96–97, 135
Act for preventing Suppressing and punishing the Conspiracy and Insurrection of Negroes and other Slaves, 56, 58
Act for preventing the Conspiracy of Slaves (1708), 89
Act for the Gradual Abolition of Slavery (1799), 57
Act to Incourage the Baptizing of Negro, Indian and Mulatto Slaves (1706), 58
Acts and Proceedings of the General Synod (1816), 113
adultery, 44, 47
Afonso I (Kongo), 42, 75
Africa, 48, 68, 140n18; Catholicism in, 39, 42–43, 74, 76
African Burial Ground report, 127, 131
African captives, 6, 20–22, 72, 140n18, 140n19, 149n59, 149n69, 154n113, 162n90
African culture, enslaved community and, 68, 71–72, 74–77, 162n87; religious practices and, 75–76, 93–94, 129, 131–132
agricultural labor. See farming
Aimwell, Absolom, 70
Albany County, 5, 66; enslaved population in, 54–57, 80; legislation in, 59
Albany, 56, 59, 67, 165n28, 166n49; built environment of, 60–61, 64, 81, 85–86; churches in, 108, 112, 118–21, 123, 127, 186n80, 188n112; enslaved population in, 80, 86; fire in, 64, 70, 91, 171n136; public spaces in, 59, 61, 64, 70–71; Synod of, 115. See also Beverwijck
alcohol, 38, 65–66, 68, 73. See also taverns
Alexander, Robert, 108, 119
American Revolution, 6, 66–67, 72–73, 86, 113, 123
Amsterdam, 20–21, 71, 174n23; Classis of, 105, 111, 114
amulets, 130–31

Anderson, Elijah, 53, 163n6
Andrade, Tonio, 17
Andries (enslaved by Jan Baptist van Rensselaer), 25–26, 152n97
Anglican churches, 105–6, 116–17, 120–121, 123, 128, 132, 182n22, 184n58
Angola, 22, 43, 75, 131, 162n87
Angola, Anthonie van, 39–40, 156n32
Angola, Christina, 52
Angola, Domingo, 51–54, 77
Angola, Dorothea, 42, 44
Angola, Emanuel Swager van, 40, 157n37
Angola, Gracia d', 13, 26, 43, 154n115
Angola, Maijken van, 31–32, 39, 42, 48, 50, 52
Angola, Manuel, 52–54, 77
Angola, Paulo, 26, 43, 154n115
Angola, Samuel, 40, 42
Angole, Emanuel d', 40, 41
Angool, Lúcie d', 39–40, 156n32
Anthonij, Anthonij, 42, 44
Antonij, Cleijn, 13, 26, 42–43, 154n115
archeology, 8–9, 80, 83, 87f, 88, 92–93, 129–32, 137n3, 177n66
architecture, churches and, 106, 117, 120–21, 124–25; changes in, 11, 81, 85, 88, 116, 120, 174n23; control and, 8, 16, 59–60, 81, 85, 89
arson. See fires
artifacts, 9, 84f, 92–94
Ashanti Adae, 76
Atlantic Creoles, 6, 48
Atlantic Ocean, 15. See also slave trade
auctions, 21–22, 38, 78–79

Bakongo, 93, 130, 190n152
balconies, 119, 121, 123
Baltus (enslaved man), 59–60
Banda Islands, 16, 17
baptism, 39–42, 44, 107–109, 111–13, 156n37
Baptist church, 105, 124
Barbados, 59, 140n18, 168n70